9|9|

LOOKING GOOD

LOOKING GOOD

MALE BODY IMAGE IN MODERN AMERICA

———

LYNNE LUCIANO

HILL and WANG

A DIVISION OF FARRAR, STRAUS AND GIROUX

NEW YORK

Hill and Wang
A division of Farrar, Straus and Giroux
19 Union Square West, New York 10003

Library of Congress Cataloging-in-Publication Data
Luciano, Lynne, 1943–
    Looking good: male body image in modern America/Lynne Luciano.
      p.   cm.
    Includes bibliographical references and index.
    ISBN 0-8090-6637-8 (alk. paper)
    1. Body image in men. I. Title
  BF697.5.B63 L83 2001
  306.4 —dc21   00-032013

Designed by Jonathan D. Lippincott

A concerted effort has been made to obtain permission for all illustrations.

WITH SPECIAL THANKS

TO DON PRINCIPE

TABLE OF CONTENTS

ACKNOWLEDGMENTS

There are many people whom I must thank for their help over the past years while I was writing this book. First, I owe a great deal to my dissertation committee at the University of Southern California: Steve Ross, Lois Banner, and Barry Glassner. The idea for the book was first developed during a seminar with Steve, and his dedication and unflagging support turned an idea into a reality. Both Steve and Lois consistently challenged me to ask the hard questions and to analyze my topic from fresh perspectives, while providing inspiring models with their own work and scholarship. I thank Barry for widening the scope of my inquiry, moving it beyond history to include a sociological perspective.

I was fortunate to have the encouragement and support of many fine scholars at U.S.C. I am particularly grateful to Frank Mitchell, Terry Seip, Ed Perkins, and Mauricio Mazon in the Department of History and Norman Mirsky at Hebrew Union College, all of whom were good friends as well as mentors. I owe a debt of gratitude to the university for providing me with a fellowship that made it possible for me to complete my graduate studies and embark upon this writing project. I am most appreciative of the university libraries and their dedicated staffs, especially Doheny Library and the Norris Medical Library.

I am grateful to E. Anthony Rotundo for his perceptive reading of my work, which has greatly enhanced it on many levels, and to Beth Haiken for generously sharing her scholarly expertise in the history of cosmetic surgery and for her marvelous sense of humor. John Broesamle and Ronald Davis at California State University, Northridge, have been staunch friends and supporters, and I offer special thanks to Marvin Klotz, who suggested that graduate school was a more worthy pastime than playing paddle tennis at Venice Beach.

At Hill and Wang, I am deeply grateful to my editors, Lauren Osborne and Catherine Newman. They shared my vision of this book and have worked indefatigably to make it a reality. I also wish to thank Niko Pfund of NYU Press for his enduring interest in this project and for the many useful and intriguing articles that he has sent me.

From the standpoint of research, I am greatly indebted to Dr. Harold Clavin, who, despite the demands of a successful practice, generously shared his expertise in cosmetic surgery, introducing me to patients and other surgeons and allowing me to observe surgical procedures in his operating room. Thanks are due as well to Dr. Randall Sword of the Sword Medical Group, Dr. John Williams of Aesthetica Surgical Center, and the Elliott and True Hair Replacement Center in Beverly Hills. Psychologists Bryce Britton, Lou Paget, and Joan Irvine provided invaluable insights into issues related to male sexuality and male-female relationships.

I am beholden to many very good friends. I offer special thanks to June Hopkins, with whom I began the journey of graduate school, and Sioux Harvey, who was waiting outside the conference room, flowers in hand, on the day I defended my dissertation. Their friendship, and their scholarly expertise, have made all the difference. And I thank Hanita Dechter, a very special person.

To my parents, Bill and Erica Paul, and my sister, Carole Vesely, I can only say that I could never have done this without your love and support, and your continual encouragement. I know you are always there for me, and I am grateful.

LOOKING GOOD

INTRODUCTION

One of the things that makes the modern world "modern" is
the development of consciousness of the self.
　　　　　　　—Warren Susman, *Culture as History*, 1973

The book you are about to read is a journey through the world of
male vanity. It is a world of steroid abusers and compulsive runners, anorectics and bulimics, men who are losing their hair and
potency, and patients getting face-lifts, buttock lifts, and silicone
implants—all in pursuit of youth, sex appeal, and success. And it's
a world that has changed decade by decade both for men and
for society as a whole. The story begins immediately after World
War II, when America emerged as the world's most powerful and
influential nation, and continues through the end of the twentieth
century.

American men spent $3 billion on grooming aids and fragrances
in 1997. They also spent nearly $800 million on hair transplants and
$400 million on hairpieces. Sales of exercise equipment and health-
club memberships raked in $4 billion. An estimated eighty-five
million Americans, mostly male, are doing some kind of weight
training. Even serious bodybuilding, once a fringe activity largely

relegated to the lower classes, has gained middle-class status as upwardly mobile men of all ages grunt and strain for the blood-vessel-constricting high known as the pump. For men who have more fat than muscle, a lucrative foundation-garment industry offers Butt-Busters and Man-Bands to flatten bulges. Men are dieting in unprecedented numbers, and an estimated one million of them suffer from eating disorders commonly thought to afflict only women.

Also surprising is men's pursuit of beauty through the scalpel: in 1996, the bill for male cosmetic surgery was $500 million. Just under $200 million was spent on the two most popular surgeries, liposuction and rhinoplasty (nose jobs), with the rest going for esoteric surgeries like pectoral implants and the creation of cleft chins, not to mention the ultimate male surgery, penis enlargement. We are clearly witnessing the evolution of an obsession with body image, especially among middle-class men, and a corresponding male appropriation of, in the words of the feminist Barbara Ehrenreich, "status-seeking activities . . . once seen as feminine."

What, then, does it mean to be a man at the dawn of the twenty-first century? The historian and philosopher Elisabeth Badinter has concluded that models of masculinity haven't changed much over the centuries. She points to four "imperatives" for today's men: first and foremost, men must be men—"no sissy stuff"; second, they must be competitive, constantly demonstrating their success and superiority; third, they must be "detached and impassive"; and, finally, they must be willing to take risks and confront danger, even to the point of violence. These four imperatives have two qualities in common: they are diametrically opposed to what is generally regarded as feminine behavior, and they say nothing about how a man is supposed to *look*.

Until World War II, it is true, male attractiveness was derived from activity; how a man behaved and what he achieved were the true measures of his worth. In the immediate aftermath of World War II, it seemed these ideals would continue along their accustomed track. The American male would provide for his family, succeed at his job, and be strong, rugged, and virile. While women labored at self-beautification, men devoted themselves to more important matters. Men were not exactly indifferent to their bodies, but any man who overly emphasized his physical appearance risked being accused of vanity. Men who wore toupees aroused amused derision at best. Although obesity among Americans had reached alarming proportions by mid-century, men shied away from dieting, despite warnings about heart disease. Exercise, which at least had the cachet of being "masculine" because it was associated with action, didn't get much more strenuous than golf and gardening. Workouts that raised serious sweat had few middle-class adherents, and cosmetic surgery was regarded as the exclusive preserve of women. As for the body's most intimate parts, a cloud of secrecy shrouded them, as well as their function (and dysfunction), from public debate and public view.

What has caused American men to fall into the beauty trap so long assumed to be the special burden of women? Does men's concern about their bodies mean they've become feminized? Have they been so addled by the women's movement that they are responding by becoming more like women? There is no simple, single answer. Rather, a confluence of social, economic, and cultural changes has been instrumental in shaping the new cult of male body image in postwar America.

The changing status of women brought about by second-wave feminism has radically reshaped how women view the male body. As long as men controlled economic resources, their looks were of secondary importance. Though feminism would have many, often conflicting, objectives, the liberal feminism that emerged mainly among professional and upper-middle-class women focused on social and legal constraints that denied women equal access to the workplace. As the role of breadwinner became a shared one, men's economic power and sense of uniqueness would be undermined.

The impetus behind the rising number of college-educated wives entering the workplace came less from the need to contribute to the family income, however, than from the diminishing attractions of the home. Avid middle-class pursuit of higher education, especially at graduate and professional levels, deterred growing numbers of young men and women from early marriage. At the same time, greater latitude for sexual experimentation made it less likely that women would marry just to legitimize sexual relations. An emphasis on the importance of self-fulfillment also undermined marriage as a priority for many young Americans. It was during the 1960s that the term "lifestyle" was first used in reference to being single: its significance lay in its suggestion of choice. Marriage was no longer expected but a matter of personal taste, as were its alternatives, divorce and cohabitation, which became ever more common.

By the end of the decade, the average age at first marriage had risen, and the marriage rate had begun to drop, and continued to drop through the 1970s. A survey of college students at that time showed that 82 percent of the women rated a career as important to self-fulfillment, whereas only 67 percent believed this was true of marriage. The *Cosmopolitan* editor Helen Gurley Brown, who had spent most of the 1960s trying to create an image of the *Cosmo* girl as mirror image of the sexually uninhibited *Playboy* man, emphatically agreed: marriage, she told her legions of female readers, was nothing more than "insurance for the worst years of your life."

Try as she might to turn men into sex objects, Brown was ahead of her time in 1962. For most women, being single was still stigmatizing rather than stimulating. And as Brown herself was quick to point out, sexual liberation didn't work without economic liberation, and that hadn't arrived yet. But as the decade progressed, single life took on new legitimacy and had wide-ranging social and economic effects. One of the most significant was that in the dating marketplace, single women were as likely to be doing the choosing—and rejecting—as men, elevating the importance of male looks to a whole new level. Why, demands the woman who works out rigorously to keep her body lean and fit, should I put up with a man who spends his leisure time sitting on a couch watching television? Or, as the feminist Germaine Greer inquired with some acerbity in 1971, was it too much to ask that women be spared "the daily struggle for superhuman beauty in order to offer it to the caresses of a subhuman ugly mate"?

Economic change wasn't limited to women's more substantial paychecks. World War II catapulted America into unprecedented power and prosperity. Lavish government spending, corporate expansion, and the development of a vast complex of technological industries based on the postwar symbiosis of military, government, and science created thousands of secure, well-paying white-collar jobs. As union wages rose, stimulated by cost-of-living increases and buffered by national prosperity, millions of working-class Americans could afford middle-class lifestyles and the accoutrements that defined them.

For nearly a quarter century, expectations of continued affluence and material progress were undimmed. But in the 1970s, America's virtually unchallenged global economic preeminence, as well as its internal prosperity, would confront foreign competition, inflation, declining corporate profits, and unemployment. In the ensuing downsizing that persisted well into the 1990s, hardest hit would be those most accustomed to job success and security—white males. To maintain an edge, it became important not just to be qualified for a job but to look as if one were; and that meant looking dynamic, successful, and, above all, young.

These changes are related to a more complex and extremely significant alteration in American life since mid-century: the rise of a culture increasingly based on self-fulfillment and the cultivation of self-esteem. Though many factors brought about this sea change, one of the most compelling was the proliferation of consumerism and its emphasis on the importance of self-image.

America's transformation from a culture of production to one of consumption was well under way by the turn of the nineteenth century. At that time, the basic needs of most middle-class Americans were being met, and manufacturers therefore sought to create desire in place of necessity. They were aided by advertisers who set out to convince consumers that their very identities depended on owning the right products, that they could be whatever they wished, as long as they purchased enough goods.

Advertising agencies appeared on the American landscape as early as the 1850s but remained on a small scale until World War I, when technological and cultural factors converged to create the modern advertising industry. New technologies like arc and neon lighting allowed ads to be displayed in more interesting and enticing ways, while advanced printing methods like lithography made it possible to copy images less expensively and more attractively. During the war, advertising and public relations joined forces with the U.S. government to generate propaganda and unifying symbols as a means of mobilizing support for the war among a fragmented and diverse population—an effort devoted more to popularizing and legitimizing the war than to disseminating real information. Afterward, products poured off booming American assembly lines, and advertisers mobilized consumer enthusiasm in much the same way. Ad agencies created personalities for their products, which were sold not on the basis of what they could do but on the basis of the image they projected—as one advertising mogul put it, they sold the sizzle, not the steak.

Advertising was helped in its crusade by the emergent popularity of psychology. Terms like "ego" and "repression" were bandied about in everyday conversation, and by the 1920s, the idea of complexes had moved out of medical circles and into the lives of ordinary people. Americans, buffeted by changes brought about by industrialization and the new public life of cities, had fallen prey to feelings of anxiety and insecurity. Magazines and self-help books asked, "Do you have an inferiority complex?" and emphasized the importance of self-scrutiny. Advertisers seized on the connection between the psychological and the physical, urging consumers to buy their products to overcome deficiencies ranging from dandruff to bad breath.

Well into the twentieth century, women were advertisers' main targets. Consumption—that is, shopping—was defined as women's work. Single women were encouraged to compete for men by buying commodities to make themselves more beautiful, and married women were encouraged to demonstrate their husbands' success by their purchasing power. But as commodities became increasingly central to defining self-worth, men, too, would be pulled into the vortex of consumerism, warned by advertisers that the wrong "look" posed a threat to career, love life, and self-esteem.

In its early days, advertising had been simply a means of linking buyer and seller by presenting basic information about a product—how big it was, for example, or how much it cost. But in an urbanizing and modernizing culture, advertising evolved from selling mere products to selling their benefits. Advertising is about image, self-esteem, and display of the self. It is *not* about what the psychologist Erik Erikson calls, in his studies of human psychological development, "the mature person's developing sense of the importance of giving something back to community and society." In a consumer society, a sense of responsibility to the larger community doesn't develop. As the sociologist Diane Barthel points out, every advertiser knows that the critical attribute of any product is "What will it do for *me*?" The line between commodity and individual has become blurred, so that we *are* what we buy. Americans have been beguiled by marketing acumen, and the body has become the ultimate commodity.

The importance of self-presentation originated early in the century, though initially it was more subtle than it is today. As early as the second decade, social critics were noting that America was shifting from a culture of character to a culture of personality. Character implies self-discipline and a sense of inner direction, whereas personality revolves around the ability to please others—not necessarily through real accomplishment but by winning friends and influencing people. While character is its own reward, personality demands external validation and appreciation.

By mid-century, the ethos of personality had almost entirely displaced older notions of character. Image is described by the historian Daniel Boorstin as "a studiously crafted personality profile of an individual . . . a value caricature, shaped in three dimensions, of synthetic materials." Like the right personality, it relies on external indicators to proclaim our personal worth and determine how others see and evaluate us. The right clothes, the right car, and even the right body and face—all can be purchased rather than cultivated.

The 1960s brought not only social upheaval but an emphasis on sexuality, self-expression, and youth. Commercial packaging of youth actually began in the 1950s, when marketers recognized teenagers' "purchasing power," a term first used after World War II. By 1959, teenagers controlled ten billion dollars in discretionary income, more than the total sales of General Motors. Teen society was grounded in a sense of acute difference from adult society and was primarily defined in terms of consumer choices, especially in fashion and music. Yet in other respects, adolescents in the 1950s appeared to want the same things as their parents: a mate, a family, a home in the suburbs. They spent a great deal of time practicing for their future by playing courtship games like going steady and getting pinned. Most girls looked forward to taking on the responsibilities of motherhood, and boys wanted to become men. As for adults, though they wanted to look attractive and have that elusive quality known as "sex appeal," they generally didn't wish to look, or behave, like teenagers. The culture of youth was distinctive *because* it was reserved for the young.

The cultural importance of youth surged in the 1970s, as prosperity continued to allow teenagers to pursue their distinctive consumerism and because so many defining aspects of the 1960s—fashion, hair, music, radicalism—had centered on young people, especially those of college age. Even the soldiers who fought in the Vietnam War were younger than those of any previous American war: their average age was nineteen, compared with twenty-four for soldiers in World War II. Although the end of the 1960s was marked by disillusionment over the decade's social and political turmoil, the desirability of being (and looking) young remained undimmed. Growing numbers of Americans, confronting the prospect of turning thirty, became determined never to leave adolescence—at least, not physically. Youth was no longer a stage of life to be passed through but one to be clung to tenaciously.

In the 1970s, the obsession with youthfulness combined with the emphasis on self-expression and acquisitiveness to create an entirely new culture grounded in the importance of self-esteem. Narcissism, identified in the 1960s by Erikson as a modern form of neurosis, was recast by the historian and cultural theorist Christopher Lasch into a theory of modern social history. According to Lasch, the bewildering array of images to which the average American was subjected led to a preoccupation with projecting the "right" image of oneself in order to confirm one's very existence. If the 1950s had been defined by conformity, the 1970s were characterized by a sense of selfhood "hopelessly dependent on the consumption of images" and consequently on relentless self-scrutiny. The marketing of commodities, Lasch cautioned, created a world of insubstantial images difficult to distinguish from reality. Within this world, images were incorporated into Americans' visions of themselves, with important implications for body image for both genders. Advertising and mass marketing held out the promise of self-fulfillment and eternal youth through consumerism—for everyone. Finally, as the historian Margaret Morganroth Gullette has observed, "the system that sells products based on fears of aging . . . turned its giant voracious maw toward that next great big juicy market, men."

In the 1990s, that "big juicy market" was the largest it had ever been—the baby boomers were entering middle age. These thirty-one million people—12 percent of the population—were beginning to experience the trauma of midlife crisis. In 1993, the National Men's Resource Center declared that all men undergo a midlife crisis and that a major manifestation of this was growing concern about the loss of physical appeal.

It's tempting to surmise that men's interest in body image, and their relatively recent concerns about physical attractiveness, along with sexualization of the male body, means they are becoming feminized. This, however, is decidedly not the case. Looking good is part of a quintessential male strategy whose ultimate aim is to make men more successful, competitive, and powerful. The means of achieving this goal may be new, but the objective is not.

Millions of American men have been transformed into body-conscious consumers of revealing fashions, seductive perfumes, and the services of hairstylists, personal trainers, and plastic surgeons. Due credit for this transformation must be given to advertisers, marketers, and self-esteem gurus, who have sold men—and all of us—a message of self-transfiguration through self-commodification. The traditional image of women as sexual objects has simply been expanded: *everyone* has become an object to be seen.[1]

LOOKING GOOD

A HISTORICAL PERSPECTIVE

Most men are conscious of the fact that they are competing not only with younger [male] competitors but with women who know how to take care of themselves.

—David Nap, marketing VP

Since the 1950s, men have been concerned about four major areas of body alteration and enhancement. They have lavished great attention on their hair, they have worried about physical fitness and body shape, they have made forays into cosmetic surgery, and they have fretted about sexual dysfunction. Men's ways of dealing with their "problem areas" have changed drastically in this century, and it is impossible to understand current practices without first looking back at men's attitudes in earlier times.

Hair

Hair frames a man's face and accents his features, and it can't be disguised by the cut of a suit. A full head of hair typically has been synonymous with youth and virility, yet 20 percent of men begin to lose their hair by their twenties, and by age sixty, most experience substantial male pattern baldness. Women have never been kind to bald men: "Is there anything more ugly in the world," asks Scheherazade in *Arabian Nights,* "than a man beardless and bald as an artichoke?" As a result, even the rich and powerful dread baldness. Julius Caesar wore his trademark ceremonial wreath to disguise his shrinking hairline, and Hannibal wore a wig into battle and kept a second on hand for social occasions.

Wigs, forbidden by the Church throughout the Middle Ages because they suggested vanity and worldliness, had become common by the fifteenth century and reached the height of fashionableness in seventeenth-century France. Louis XIII, balding by the age of twenty-three, made wigs immensely popular at the French court, and they soon spread throughout Europe. These wigs, worn by both women and men, were lavish creations that transcended efforts to enhance physical appearance and became symbols of wealth and status. In his later years, Louis tottered about under enormous white-powdered wigs. So did everyone else in court because, as one courtier explained, "everyone wants to look old, for that is to appear to be wise." Wisdom, however, seems to have been more admired in seventeenth-century France than in twentieth-century America.

In eighteenth-century America, wigs were an essential fashion accessory, though, in keeping with American egalitarianism and aversion to flamboyance, they were never as ostentatious as at the French court. Still, they signaled the status of their wearers: styles indicated professions and social levels, as well as personal standing—hence, the origin of the term "bigwig." Virtually every man wore a wig; even slaves, who couldn't afford to buy them, made them from whatever materials were at hand, including animal hair and plant fibers. By the nineteenth century, wigs had fallen out of vogue, metamorphosing into dust mops and rags. For much of the twentieth century, the average man, afraid of being considered vain and effeminate, felt as comfortable visiting the toupee maker as a house of ill repute.

Potions, lotions, and elixirs claiming to stimulate hair growth also have a long history. Egyptian remedies dating as far back as 1500 B.C. prescribed potions made of ibex, crocodile, lion fat, human nail clippings, and singed hedgehog bristles. Hippocrates, obsessed with his own hair loss, mixed opium with floral essences, wine, and pigeon dung. Roman physicians prescribed weekly applications of boiled snakes, and Roman men painted locks on their bald heads, presaging twentieth-century scalp-spraying methods. Monks and alchemists searched for baldness cures throughout the Middle Ages and jealously guarded these "secret" remedies, even though none of them worked. Seventeenth-century English noblemen rubbed a mix of Indian tea and lemon onto their bald scalps, while the less noble used chicken droppings. In the nineteenth-century American West, tough and supposedly image-indifferent cowboys lined up at medicine shows to buy snake-oil concoctions. Indians worried about losing their hair, too; they used yucca and chili pepper oil. Before becoming a director, D. W. Griffith hawked a yucca-root-based tonic called Yuccatone as a baldness remedy.

Despite the emotional distress caused by hair loss, American men in the twentieth century have been expected to be indifferent to balding and to regard efforts at remedying or disguising it as shamefully vain. As for hairstyles, the truly masculine man was to have well-groomed hair unequivocally shorter than women's. Clean, healthy hair was an indicator less of sex appeal than of neatness; advertisers promised that using the "right" products would give men's hair a "rich, glossy, refined and orderly appearance." Hair was to be parted on the side, because center parts were considered feminine. Wavy hair was frowned upon for the same reason until well into the 1940s. Waviness was produced by dipping a comb in water or by going to a professional stylist, but only surreptitiously. As for hair length, a nineteenth-century observer of American society concluded that though there wasn't anything specifically unmanly about long hair, its upkeep demanded time and attention "unworthy of a man." Etiquette manuals warned men that publicly fussing with their hair, or even carrying a comb, was "irreconcilable with all nicety of manner."

Disdain for long hair on men has deep roots in American history. In the seventeenth century, the Harvard College Book left students in no doubt about appropriate hair length by designating long hair an abomination "uncivil and unmanly," suitable only for "Ruffians and barbarous Indians." As the United States expanded, a variety of masculinities emerged to displace the Puritan Yankee ideal. Among these were the rough-and-ready frontiersman, the Southern gentleman, and the cowboy, many of whom sported long hair, often accompanied by a beard or mustache. The era of longest hair for American men was from 1840 to 1860; thereafter, the industrialized urban society of the North set a new standard of businesslike sobriety that brought both long hair and facial hair into disfavor. These constraints extended through the first half of the twentieth century, which has been designated by the fashion historian Richard Corson as "the least colorful period in history for men's hair styles." They carried particular weight during the politically and socially conservative 1950s, when any departure from middle-class norms of appearance or behavior was frowned upon. A decade later, changing attitudes, and changing technologies, would revolutionize the way men thought about their hair.[1]

Physical Fitness and Body Shape

Long before the explosion of aerobic exercise and health clubs in the 1970s, American men worried about physical fitness. Before the Civil War, fitness movements recognized the need for exercise but generally subordinated it to diet and sexual restraint. Antebellum fitness was also reflected in Muscular Christianity, a doctrine that originated in England in the early nineteenth century and linked physical perfection to spiritual health and morality. Muscular Christianity was both a religious and a cultural ideal: in a society where urbanization and rapid social change were creating great dislocation, especially for young men, physical exertion could redirect misplaced passions and ensure social order. Exercise gained new urgency as Gilded Age America struggled with the evils of urbanism and sedentary lifestyles. Half the population of the Northeast lived in cities and towns, removed from fresh air and lacking opportunities for exercise. Playgrounds, YMCAs, and organized sports programs aimed to offset the enervating effects of city life. They catered to all classes, but their primary target was the middle class: workers, after all, sweated enough on the job.

Religion and health conjoined to promote fitness as a means of saving America from national and international crisis. Many responded by venturing wholeheartedly into what President Theodore Roosevelt exalted as "the strenuous life," shaping and strengthening their bodies through physical activity and healthful living. At the extreme, physical strength was held up as a duty not only to country but to race, as the American stock appeared in danger of being overwhelmed by waves of immigrants, most of whom enjoyed the "advantage" of doing manual labor instead of white-collar paper pushing.

By the turn of the century, the genteel tedium of gymnastics, introduced in mid-century by German immigrants fleeing the 1848 revolution, had given way to an obsession with sports. College athletics became enormously popular. They were seen as more manly than gymnastics and, in a tough new imperialist world, appropriately aggressive. Athletics not only developed strength and agility but were believed to cultivate sportsmanship and to prepare men for leadership in the business world. Increased leisure time and discretionary income, especially among white-collar workers, made spectator sports accessible to millions of Americans. The display of physical prowess and the athletic body at such events created new models of virility for mass consumption.

American men flirted with bodybuilding and weight lifting at the turn of the century, but muscular self-improvement had much the same rationale as team sports: it was a means, if only symbolic, of asserting national superiority and the ability to resist foreign aggression. Strongmen traveling with carnivals and fairs were pop-ular. Crowds gasped in appreciation of their awesome strength and enjoyed the flexing, posturing, and fake leopard skins as well. It was this element of spectacle that doomed bodybuilding to lower-class status, since few middle-class men could be persuaded to flaunt their near-naked bodies (with or without leopard briefs).

Strength has always been a prized American attribute, thanks to a frontier mythology that lingered long after most of the frontier had been supplanted by industrial smokestacks and crowded cities. Two sports that fitted well with ideals of strength and national power were boxing and weight lifting, but boxing initially had a hopelessly disreputable image because it was so violent. Boxers fought bare-fisted, gouging, biting, and raking each other with fingernails until somebody fell down and couldn't get up. The Marquis of Queensberry, an early patron of English pugilism, cleaned up the sport in 1867 and made it less lethal by requiring gloves and replacing fights to the finish with three-minute rounds. Though it eventually gained sufficient cachet to be taught at Harvard in the guise of "the manly art of self-defense," boxing couldn't entirely shake off its association with brutality or with working-class ruffians. Weight training lacked boxing's aura of violence but was perceived as equally proletarian: hoisting barbells wasn't all that different from manual labor.

Weight lifting preceded bodybuilding and differed from it mainly by emphasizing how much a man could lift, as opposed to how he looked while lifting. "Cosmetic" muscles were sneered at until the irrepressible Prussian-born Eugen Sandow arrived in America via a vaudeville act and began marketing his magnificent muscularity as the ideal of male perfection. Sandow promoted himself through nude photographs until well into his sixties. He got away with this very un-Victorian behavior by striking poses that resembled classic Greek statues, complete with a fig leaf—a ploy that tied self-display to high culture. Sandow emphasized not only how a man looked but how healthy he was: his genius was to transform muscle and strength training into a miracle cure for the ills of a sedentary and stressed male population. More than just staving off debility, Sandow claimed, cultivating a muscular body could heal existing conditions, including declining virility.

Sandow was joined in his aggressive promotion of the benefits of bodybuilding by Bernarr "Body Love" Macfadden, whose magazine *Physical Culture* was the first publication totally devoted to physical development. Macfadden's program for achieving muscular masculinity combined deep breathing, barbell exercises, and regular intake of his breakfast cereal, Strengtho. He even invented a peniscope, a vacuum device designed to enlarge flagging male organs. The middle class couldn't resist role models like these. But as new sources of popular amusement became available, especially ones men and women could enjoy together—bicycling, for example, which soared in popularity at the turn of the century — bodybuilding sank back into comparative oblivion. When Muscle Beach in Santa Monica, California, became a haven for bodybuilders in 1939, the local chamber of commerce wasn't sure whether to be proud or embarrassed. The first Mr. America contest was held that same year and over the next thirty years would draw thousands of spectators, but winners rarely earned more than a thousand dollars for all their hard work and self-cultivation. When Arnold Schwarzenegger took first place in the Mr. Olympia contest in 1976, he won only fifteen hundred dollars.

If attitudes about bodybuilding fluctuated with the times, so did those about body weight. In the mid-nineteenth century, the health reformer Sylvester Graham proclaimed gluttony the greatest threat to both diet and morality in America. Health reformers estimated that there were three million gluttons in the country out of a total population of eighteen million. Gluttony was blamed for causing weakness, dyspepsia, a host of other physical ailments, and the more grievous sins of lust and sexual excess. Only alcoholism represented a threat of similar magnitude—and a considerable amount of alcohol was consumed not to get drunk but to aid digestion of the rivers of grease that Americans took in with each meal. Commenting on the American diet, a visiting Frenchman lamented, "Mon Dieu! What a country! Fifty regions and only one sauce—melted butter."

Vegetarian diets were recommended because they were believed to dampen the flames of passionate excess. Graham, a vocal critic of meat, was an equally vocal proponent of bran; he had absolutely no knowledge of its vitamin and mineral content but was obsessed with bowel regularity and lauded bran's laxative effects. Like other health reformers, he promoted an abstemious and morally upright diet as a means of fashioning a healthy and functional internal body rather than a sleek external one. Ultimately, such diets never took off because vegetarianism couldn't compete with the established preference for meat.

During America's Gilded Age, fat men enjoyed a flurry of popularity: plump bodies were equated with plump wallets, while thinness, in this age of excess, was associated with poverty. Millionaires were depicted with bulging waistcoats, gold watch chains stretched across their ample midriffs, their size reflecting their power. There was even a Fat Man's Club founded in 1866. Extravagance and overindulgence found their highest expression in Diamond Jim Brady, a railroad-equipment salesman whose voracious appetites were paid for by a lavish expense account. For Brady, a typical meal might include three dozen oysters, six crabs, soup, a half-dozen lobsters, two ducks, steak, vegetables, and a platter of desserts, followed by a two-pound box of candy. When he died of stomach trouble at the age of fifty-six, an autopsy showed his stomach to be six times the size of a normal man's. The fat man as positive model didn't survive the nineteenth century. In 1903, the Fat Man's Club went under, and William H. Taft, who weighed 355 pounds when he took office and endured the indignity of getting stuck in the White House bathtub, would be the last fat president.

There were a number of reasons for this abrupt reversal of thinking. A rising tide of resentment against immigration associated fatness with being lower-class and foreign. The poor, especially immigrants, had formerly been viewed as scrawny and ill nourished, but in the 1920s they were seen as stocky and overweight. This was especially true of women from southern and eastern Europe, the areas least favored as sources of immigrants by an increasingly xenophobic native white population. Politics notwithstanding, Americans were also becoming more image-conscious, thanks to the rise of a major new industry.

In the first decade of the century, motion-picture companies began to migrate from the East Coast to California, where weather conditions offered the opportunity for nearly year-round shooting. By the early 1920s, Hollywood was symbolized by movie stars who radiated youth, good health, and sex appeal. In the perpetual California sunshine, bodies were exposed as they had never been on the East Coast. For bodies to look beautiful on film, actors and actresses had to be slim, because cameras automatically added twenty pounds to actual weight. Slimness was also essential for the performance of derring-do like horseback riding, often for repeated takes. As the foremost medium of the early twentieth century, movies played a major role in transmitting ideals of bodily perfection to ordinary Americans.

Of the plethora of manly models, what constituted the ideal body? In 1940, the Harvard psychologist William H. Sheldon tackled this question and came up with three basic body types: the portly endomorph; the middle-of-the-road, muscular meso-morph; and the thinner, more slightly built ectomorph. With no empirical evidence, Sheldon even attached personality traits to his body types. He described the endomorph as warmhearted and convivial but prone to gluttony and laziness. The ectomorph was likely to be intelligent and sensitive but tended toward nervousness and secretiveness. Nearly everything about the mesomorph, however, was positive. These perceptions about body image would prove remarkably enduring: for the rest of the century, men and women asked to attribute personality traits to silhouettes of meso-morphic bodies consistently came up with qualities like strength, masculinity, self-reliance, energy, and youthfulness. Virtually every study of body image still confirms that for women the medium, V-shaped, athletic physique of the mesomorph represents the masculine ideal.[2]

Cosmetic Surgery

It may seem, in view of the publicity given to aesthetic surgery in the past twenty years, and the huge amounts of money Americans are spending on it, that it is a modern phenomenon, but this isn't so. The Vedas, the ancient Indian sacred books of knowledge, describe rhinoplastic and earlobe surgeries performed in 600 B.C. by the eminent brahman Sushruta, designated by modern physicians as the father of plastic surgery. The first historical reference that connects plastic surgery to body image dates to the seventh century, when the great Byzantine surgeon Paul of Aegina targeted gynecomastia, a benign and fairly common enlargement of the male breast. It is an ancient condition: statues of pharaohs in the thirteenth century B.C. have enlarged breasts, and Aristotle commented on gynecomastia. When Paul was approached by a young man who implored him to correct this condition, he agreed: here, he proclaimed, was a true deformity because it made the man look effeminate and as such constituted an assault on his self-esteem.

Of all the strategies for self-beautification that men have adopted, cosmetic surgery is perhaps the most unusual because it has traditionally been considered a female prerogative. For hundreds of years, improving self-image remained secondary to reconstruction necessitated by serious physical problems, but it was never altogether absent from male surgeries. In the mid-sixteenth century, Gaspare Tagliacozzi, a professor of surgery at the University of Bologna, operated on a young Italian nobleman who had lost part of his nose in a duel. A replacement nose made of silver and secured to his face by an elaborate arrangement of threads and strings had proven aesthetically and functionally inadequate. Tagliacozzi's notes on the case leave no doubt that his patient was distressed by the aesthetics of his condition, and the surgical methodology also showed concern for appearance: to avoid facial scarring, Tagliacozzi attached the graft to the patient's arm rather than to his forehead. The operation's success lent legitimacy and prestige to both the surgeon and his specialty; but prestige couldn't protect Tagliacozzi from censure for performing procedures tinged with vanity—on the basis not only of effeminacy but of heresy. After his death, the Church charged him with blasphemy for meddling in God's handiwork and ordered his body exhumed from the Covenant of St. John the Baptist in Bologna and unceremoniously placed in unconsecrated ground.

Religious strictures against altering the body waned as society became more secular, but well into the twentieth century cosmetic procedures for men continued to focus on acute injuries or functional restoration of diseased or damaged body parts. These surgeries often combined reconstructive and aesthetic techniques, since many injuries weren't incapacitating but simply unattractive. But "unattractive" is a relative term and prior to modern times referred not to small imperfections but to serious featural distortions, like missing noses. Until relatively recently, even general surgery had a dark reputation: lack of anesthesia and proper sanitation methods meant it was accompanied by appalling pain and suffering. In dirty hospitals and on contaminated battlefields, blood mingled with bacteria, leaving surgical patients with only a fifty-fifty chance of survival. Under such conditions, few people welcomed even necessary surgery, much less operations for purely cosmetic reasons.

By the late nineteenth century, presentation of the self, especially in urban settings, had become more important. Doctors began to show greater awareness of the mental discomfort caused by unattractive facial features, such as saddle nose. Characterized by a severe depression in the nasal bridge, saddle nose was a common effect of syphilis, which was widespread in the days before penicillin. To correct saddle nose, surgeons experimented with various materials as filler, including precious metals and ivory. One of the most innovative approaches was Dr. Robert Weir's use of a duck breastbone, which he believed would be more functional because of its organic origin. It soon became abscessed, however, and had to be removed. In 1887, Dr. John Roe wrote on the subject of correcting pug noses for cosmetic reasons, and in 1898, Dr. George B. Monks specialized in treating a nasal deformity referred to as "toper's nose," distinguished by broken blood vessels and often associated with excessive drinking. In the late nineteenth century, medical journals were publishing accounts of procedures performed to shorten long noses and eliminate excessive arches to make noses look more attractive.

Doctors defended aesthetic work by citing the mental anguish suffered by the possessors of unattractive features—not only because the features were physically unattractive but because they indicated flawed character, resulting as they did from sexual and alcoholic excess. For men, correcting physical evidence of self-indulgence was related more to displaying character than to beauty. As far back as Aristotle's time, facial features were believed to indicate character or temperament. Bulbous noses, Aristotle informed his students, denoted a swinish temperament, while sharp ones indicated irascibility. Leonardo da Vinci believed that in the nose resided the entire character of the human face. Character was less important for women, although the belief that the shape of one's nose determined temperament influenced prospective suitors. The nineteenth-century "science" of physiognomy categorized noses primarily according to masculine qualities: the Roman nose was believed to indicate executive capability, while the unfortunate snub, or pug, nose suggested weakness. Surgery could also help patients shed evidence of immigrant backgrounds by ameliorating "ethnic" features like the "Semitic" nose.

In 1914, the profession would gain new prestige and techno-logical enhancement from an unexpected and very masculine source—World War I. With its machine guns, aerial bombs, and high-explosive shells, the war opened a new era of devastation: fifty-six million men went into battle, and twenty-six million became casualties. Ninety percent of wounds were caused by shell fire, which drove metal fragments along with mud-soaked pieces of clothing and equipment into bodies—and faces—with ghastly results. Soldiers scrambling out of trenches were at especially high risk of being hit in the face or head. Pressing need for body and facial reconstruction created by these horrors gave tremendous impetus to the development of the plastic surgery profession.

The battlefield had long been a place for developing recon-structive procedures; prior to the eighteenth century, virtually all aspiring surgeons were required to serve in the military to learn their craft. Aesthetics were a secondary consideration: speed was of the essence, and most soldiers who fell in battle died even with immediate surgery. Practicality did play a role, as in the case of the sixteenth-century Paris surgeon Ambroise Paré, who designed inventive prostheses for battle-ravaged soldiers. Among his cre ations were an iron arm made for a French army captain and an array of artificial penises designed for soldiers who had "had their yards cut off close to their bellies." Paré's writings suggest that his phallic creations were valued less for their aesthetics than for allow-ing men to urinate without having to suffer the indignity of sitting down like women.

The sheer number of injuries inflicted in World War I and the proportion involving disfigurement raised surgeons' consciousness about the need to cope not only with orthopedic rehabilitation but also with psychic and aesthetic devastation. The preeminent reconstructive surgeon was Sir Harold Gillies, whose work on mutilated soldiers became legendary. Gillies began his medical career as an ear, nose, and throat specialist before service as a regi-mental medical officer in the Royal Army Medical Corps exposed him to the horrors of the battlefield. Hearing of work being done in Paris on skin- and bone-graft reconstruction, Gillies obtained permission to study this technique. Though the Paris surgeons were relatively unsophisticated—plastic surgery was not an official specialty at the time—Gillies was impressed. When he returned to Britain, he persuaded the influential physician William Arbuthnot Lane to designate him the first specialist in plastic surgery in the British forces. Beyond the few cases he had studied in Paris, Gillies had no knowledge or real experience of plastic surgery, making his contributions all the more extraordinary. His self-proclaimed objective wasn't to create beauty but to restore normalcy in both function and appearance.

Like many surgeons at the time, Gillies was especially concerned about facial injuries, and he convinced the British War Office to send all these casualties to his hospital in southern England, which was devoted solely to cosmetic surgery of the face. In reality, of course, all parts of the body were at risk: writing about the British experience in World War I, the historian Joanna Bourke notes that 60,500 British soldiers were wounded in the head or eyes, 89,000 sustained serious injury to their bodies, and 41,000 needed to have their limbs amputated.

Advances brought about by wartime reconstructive surgery could be readily applied to non-battle injuries and made a significant contribution to general surgery. Use of very fine catgut and silk sutures had by then become a specialty of the plastic surgeon, as had extremely gentle handling of tissues and precise alignment of wound edges—practices distinctly at odds with prevailing standards of battlefield medicine. Improved techniques were especially apparent in orthopedic surgeries; conventional surgery was somewhat haphazard in its approach to amputations, most often concerned with wielding the scalpel quickly to prevent excess bleeding. As surgeons turned their attentions to restoring shattered faces, they paid more attention to details—recognizing, for instance, that when restoring noses, it is essential not only to rebuild the outer structure but to reconstruct interior mucous linings. All these improvements passed into general surgical use after the war and contributed substantially to changing attitudes about plastic surgery. Furthermore, by recording the effects of surgeries on soldiers' morale, Gillies and his fellow practitioners showed that a restored physical appearance carried valuable social, and even economic, benefits.

Men returning from the battlefield needed jobs, which were difficult to find for those who were physically incapacitated or badly disfigured. Yet however grateful they may have been for what wartime surgery did to restore them to normalcy, few men considered taking advantage of the accompanying advances in general cosmetic surgery. Practitioners were addressing this issue and trying to enhance the validity of their specialty as early as the 1930s, when Dr. Jacob Sarnoff suggested that plastic surgery could prevent crime—a subject of interest to Americans in the midst of Prohibition-era gangsterism. Sarnoff believed that people with substantial facial disfigurements were candidates for inferiority complexes that could cause them to withdraw from normal social intercourse, fall in with bad company, and head down a path of crime. But even to other medical practitioners, plastic surgery seemed to have a dubious future, resting primarily on the increased frequency of serious road accidents, as well as on what surgeons condescendingly referred to as female whims. In 1926, Dr. Otto Barnes of Los Angeles linked cosmetic surgery to a collapse of the American character and the "development of a pleasure-loving race in place of the more serious types of the past." Until recently, any surgeon who found men in his waiting room assumed they were either aging actors or, as one Manhattan doctor delicately put it, "gay birds." Though it had become quite sophisticated by the twentieth century, plastic surgery as a profession achieved legitimacy slowly and with difficulty.[3]

The notion that purely aesthetic surgery was only for women was so prevalent that articles published in professional journals like

The Journal of Plastic and Reconstructive Surgery automatically referred to patients as "she." Examples of such gender bias abound; in an article for *Aesthetic Surgery,* the surgeon S. J. Aston began his description of a typical office visit by writing that "the patient arrives and is met in the reception room . . . After filling out her medical history form, the patient is given a complete information sheet." Describing a new "mini-lift" procedure in 1971, doctors cautioned the media against overly optimistic reports about the operation's success because the prospective patient was often "extremely gullible, looking for a quick fix for improving her aging face." A particularly lyrical example of gender bias is offered by one surgeon who described a typical patient for blepharoplasty (eyelid surgery) in verse:

> *Resolute and committed, we stand at the head*
> *While the patient lies there on the surgical bed,*
> *She looks rather calm, disguising her dread . . .*

Of all cosmetic surgery procedures, the one most purely dedicated to erasing signs of age is the rhytidectomy, or face-lift. Though widely accepted and freely discussed in Europe at the turn of the nineteenth century, face-lifting was slow to gain acceptance in America. When Dr. Earl Calvin Padgett wrote his 1948 textbook on the profession and practice of plastic surgery, he devoted less than three pages out of a total of one thousand to face-lifting. But as the face became an advertisement for its owner's attributes—and age—face-lifting would gain in popularity among men.

The correlation between sagging faces and sagging incomes was tied not only to workplace competition but to fundamental occupational shifts. Jobs in which looks were largely unimportant, like farming or assembly-line work, declined precipitously in the twentieth century, while white-collar jobs that placed a greater emphasis on personal appearance and presentation of the self became more numerous. At mid-century, white-collar employees outnumbered blue-collar workers for the first time.

"Lifting" the face is a process of surgically removing superfluous skin to create a firm, youthful appearance. Early face-lift operations cut a small piece of skin from in front of the ears, then pulled the face back. Although this procedure enjoyed a flurry of popularity, its effects lasted only a few weeks. The skin was simply sutured without undermining—that is, separating it from the underlying musculature and fat. If this separation isn't done, the weight of these understructures drags the skin back down. Early operations could therefore more accurately be called "skin-lifts" than "face-lifts."

Face-lift technology radically improved in the twentieth century with the development of a single long, continuous incision from the temporal region of the head to under the earlobe. This procedure allows the face to be lifted off its underlying musculature while the surgeon uses retractors to hold the fragile skin away from its bloody underpinnings. Extreme delicacy is required, and blood supply to the skin is critical. If too thin a layer of skin is pulled away, blood supply will be jeopardized. If too much is taken, underlying nerves and muscles can be irretrievably damaged. Excess fat is then trimmed and reshaped, key muscles are given a final tightening, the new underface is sewn up with self-absorbing stitches, and, finally, the external face is redraped over its foundation.

Well into the postwar period, face-lifting was regarded as a female surgery, and male requests for it were viewed with caution. A 1957 article on face-lifting in *Good Housekeeping* compared the doctor to a dressmaker and the patient to a wool jersey dress whose seams had stretched. Such an analogy wouldn't have made much sense to the average man, but any woman was expected to understand it completely (although the suggestion that a face-lift was no more complicated than opening a few seams and pulling the fabric back into place represents medical understatement at its best). The feminization of cosmetic surgery was understandable, commiserated one of its prominent practitioners, since women were "deprived of the many sources of gratification available to men in terms of achievement" and therefore reliant on "us[ing] and valu[ing] their bodies . . . to please themselves and others."[4]

Sexual Dysfunction

Well into the 1960s, women bore most of the responsibility for sexual dysfunction. Impotence, though recognized, was almost always regarded as being the "fault" of women.

The term "impotence" refers to several, often related conditions. Its two primary forms are premature ejaculation and erectile failure, the latter defined as either inability to achieve an erection or inability to maintain it until orgasm. Of the two forms of impotence, premature ejaculation is more subjective, centering on the ability to control the timing of ejaculation. This subjectivity makes the definition of "impotence" more complex; for much of history, having an erection was proof of virility, and its duration was of little importance. In postwar America, Dr. Alfred Kinsey determined that as many as three-fourths of all men reached orgasm within two minutes of beginning sexual relations, a fact he didn't regard as problematic, although many women might. Worse yet, Kinsey observed that for many men climax was reached within ten or twenty seconds after penetration. In comparison to other primates, however, the average human male looks good: male gorillas last about a minute, while chimpanzees clock in at about eight seconds. As a zoologist, Kinsey pragmatically viewed quick ejaculation as a positive trait for mammalian survival because it enabled the male to service larger numbers of female partners more quickly. It would be difficult, he concluded, "to find another situation in which an individual who was quick and intense in his responses was labeled anything but superior."

In cultures where impregnation was the main objective of sexual activity, failure to satisfy the female was given little importance. In modern America, however, the penile property most in demand (next to size) is endurance. This has been an ideal at odds with reality for many men. In the early twentieth century, as Sigmund Freud and the study of sexuality focused greater attention on human desire and sexual fulfillment, sexologists advised that women needed a minimum of twenty minutes of sexual activity to become fully aroused. The revelation was not a pleasant one for many men. Today, an estimated one-third of American men suffer from inability to control ejaculation. Even more devastating is complete erectile failure. From earliest childhood, the connection between having an erection and being a man is hammered into boys. The penis is the heart of the male sexual being, and the sexual penis is by definition erect. Masculinity and potency are inseparable, making the term "impotent man" a terrible contradiction in terms.

Impotence isn't a modern phenomenon, and explanations for its origin have varied over the centuries. Though many ancient peoples (and, more recently, colonial Americans) blamed erectile failure on divine curse, medieval Europeans attributed impotence to witchcraft. It was believed to be brought about by a magical process in which knots were tied in threads or leather strips, which were then secreted away. The number of knots determined whether a victim was rendered partially or totally impotent, or even sterile. A man could be cured only if the knots were discovered and untied or if the witch was forced to retract her spell, often by violent means.

Virtually every culture and era searched for aphrodisiacs, ransacking entire continents for spices believed to increase potency like cloves and cinnamon. In the sixteenth century, French and Spanish explorers plundered the New World in search of chocolate as well as gold. The quest continues today despite expert consensus that no true aphrodisiac exists.

In early America, the understanding of impotence was undermined by its being viewed as a fertility problem, similar to barrenness in women. This confusion explains why George Washington, because he wasn't impotent, considered himself fertile—even though he failed to produce any offspring with his wife, Martha, who had four children from a previous marriage. In view of the emphasis on procreation over sexual pleasure, this misunderstanding isn't surprising. Influenced by the religious tenor of colonial society, people understood impotence as a "mysterious interference of heaven" rather than a treatable malady.

In the nineteenth century, with the separation of reproduction and sexuality, impotence was identified as a male sexual disorder—and a moral problem. In conjunction with fears about over-civilization and the sapping effects of city life, gaining control over the body became a central theme of American masculinity. In a world that seemed out of control as it lurched into its industrial future, self-control became essential. These concerns paralleled a general shift away from the spiritual and toward the physical and were buffered by Darwinism, a scientific theory that was often manipulated to fit social parameters as well as biological ones. In the view of social Darwinists, some humans, just like the birds and reptiles of the Galápagos Islands, stop evolving; they remain uncivilized and incapable of proper behavioral and moral restraint, especially sexually. Lower-class white men and all black men were particularly susceptible, while the middle-class white male was held up as a model of decorum and self-control. Unfortunately, this paragon of evolutionary perfection was also more prone to ailments to which the lower orders were largely immune—like impotence.

In trying to understand impotence, people paid particular attention to masturbation, considered not only depraved but dangerously enervating to the already-threatened modern male. The health reformer and cereal czar John Harvey Kellogg, a fanatic foe of self-abuse, recommended remedies for this most emasculating of vices that ranged from bandaging the genitals to suturing the foreskin to prevent erection. Self-help books offered "true" stories about the perils of masturbation; a favorite chronicled the decline and fall of a university professor who so enfeebled himself that he ended his days cleaning hotel toilets. Impotence was also linked to promiscuity, which was heavily frowned upon by upstanding Victorians, and as a preventive measure health experts advised extreme moderation in sexual relations—in some cases, a maximum of one encounter per month.

By the turn of the century, psychoanalysis identified sexual dysfunction as the result of "intrapsychic conflict rooted in infantile or childhood experience." Freudian emphasis on the importance of expression over inhibition led to the belief that restraint, rather than passion, should be blamed for impotence. Masturbation was exonerated; in the new light shed by Freud, impotence could be blamed on castration anxiety, unconscious homosexuality—or fear of women.

Victorian women were viewed as sexually passive. Female sexual desire was perceived as a dangerous aberration, posing a threat to the solidity of civilization. White middle-class women were expected to be modest and restrained, "awaiting the awakening of desire in response to the approaches of men." As Americans moved away from Victorian strictures and toward a more open erotic life, recognition of female desire led to greater interest in female sexuality, which in turn led to an increased emphasis on female sexual pleasure within marriage.

This change was influenced not only by Freud but also by the youth culture that emerged in the 1920s. Prosperity stimulated by the industrial revolution contributed to the formation of a large middle class, for whom higher education became important. Young people stayed in school longer and formed a peer-related culture in college centered on fashion, leisure, and dating, quite distinct from the more conservative social ethos of their parents. The greater freedom, combined with mass entertainment and the automobile, which offered new opportunities for privacy, intensified the sexualization of American society. At the same time, the trend toward smaller families, well under way in the white middle class, contributed to a new concept of male-female relations known as the companionate marriage. Instead of worrying about exhausting their vigor by expending too much sperm, men turned their attentions to the mutual pleasures of the bedroom. Well into mid-century, however, mutual pleasure was often hampered by what was regarded as the major sexual "problem" of America, frigidity.

In 1912, Dr. William Robinson, chief of genitourinary surgery at Bronx Hospital and author of more than a dozen books on sexual matters, coined the term "frigidity." Robinson placed the blame for male sexual dysfunction squarely on women, whose unresponsiveness failed to "call out [male] virility." Women's "virginal reserve," he cautioned, might initially be attractive to men but should quickly be abandoned in the interests of a more forthright marital relationship. This may have been wise advice, but it wouldn't prove easy to do away with long-standing ideals of demure female behavior. A great gulf existed between the premarital experience of men and women, leaving the latter heavily dependent on the former for sexual enlightenment.

To close the gulf, an abundance of marriage manuals offered advice; but the persistence of a double standard that insisted on female chastity while celebrating male proficiency proved a major stumbling block. Ideals of mutual satisfaction notwithstanding, lovemaking texts were almost exclusively addressed to men, who were charged with the role of instructors in the art of "joyous mating." Typical was Dr. Theodore van de Velde's best-seller *Ideal Marriage*: first published in 1926, the book sold over a million copies and was still widely read in the 1950s. Van de Velde decreed that women needed to have orgasms—not for pleasure but for health reasons. Orgasm relieved "congestion" produced by intercourse, which if left unresolved would lead to a host of gynecological problems. The husband was assigned the responsibility of averting these potential medical difficulties; wives were simply passive recipients.

As couples scrambled to adapt to the new standards, the penalty for failure was to be labeled frigid. By the 1920s, the sex expert

Wilhelm Stekel declared that as many as half of all American women were frigid, especially those of the "higher cultural levels." Frigidity, in keeping with the contemporary enthusiasm for psychological interpretations of behavior, was defined as a neurosis that prevented a woman from experiencing vaginal orgasm during intercourse. While the impotent male was regarded as wanting sex but unable to perform, the frigid woman was totally lacking desire, turning her back on sex and, by extension, her husband. Sexual passivity, so desirable in the Victorian woman, had become a threat to the post-Victorian male. As women were invested with more responsibility for men's sexual performance, they would also carry more blame for men's failures.

Prior to the twentieth century, the term most commonly used to describe a man physically was "manly." For most of American history, the very handsome man was likely to be seen as defective, his good looks undermining his masculinity. If the woman who was careless about her looks seemed to lack femininity, the man who cared too much about his was putting his masculinity at risk. Since World War II, a great change has taken place. According to the anthropologist Geoffrey Gorer, the body has become "a palpable symbol of its owner's relative position in the competition of life." The pressure to look good is no longer put only on women. For the American middle-class man, too, the body is an icon of personal achievement and an unambiguous statement about where he stands in the competitive game of modern life.[5]

2

THE ORGANIZATION MAN

MEN IN THE 1950s

A woman carries a vanity case and a man carries a briefcase.
—*Saturday Evening Post,* 1954

Open the pages of nearly any contemporary women's magazine, and you're likely to find an article about what women notice or admire about men's bodies. Women confess to yearning for "sweetly curving" buttocks, washboard stomachs, and virile chests. One confesses to a weakness for sensuous mouths, and another admires the articulation of rippling deltoids. The way men's bodies look is associated with sex appeal, virility, and potential ability to please a woman. And women don't limit their observations to positive commentary; male bodies that fail to measure up are derided.

Forthright discussion of male bodies would have been startling, if not appalling, to women in the 1950s. The difference is evident in a 1951 *Ladies' Home Journal* article, "What Women First Notice about Men." Respondents rhapsodized about self-possession, neatness, and well-kept hands. Men's eyes aroused considerable discussion, less because they were sultry or long-lashed than because of what they suggested about character. Physical features said less about sex appeal than about a sense of purposefulness and good grooming, and women's attitudes said less about what women wanted in a man's body than about what they wanted in a man.

According to Katherine Orr, the publisher of the Harlequin romance novel series, what women really wanted in the 1950s was the alpha man. The traits associated with this paragon were expressed through adjectives like "strong," "imposing," and "brooding." Doctors were prototypical examples of masculinity because they were "mysterious . . . [and] under a lot of pressure"—hence, brooding. And, Orr adds, alpha men were "always wealthy." Of course, she is talking about fictional romantic heroes, but they reflect the value system of their times. The hallmarks of the alpha man and postwar masculinity haven't been entirely displaced, but they carried a lot more weight a half century ago. Men, then and now, pursue what gives them power. In the 1950s, being a good provider was often enough and made it less likely that anyone would be concerned about a man's other attributes. The power inherent in the breadwinner role was reinforced because few women could hope to challenge men in the workplace.

A white middle-class man who pursued a middle-of-the-road course of education, work, and familial responsibility was assured a relatively predictable path to success. Rapid economic growth was the keystone of postwar American prosperity: between 1945 and 1960, the number of businesses increased sevenfold, and the gross national product and average family income more than doubled. Amid this national affluence, the identity of the American male was tightly bound up with his job, and it was here that his appearance mattered most. The paradigmatic postwar workplace was the corporation, and for the corporation man, work was more than just a means of earning a living: it was a way of life.[1]

The Organization Man

The corporate workplace, molded by the rise of massive trusts, was well on its way to becoming bureaucratized at the beginning of the twentieth century, and the white-collar worker was quickly becoming as much a victim of workplace routinization and anonymity as the factory laborer. With the enormous expansion of postwar industry and government, the modern-day corporation had come into its own by the 1950s. Alfred P. Sloan, the chief executive of General Motors, worshipfully described the corporation as a "pyramid of opportunities" for advancement and success; less enthusiastic observers compared corporate culture, with its dense hierarchical layers and rigid chain of command, to the army. This analogy contained more than a kernel of truth: corporate recruiters tended to be impressed by military service on an applicant's résumé because it suggested he'd been conditioned to work within a hierarchy. Men even wore uniforms: the man in the gray flannel suit, immortalized in Sloan Wilson's best-selling novel, stands as the prototypical male image of the decade.

The self-made single proprietor had nearly vanished by the turn of the century. In 1800, four out of five American men had been self-employed, but this proportion had fallen to one in three by 1870 and continued to drop throughout the twentieth century. In the mid-1950s, a study of executive career patterns revealed that only one in ten men in executive corporate positions had run their own businesses before becoming company men.

Big business, not government, invented bureaucracy. In 1870, white-collar office workers represented only 1 percent of the total American workforce. By 1950, the ranks of white collar workers—clerks, salespeople, managers, and professionals—had grown to 37 percent. Supervision and organization of the burgeoning numbers of white-collar employees required a vast expansion in the ranks of management. Within the corporate bureaucracy, the most notable growth came in what was called middle management, described by the historian Olivier Zunz as being "neither powerful nor powerless, rich or poor"—but decidedly middle-class. Many middle managers were recruited from the supervisory levels of the working class. Several of the tasks and responsibilities once allocated to skilled workers became functions of management and a new army of technicians, shifting traditionally blue-collar work into the swelling white-collar ranks and contributing to the expansion of the middle class after World War II.

The surge of technology during the war also contributed to changes in the postwar workplace. As physical work was replaced with brain work, interpersonal dealings were suddenly crucial. Cooperation replaced independence, and administrative skills became as important as entrepreneurialism. The fate of the white-collar employee depended on his ability to please others, forcing him to develop a whole new social character in which his personality and appearance mattered most. When fifty of America's top business leaders were asked in 1947 to share the secrets of their success, their answers included traits like enthusiasm, confidence, and tolerance—not moral integrity and initiative, which would formerly have been considered essential. These vague qualities were quintessentially white-collar: for factory workers, they would have had little practical application.

The elevation of personality over accomplishment would have confusing implications for masculinity. White-collar office work was demasculinizing in its retreat from the physical to the sedentary. Physical strength was suddenly irrelevant. Though the 1950s have been roundly criticized for relegating women to domesticity, men, too, were rigidly cast into roles—as breadwinners, workaholics, and cogs in organizational wheels. But if the type of work men were doing wasn't ideal for expressing masculinity, work itself continued to be. Only under the most exceptional circumstances could any man be self-respecting or enjoy the respect of others if he didn't have a job.

If it was clear how middle-class men were supposed to behave, it was equally clear how they were supposed to look. Physical appearance was centered less on physical attributes than on what the social critic Vance Packard called a "successful package." In *The Pyramid Climbers,* his best-seller about the mad scramble up the corporate career ladder, Packard stressed the importance of having The Right Look—but what was this look exactly? Here he became vague; his parameters applied more to the creation of an impression than to precise physical qualities. For example, he suggested that executives should look like "symbolic fathers." What he did not say is that they must look unlined, fresh, and young. Men weren't expected to *be* in the executive suite unless they had acquired experience—and, in the process, a few wrinkles.

Amid these murky notions about physical appearance, men did receive a few clear signals. Height was desirable because it conveyed dominance; Packard suggested that the "well-packaged executive" should be tall because size commands attention. Politicians in particular have always benefited from height; until 1968, every president elected in the twentieth century was the taller of the candidates. The advantages of height weren't limited to politics and the executive suite: most women want a man at least 6 inches taller than they are, and nearly all want one at least 4 inches taller (the average American man is 5.4 inches taller than the average woman). Some of the less lofty creatively obtained their desired height by wearing elevator shoes, ordered from the back pages of *Playboy* or *Esquire*.

Strong facial features were the ideal complement to a full frame and gave an additional professional edge. A personnel tactic called the Merton System of Face-Reading enjoyed some popularity in the 1950s. Based on 108 facial "check-points," the Merton method presumably selected good staff men by the angularity of their faces. But still, the most common parameter for determining access to the executive suite was perfectly natural given the tenor of the times: being clean-cut and looking like the fellow next door—who was assumed to be white, Anglo-Saxon, and altogether average.[2]

Toupees and Crew Cuts: Men's Hair in the 1950s

When Elvis Presley applied for a job as an electrician's apprentice before his musical career took off, the employment office warned prospective interviewers that they might find his appearance off-putting—not only because of the length of his hair but because he clearly spent so much time arranging it. Not only would Elvis shock America with his pelvic gyrations, adopt black music stylings, and wear flamboyant "Negro" clothing, he would blur the physical distinctions between men and women with hair that demanded a complicated regimen of fussing and combing. He even had his coif styled in a beauty parlor instead of a barbershop.

An inappropriate hairstyle wasn't just feminizing or a rejection of standards; it could transform the most wholesome young man into a potential threat to the social order. Ricky Nelson, of *Ozzie and Harriet* fame, was the quintessential boy next door as a preadolescent but evolved into a greaser when he entered his teens. He achieved this status mainly for the way he styled his hair: divided into eight parts, topped with an imposing crest that fell over his forehead, and larded with brilliantine. Even if they didn't seem threatening, men who wore their hair too long and lavished too much attention on it couldn't be taken seriously—as in the case of Edd "Kookie" Byrnes, whose inseparability from his comb made him a television star but also an object of amusement, clearly distinct from men who had more important things to worry about than their hair.

The dreary state of male hairstyling and fashion in the 1950s was a continuation of the trend set in motion after the Civil War, when Gilded Age businessmen weren't expected to have time for the frivolity of excessive grooming. The unmanliness of long hair was intensified by a general retreat after World War II to the rigidly separated gender spheres typical of the Victorian age. The definitive male hairstyle of the decade was the crew cut, which had strong masculine roots in the war. To eliminate lice, the army required soldiers to keep their hair trimmed to no more than an inch, and after the war men brought the style home and made it the American norm. Whether or not it could be considered attractive—one fashion arbiter dismissed it as suitable only for convicts—the crew cut, like the gray flannel suit, proclaimed its wearers members in good standing of a respectable middle-class majority.[3]

Aside from negotiating the aesthetics of the crew cut, men confronted the distinct possibility of going bald. Serious research into hair health began in the late nineteenth century and made its greatest advances in understanding scalp hygiene. The demise of wig wearing and the greater availability of hot water and soap made major inroads against bacteria, lice, and dirt, all of which were harmful to the scalp. Researchers found that unhealthy scalps could cause some forms of baldness and developed effective treatments for many disorders, including dandruff. A postwar explosion of personal care items disseminated these discoveries, brightly packaged and heavily advertised, into millions of American homes. Curing dandruff, of course, is one thing; curing baldness is quite another.

The only viable solution to baldness was a hairpiece, but wearing one aroused ambivalence. Like applying cosmetics, putting on a toupee was seen as a deliberate effort to improve appearances. Hairpiece technology wasn't well enough advanced to ensure undetectability, so men who wore toupees were advertising their vanity. The toupee maker Herb Yerman remembers that men were often late to appointments because they would walk around the block wrestling with the decision of buying a hairpiece.

Toupees, unflatteringly referred to as "divots," "rugs," and "wall-to-wall carpeting," depending on how much area they covered, not only were stigmatized for their narcissistic implications but posed a multitude of problems, including cost, inconvenience, and upkeep; moths were the deadliest of a host of enemies. Men worried about whether they would be ridiculed if a toupee came off at an inauspicious moment and about whether it would look natural. On both counts, they had good reason to worry: humorists found inexhaustible material in visions of toupees floating away in swimming pools or skimming across city streets in high winds, and as for naturalness, most hairpieces were so detectable that they drew attention to baldness instead of disguising it.

Hairpieces got a boost with the arrival of television. Unforgiving studio lights highlighted the glare of bald heads, sending news commentators and actors scrambling to toupee makers. The number of TV and film personalities known to be toupee wearers (an estimated one out of ten actors over thirty-five wore a hairpiece of some kind by mid-decade) helped spur the acceptance of hairpieces, but manufacturers continued to approach ordinary men with caution. When Sears, Roebuck and Company launched a promotional campaign for its toupees, it shrewdly linked the wearing of "career-winning" hairpieces with professional success to help potential clients overcome worries about appearing vain. Clients sent Sears measurements and pencil outlines of their bald areas for custom-made toupees. This "hair-mail" campaign was a hit: "We've put across the idea," claimed a delighted Sears representative, "that a man is not completely dressed without hair." Clever marketing transformed the hairpiece from an embarrassment into an adjunct to dressing for success.

Baldness could be a liability in the work world. Sales executives confirmed that bald men were less likely to get past front-desk receptionists. Bald salesman were also less successful when dealing with the public: the sales director of a major appliance company discovered that between two home demonstrators, equal in intelligence, personality, and general physique, the man with hair invariably sold more products, and so he provided his bald salesmen with toupees. Yet despite heartwarming testimonials like the story of the businessman who sobbed with joy as he left the toupee maker, doubts about hairpieces lingered.

Negative attitudes were reflected in the advertising of two major American men's magazines, *Playboy* and *Esquire*. Even after overcoming advertisers' initial skepticism about the appropriateness of *Playboy* as a marketplace, the magazine refused to advertise any products that would intrude on the euphoric illusion it created of a wonderland where gorgeous naked women frolicked with handsome, successful men. Some ads for hair-grooming products were allowed, like contour waxes for crew cuts and Vaseline hair tonic. These, however, were intended to improve something that was already all right, not to fix something that was radically wrong. Hugh Hefner didn't want readers to open his magazine and find ads reminding them they were losing their hair. In *Esquire,* ads for "Instant Hair" wigs and "undetectable hair filler" were relegated to back pages and sandwiched between equally small ads for elevator shoes and hat-shaped hangover ice-bags. These shameful products, and information about them, were mailed in plain brown envelopes.

As much as they may have shrunk from addressing the reality of losing their hair, more than 350,000 American men were wearing toupees by the end of the 1950s. Manufacturers had persuaded many men that opting for artifice was all right, as long as it was connected with getting ahead on the job. With more stylish and less detectable products to choose from, the demographic composition of toupee wearers shifted toward much younger men, attracted by new no-part models that looked more natural. One of the largest makers of hairpieces targeted every conceivable potential buyer: men with thinning hair, men with no hair, graying older men who wanted to look younger, and even G.I.'s trying to disguise regulation haircuts while off duty. Ads for Lancelot toupees slyly reminded stubborn holdouts that scientists had debunked the myth of baldness as an indicator of virility. Toupees were even designed for corpses.[4]

As for sex appeal, women preferred men with full heads of hair. But most men were comfortably married before their hair began to fall out, and dependent wives were unlikely to leave their husbands on the basis of receding hairlines. Marriage and family life fostered complacency, allowing men to accept signs of aging and physical shortcomings without undue panic. But by mid-decade, the male body had come under scrutiny for an altogether new reason that had little to do with vanity but a great deal to do with health.

Digging His Grave with His Teeth: The Overweight Executive

In 1953, *Time* magazine announced that America was becoming a nation of fat people. Nearly half of women and one-quarter of men were categorized as overweight. Despite these alarming statistics, men tended to be complacent about excess weight. Their complacence, however, was about to be dealt a heavy blow by a new guru of health and diet.

Though insurance companies had long warned of the health risks associated with excess weight, little attention was paid until Dr. Louis Dublin, the head statistician for the Metropolitan Life Insurance Company, addressed the American Medical Association in 1951. Armed with charts, graphs, and pithy catchphrases like "We are digging our graves with our teeth," Dublin painted a grim portrait of the potentially fatal consequences of obesity. He was addressing the health of all Americans but targeting men because of their greater propensity for coronary disease, which was directly related to being overweight. Extremely obese men, according to Dublin's statistics, had a 70 percent greater mortality rate than men of average weight, and even those who were only moderately overweight were nearly twice as likely to drop dead.

Dublin accompanied his warnings with charts listing ideal weights for men and women with medium frames. His innovation was to focus on "ideal" rather than "average" weight, thereby greatly increasing the number of Americans categorized as too fat. Because Dublin defined overweight as 10 percent higher and obesity as 20 to 30 percent higher than the ideal, America was suddenly wallowing in an epidemic of obesity. A year after Dublin dropped his bombshell, the National Institutes of Health proclaimed obesity the primary nutrition problem in the country, taking that distinction away from vitamin-deficiency diseases. These widely publicized findings caused potential employers to cast a jaundiced eye on fat men.

Companies began to issue warnings to employees, especially those at the management level, if they were becoming unacceptably plump, as in the case of a major corporation that sent a top executive for a thirteen-week management program and advised him to use the time to lose thirty pounds. To preserve the health and lives of valued executives, lunchrooms served lighter meals, and many companies devised expensive in-house programs offering everything from annual physical examinations to cardiac workouts.

Some of the prejudice against excess weight stemmed from legitimate concerns about potential health problems. Companies weren't anxious to hire obvious candidates for lost work time and diminished performance. But fat also implied a lack of character and self-control fatal to a businessman's image. When a national news magazine designated the beer belly as "the kiss of death to any man who seriously wants to get ahead in his career," it was referring not to literal death but to how men with flabby bodies projected a lack of accountability. Companies who already had overweight employees began designing programs to help them shed pounds, based on the philosophy that for every dead executive it cost double his annual salary to train a replacement. An additional benefit, of course, was that expense accounts shrank dramatically as businessmen downed Metrecal, the preeminent dietary supplement of the era, instead of Scotch and steaks. Some companies even offered cash bonuses for executives who achieved weight-loss goals by a specified deadline.

To get their bodies into shape and shed deadly excess pounds, why didn't men exercise? At their most extreme, companies allowed executives to mix business, pleasure, and good health by sending them off to costly watering holes like Rancho La Puerta in Mexico and the Golden Door Spa in California, which offered a Man's Week program tailored to overworked executives. But these were centers for socializing and relaxing, not for serious exertion. The Golden Door's philosophy was clearly articulated by its founder, Hungarian-born Edward Szekely, who considered exercise "very boresome" and claimed that every time he felt impelled to exercise, "I lie down and wait for the urge to pass." The spa, in other words, wasn't about dieting or working out but about being pampered and restored to health and vigor without effort. Physical fitness was supposed to be fun, not drudgery. Dressed in fashionable gray sweats, men took leisurely walks on country roads; and every morning, before heading for the tanning machines, they held group discussions about health in heated pools while wrapped in herbal dressings. The most notable feature of the Golden Door's menu was that executives were served their meals in bed.[5]

Exercise was more than boring: it was hard work. Postwar America was the first society in the history of the world to become so materially advanced that human beings no longer needed to expend much physical effort to survive comfortably.

But exercise was only part of what was necessary to lose weight; men were also told they had to abandon their meat and potatoes. Despite the concern aroused by findings about fatty diets and excessive cholesterol, however, few guidelines were developed on what to eat. Businessmen were advised to space predinner highballs at least forty-five minutes apart, limit after-dinner drinking, and have wine with meals—not because wine had any nutritional value but because a table set with wineglasses was pleasing to the eye and therefore good for digestion. Another suggestion: men whose weight was above average (not, as Dublin's charts had stressed, above ideal) should lose one pound per year until they retired.

And who was responsible for overseeing the new dietary regimens? The wives. Dublin, citing the example of an overweight husband who toppled to his death from a roof while making repairs, blamed the wife who had failed to keep him slim. Prior to the alarm generated by Dublin's warnings, women had focused dieting on themselves, while serving their husbands hearty meals. The message had been clear: women always had to be at least thinking about being on a diet, if not actually on one, while men were free to eat as they chose—indeed, should be indulged at the dinner table (although, in extreme cases, it was advisable to remove the gravy boat surreptitiously after one helping).

With the awful revelations of the association between fatty diets and male mortality, women were besieged with advice on "the care and feeding of business executives" and, for those whose husbands might not be executives, "how to keep a husband alive." A conscientious wife could accomplish these things by proper feeding and by making sure her husband got his daily exercise—for example, a stroll to the train station. Because being told what to eat could be stressful to men, wives were cautioned to avoid unpleasant scenes by trimming objectionable fat from meat before it reached the table. Above all, a wife should not disrupt the dinner hour by burdening her husband with her problems, at least not until he had had time to relax with a drink.

To help women keep husbands healthy, though not necessarily slim, women's magazines rallied with an avalanche of recipes and menus. Advice was often questionable, like the eat-all-you-want diet for men that recommended three servings of meat, plenty of fat, and a half-hour prebreakfast walk every day. Even Dublin, while placing strict taboos on carbohydrates, advised wives to ply their husbands with steaks and chops. If such a meat-heavy diet imposed a financial hardship, then hearty doses of eggs and cheese could be served as alternatives.

The inability of physicians or anyone else to provide rational advice about what, and how much, men should eat starkly contrasted with the plethora of diet-oriented magazine articles directed at women. A few important exceptions to female-centered diet advice, however, did appear. In 1951, Elmer Wheeler, a forty-seven-year-old salesman who weighed 234 pounds before embarking on a weight-loss program, published a successful diet book for men, *The Fat Boy's Book*. Wheeler included generous allowances for alcoholic beverages as long as they weren't made with high-proof liquor and a system of balancing caloric intake over three-day periods to allow restitution for bursts of overindulgence. The most innovative aspect of the Fat Boy diet was its Slide Rule for Reducing, a pocket-size chart listing the caloric content of popular foods. The technical overtones of this "scientific" device helped assuage male resistance to dieting. Men may have found the diet tips amusing, but there is little evidence that Wheeler's slide-rule techniques did much for weight loss.

A more dubious entry into the male weight-loss arena was the Drinking Man's Diet. Created by Robert Cameron, a San Francisco bar-accessories salesman, it was supposedly derived from the Air Force Academy's high-protein diet, a claim loudly denied by the Air Force, which stressed that alcohol was not part of cadets' regular diet. At the heart of the Drinking Man's Diet was the proviso that no more than sixty grams (about two ounces) of carbohydrates could be consumed daily. Since alcohol wasn't a carbohydrate, generous amounts were permissible. Calories from alcohol somehow didn't count; they would mysteriously be absorbed by the body.

The appeal of the Drinking Man's Diet was its masculinity. Here was a manly path to weight loss, unfettered by leafy vegetables and artfully arranged tomato slices. A typical meal began with two martinis served with pâté, proceeded to a steak with all the trimmings, accompanied by two glasses of dry wine, and concluded with brandy for dessert. Aside from avoiding unwanted calories, executive bons vivants would benefit from alcohol's relaxing qualities. Cameron's book had a brief but lucrative popularity. It also aroused the fury of physicians, who warned that any man who resorted to the Drinking Man's Diet would end up not only fat but drunk.

In addition to alcohol, other questionable substances were promoted as dietary aids, including amphetamines like Dexedrine and Benzedrine. Amphetamines came into medical use in the 1930s to treat depression but were soon found to suppress the appetite. Though these "mother's little helpers" have most often been associated with bored housewives, who in fact were gulping them down in prodigious quantities by the late 1950s, men weren't immune to their lure—primarily because they were the most masculine reducing aids in the drug pharmacopoeia. They promised not only to suppress appetite but to make men alert and energetic. Even their side effects, sleeplessness and overstimulation, suggested action.

Many men first encountered the drugs during World War II. The U.S. Army didn't legitimize issuance of amphetamines to servicemen until the Korean War, but Benzedrine was handed out to Army Air Corps fighter pilots to keep them alert and combat-ready. U.S. medics gave the drugs to anyone who wanted them, to the tune of an estimated 180 million tablets over the course of the war. Small wonder, then, that returning soldiers embraced amphetamines as dietary aids. By the 1970s, they had become the drug of choice in obesity treatment, prescribed by an astonishing 92 percent of doctors, despite warnings that they were potentially more dangerous and addictive than heroin. Patients became both physically and emotionally dependent on them, and amphetamines proved effective as appetite suppressants for only three to four weeks, after which time dosage had to be increased to maintain effectiveness. Once they stopped taking the drug, users generally gained back all of the weight lost.

Unfortunately, diets based on alcohol or pills, manly though they may have been, weren't very effective and left many men wrestling with spreading girths. At the end of the 1950s, and well into the next decade, many successful men were still overweight (although their wives rarely were, and few successful career women were carrying extra pounds). Confronted by facts about the dangers of excess weight, it seems baffling that men would be so intransigent. If they took any action at all, overweight men were most likely to "cut back." For many, "leaving a little on the plate" passed for serious dieting. People did believe that being overweight shortened life; the problem was they didn't believe it shortened life very much. "Most people think it shortens life by maybe five minutes," concluded research conducted by the company that manufactured Metrecal.

Men trying to lose weight were dealing with issues deeply rooted in the male psyche. Many admitted to fears that weight loss could lead to loss of strength and a decline in virility. If it were possible to convince them that being lean led to increased sexual potency, dieting could have been made infinitely more popular. But most seemed to make precisely the opposite connection, equating leanness with illness, weakness, and even asceticism.[6]

Regulating food intake to control weight was considered more natural to women, who were expected to be lighter eaters than men for reasons of feminine politesse (and because they were smaller). For women, food was an implacable enemy against which they had to be eternally vigilant, while for men, gobbling down half a chocolate cake at one sitting was nothing more than a display of robust masculinity. Dieting was a full-fledged pastime for millions of American women, but with social and psychological currents running so strongly against male dieting, it's not hard to see why men resisted counting calories.

By mid-decade, men had a new excuse for not dieting. Heart disease, scarcely remarked on in the 1920s, had risen to levels described by physicians as epidemic, and statistically men were three times as likely as women to become victims. Though cholesterol was identified as the official cause, doctors also blamed lifestyle—specifically, the lifestyle of the overworked, overstressed male executive.

In 1956, the Montreal endocrinologist Hans Selye published a work hailed as "the greatest single contribution to the realm of biology and medicine since Pasteur." Selye's great breakthrough was to identify stress as the true source of disease. Victims of stress had something called a Type A personality. Type A people were competitive and aggressive, felt constantly pressured and challenged, and were most likely to be ambitious men in their mid-forties or mid-fifties.

A much-publicized three-year study of 3,411 healthy men aged thirty-five to fifty-nine concluded that nearly three-quarters of those with classic Type A behavioral characteristics were likely coronary-disease victims. Stress was quickly blamed for almost all male health problems: for example, noting that the incidence of male deaths from lung cancer had increased fivefold in the past twenty-five years, some doctors suggested that a high-pressure lifestyle was the cause. Prior to the discovery, or creation, of the Type A personality, men who were not successful because they weren't aggressive and competitive enough lacked self-respect and social respect. Now the more successful a man was at passing all the tests of masculinity, the more likely he was to die prematurely.

Getting men to lose weight after the discovery of stress became a greater challenge. Many shrugged off dieting as hopeless, since a tough day at the office could kill them whether they were fat or thin. Psychiatrists advised that it was better to live with fat than to subject oneself to the stress of trying to reduce. Eating, they argued, could provide a release from anxiety, making it a bad idea for companies to push employees into weight-loss programs. Naturally, wives were expected to protect men from dangerous stress levels by creating a soothing home environment. If women made life more pleasant for their hardworking spouses and made them feel important, men would prefer coming home to spending long hours at the office—an analysis that went beyond placing men's physical health in the hands of women to actually blaming them for its deterioration. Some critics even accused women of being the primary sources of male stress because of their acquisitiveness and admonished them to live within their husbands' means.[7]

Fat, stress, amphetamines, spas—all the doctors' warnings in the world, and even the 1955 heart attack of President Eisenhower, couldn't overcome the conviction that the fruits of material success and middle-class prosperity were a groaning table and time for leisure, not sweating and straining for the sake of health. But if men could not be convinced to diet and exercise for the sake of their bodies (and lives), perhaps they could be convinced to do so in order to keep the world safe for democracy.

"A Bulging Bicep Means a Muscle in the Arm of Democracy!"

Beginning with Dwight D. Eisenhower's presidency in 1953 and continuing through John F. Kennedy's administration, physical fitness received national attention. When Eisenhower came into office, physical education in American schools increasingly had been emphasizing fitness and fitness testing for students. A variety of methods were used in the testing process, including the Kraus-Weber test that compared the fitness of American and European schoolchildren. Of the 4,458 American children tested, 56.6 percent were unable to meet even the minimum standards, compared with a failure rate of only 8 percent for the 1,987 Italian and Austrian children. Nearly half of the Americans failed one or more of the flexibility tests, and more than a third were unable to pass tests measuring muscular strength, which only 1 percent of Europeans failed. When the results of the Kraus-Weber test were published, Americans were appalled to find they were physically inferior— and to those who had been prostrated by the war that America had won! A few years later they would be further dismayed by studies showing that Japanese girls were as much as 50 percent better in arm strength than American girls.

A key theme during the decade was softness, most often applied to one's reaction to communism. Now the same word was being applied to the American people themselves, and a soft people could hardly be expected to withstand a hostile world. As fitness was linked to America's defense capability, not only national pride but national security seemed to be on the line. Eisenhower, alarmed by deteriorating American vigor, embraced the idea of a national commitment to physical fitness. In his view, sports and fitness wouldn't just prevent Americans from physical deterioration but would also build moral fiber; young people who participated in athletics, he believed, would be better able to resist "juvenile temptations," making fitness a deterrent to that bête noire of the 1950s, delinquency.

Though prosperous and stable, America was plagued by fears about national security and the looming menace of communism. After the Soviet Union exploded its own atomic bomb in 1949, Americans looked anxiously at any hint of one-upmanship. The 1957 launching of *Sputnik* was a devastating blow to national self-esteem and prompted an avalanche of funding to enhance math and science education in American schools, seen as lagging disastrously behind the Soviet educational system, and an increased concern about physical fitness.

National defense raised the most compelling argument for a fit population. Testifying before a congressional committee on the state of American fitness and health, Brigadier General S.L.A. Marshall claimed that "loss of power in the legs," which he blamed on the proliferation of automobiles, caused a concomitant loss of "moxie," with potentially dire consequences for American fighting forces. Studies conducted among West Point cadets showed that those with the lowest physical fitness ratings also had the highest number of psychiatric problems and were most likely to resign from the academy. Worst of all, fully half of the men called for preinduction into the Korean War were rejected for mental or physical deficiencies.

A White House meeting, chaired by Vice President Richard M. Nixon in July 1955, was called to discuss what should be done, and the following year, the President's Council on Youth Fitness was established to awaken the nation to the need for physical fitness. The council's guidelines recommended at least fifteen minutes per day of "vigorous" activity for children. To ensure that this vaguely defined but essential activity took place, mass fitness programs were developed. Programs were heavily group-oriented, with little individual instruction or allowance for different ability levels. Typical activities were group calisthenics and obstacle courses—which most children hated and found boring.

Despite national publicity and hand-wringing on the part of everyone from government to parents, no one seemed able to define precisely what "fitness" meant. Physical fitness programs offered blurry explications such as "the amount of strength and endurance needed to meet the needs of everyday life" or "the ability to perform some specified task requiring muscular effort." Norms and standards set by the Youth Fitness Test proved problematic because, like the exercise programs themselves, they gave little attention to individual differences. Keeping accurate records on such an enormous scale was costly and difficult. Determining whether participants had improved over a given time period also proved elusive. The achievement of "fitness," however defined, was essentially buried by the emphasis on ends rather than means: poor test scores were an indictment not only of the school system but of the American democratic system. In addition, a great drawback to these government fitness programs was their almost exclusive focus on youngsters. Anyone over the age of nineteen was expected to fend for himself.

Undeterred by the confusion surrounding government fitness programs, John F. Kennedy declared the physical vigor of America's citizens a precious national resource and promptly expanded the fitness agenda to include flex-and-stretch classes in high schools. By the beginning of his third year in office, Kennedy had begun promulgating a doctrine of fitness no longer limited to schoolchildren. In a progress report to the American people, he pointedly remarked that national security could not be sustained by technological superiority alone but rested as well on "the hardihood and endurance, the physical fitness," of American soldiers.

Eisenhower and Kennedy weren't the first presidents to promote physical fitness. Harry Truman had taken brisk daily walks that left members of the press and his staff panting in his wake.

Even earlier, in 1908, Theodore Roosevelt devised fitness standards, which were lost for many years and resurrected during the Kennedy administration by Marine Commandant David Shoup. Shoup applied Roosevelt's fitness standards to his own officers, who passed easily, although it is doubtful that the general population would have: the regimen began with a three-day, fifty-mile hike carrying twenty-four pounds of equipment and ended with a lap of two hundred yards of jogging, a thirty-minute rest, a three-hundred-yard jog, then a one-minute rest, and a final two-hundred-yard run at full speed.

Not everyone took Kennedy's rhetoric on fitness seriously or was convinced that a grown man should be so obsessed with physical development. Exercise remained a low priority in American life; the only exception seemed to be Eisenhower's popularization of golf. At the end of the 1950s, a Gallup poll showed that one in four American men engaged in no sports activities at all—"not even," the report stated with no apparent sense of irony, "swimming, golfing, or . . . dancing."[8]

Everyone seemed to agree that keeping fit was important—if not for personal health and attractiveness, then for national security. But the simple truth was that nobody wanted to do it. For most Americans, the only acceptable means of staying fit in the 1950s was exercise without effort, a philosophy that spawned a vast and strange industry.

Even Dr. Louis Dublin dismissed exercise as hopeless: to take off just one pound, he said, a man would have to walk thirty-six miles or climb the Washington Monument forty-eight times. Dublin's exercise—or, more accurately, non-exercise—advice paled in comparison to that of Dr. Peter J. Steincrohn, who throughout the 1950s issued shrill warnings about exercise's deleterious effects. Muscles, Steincrohn proclaimed, were for the young, and doing daily sit-ups would "take the zip out of life," leaving men exhausted and debilitated. For men of any age, sensible fitness routines could include walking, sailing, and gardening. For those over forty, exercise was the worst possible assault on "creaking joints and beat-up circulatory systems," and under no condition should they even contemplate playing a set of singles or more than nine holes of golf.

Another purported expert, Dr. Frank P. Foster, didn't think even *young* men should engage in strenuous physical workouts and came out strongly against forcing high school students to do sports or even calisthenics. Instead, they should turn their talents to more useful hobbies like bird-watching, practicing music, or studying. The most important physical needs of the average young man, Foster concluded, were muscles sufficient for a firm handshake and "a head hard enough to withstand noontime martinis." Dr. Leonard Larsen, chair of the Department of Physical Education at New York University and someone who might be expected to value fitness and exercise, claimed that at age forty-six he kept fit by exercising for ten minutes every day. For the average sedentary man, however, Larsen cautioned against so vigorous a routine, suggesting a Finnish sauna instead. Other doctors told male patients to keep fit by dangling their hands to the floor until they tingled, taking deep breaths two or three times a day, or getting a massage. Dublin, however, warned against massage because "it just makes the fat parts larger." After these exertions, men could relax with a few ounces of well-deserved liquor just before retiring.

Yet men realized that they had to get *some* exercise, especially if they worked in sedentary office jobs. What set exercise in the 1950s apart from anything that had gone before, or would come after, was men's passionate devotion to doing it without expending any effort.

One of the earliest and most successful no-effort products was the Relax-A-cizor, a gadget that claimed to effect changes in body weight and shape without exercise or dieting and so was as easy to use as a television set. Introduced in 1951, the device claimed to improve muscle tone and produce tight, firm flesh. It accomplished these miracles by causing muscles to "exercise" by alternately flexing and relaxing. While the machine performed its electrically charged miracles, the user could relax, even take a nap.

Flush with success in a marketplace largely geared to women, the Los Angeles–based company began producing a version in the 1960s especially targeted at men. Dubbed "The Executive," the masculinized Relax-A-cizor wasn't much different from the original except in its advertising copy, which made the product sound "efficient, authoritative, and important"—something a real man would buy and could use while reading or talking on the phone instead of wasting time in conventional exercise routines. Since it was expensive as well, costing as much as $450 for the luxury edition, men were encouraged to think of it as an investment. The Relax-A-cizor was given added appeal by claims that it could be used to reduce tension. Instead of placing its little pads on areas that needed to be trimmed and slimmed, the stressed-out executive put them on areas that needed to be relaxed, which could be conveniently done in the office.

The greatest drawback to the Relax-A-cizor was that it didn't really do anything; the best that could be said was that the currents might lull users into a state of relaxation. In 1966, the Food and Drug Administration ordered all electrical reducing devices banned from the market. The Relax-A-cizor, it turned out, was not only useless but dangerous: if electrical current entered the heart at a critical time in its cycle, heart rhythm could be upset, and the current could cause heart damage. Despite a flood of consumer complaints and medical records of physical harm, it proved incredibly difficult to eliminate the offending device. For four years after the government filed its injunction, the Relax-A-cizor was still being produced, and the ensuing trial cost taxpayers more than a half million dollars. Manufacturers often would make a small adjustment in the product and reissue it under a new name, in a new package. But by then, a number of alternatives had emerged to help Americans keep fit without undue strain.

No-effort fitness products worked on the assumption that developing muscle tone, as the Relax-A-cizor claimed to do with its multiple tiny currents, would somehow cause flab to vanish. For users who demanded absolute freedom of movement, there were wearable reducing aids like the Tone-O-Matic, a leatherette belt lined with compartments stuffed with ten pounds of lead granules. Its sheer weight was supposed to slim and tone by forcing abdominal muscles to push against the belt in a precursor of isometric exercise. The belt could be worn underneath regular attire, making it popular with men who slipped it on while working at their desks. In reality, a six-foot-tall man weighing two hundred pounds would have to wear the Tone-O-Matic eight hours a day for forty-five consecutive days to lose a single pound. In 1971, the Federal Trade Commission ordered production of Tone-O-Matic suspended after it was found to cause back problems and hernias.

There seemed to be no limit to inventiveness: Trim Twist Exercise Joggers forced up users' knees, ostensibly providing the equivalent of a one-mile jog in six minutes. Smartbels, which looked much like ordinary barbells, claimed to generate "gyroscopic forces" equivalent to use of a 110-pound weight. The Disco-Shaper, an eleven-inch round plate, promised to burn up more calories, fat, and flab than a game of tennis; all the user had to do was sit on it and twist around. For those prepared to exert a bit more effort, there was the Yoga Slim Wheel, a medium-sized wheel with handles protruding from either side over which users draped their bodies and rolled back and forth. This "unique rolling movement" purportedly firmed sagging stomach muscles and prepared executives for their daily rigors. One of the most popular items sold at Abercrombie & Fitch's "Think Thin" boutique, the wheel was reportedly used by Spiro Agnew and Ronald Reagan, causing the latter to feel, after his initial workout, as if he'd been "hit by a truck."

Undeterred by the irrationality of their products, manufacturers forged ahead with ever more sophisticated technology. Whether shaped like belts (the Fabulous New Sauna Belt), hot pants (Trim-Jeans), or girdles (Waist-Away), all worked in the same way: each gadget was wrapped around offending areas of the body and inflated with a small pump; the operative element was a set of thermal packs. Once wrapped, pumped up, and thermally activated, users performed several mild exercises that, in combination with the generated heat, supposedly sped up the process of melting off inches by breaking down fatty tissue. Trim-Jeans prescribed a set of "Magic Torso" movements that required about ten pleasant minutes to complete; then, after the wearer spent another twenty minutes relaxing around the house, reading and smoking a pipe, the jeans—and hopefully an inch or two—came off. Slim Skins were plastic shorts with a built-in hose that, when attached to a vacuum cleaner, massaged and purportedly toned and slimmed the body from waist to knees. The most passive of all methods was spontaneous reduction, a form of human shrink-wrapping in which naked clients were swathed in strips of linen cloth, then laid on plastic couches and drenched in a mysterious secret formula (which turned out to be saltwater). They were zipped into tight plastic suits for a ninety-minute trimming session. The oppressively tight bindings squeezed off excess fluid, along with a substantial amount of blood circulation; any weight loss not brought about by profuse sweating or skin shrinkage from the effects of the saltwater was attributable solely to the imagination—or to sheer fright at being subjected to so grotesque a procedure.

While they demanded slightly more effort than spontaneous reduction, reducing aids like Hot Pants were enormously appealing because they were so easy to use and because of their technological sophistication. Hot Pants manufacturers boasted that their thermal packs had been developed by a scientist from California Polytechnic Institute; the pants were promoted, with a militaristic flourish, as "a bomb that explodes all existing time barriers in slenderizing."

The Russians and the Chinese may have had atomic devices, but they didn't have *this* miracle of technology. Furthermore, like the popular new TV dinner, these reducing devices promised not only effortlessness but instant results. They were superbly efficient: instead of exhausting oneself working out the entire body, one could target specific problem areas; "we like the idea of exercise working exactly where it's supposed to work," Relax-A-cizor ads proclaimed. Men proved especially susceptible to advertising that told them they could shed pounds without giving up favorite foods or wasting time; ease of use obscured the fact that these products did nothing to tone the body or develop stamina or endurance. Nonetheless, the yearning for easy exercise poured $100 million a year into the pockets of makers of belts, wheels, shrink-wrapping, and battery-operated electrical reducing aids.

Clearly, no-effort exercise couldn't sculpt men's bodies into a state of perfection, either visually or from a health standpoint. Men's unflagging resistance to dieting didn't help matters, either. While the average weight of American women between the ages of forty-five and fifty-four decreased five pounds between 1941 and 1963, the average American man in that age-group gained six pounds. There was one arena, however, in which at least some men were willing to forgo no-effort workouts and pay serious attention to shaping their bodies.[9]

Despite its decline in popularity among middle-class men early in the twentieth century, bodybuilding continued to be popular among teenage boys sensitive about their gawky, changing bodies and anxious to find a way of projecting the illusion of power. A disproportionate amount of its advertising appeared in comic books. Laborers, clerks, farmers, and a substantial number of prison inmates were also avid enthusiasts. In the 1950s, most were subscribers to mail-order physique courses created by the best-known precursor to Arnold Schwarzenegger, Charles Atlas.

Born Angelo Siciliano in 1894, Atlas is best remembered for his innovative ads showing sand being kicked in the faces of under-developed wimps. The legendary sand-kicking episode really did take place on Coney Island, and the ads ran virtually unchanged through the 1980s. Atlas used his splendid body less as a strongman than as a visual object, in order to sell a worldwide message of ideal manhood. Like his nineteenth-century predecessors, he emphasized a healthy diet and clean living—"live clean, think clean, and don't go to burlesque shows," he advised admirers who asked for the secret of his success.

Before he began marketing his courses, Atlas worked as a model and became extremely popular because his great strength allowed him to hold flexed poses for long periods. He attributed his strength to "Dynamic-Tension" (which would be resurrected in the 1960s as isometrics). Atlas claimed to have come up with the idea for Dynamic-Tension while watching a lion in the Prospect Park Zoo stretching and pitting one muscle against another. He introduced his philosophy of transforming ninety-seven-pound weaklings into walking powerhouses in 1921, and by the 1950s the Charles Atlas Course had been translated into seven languages as well as Braille. Hundreds of letters from grateful clients poured into Atlas's New York offices every day, making "Mr. Charles" into what one biographer calls "the Ann Landers of the healthy, handsome body, the Miss Lonelyhearts of strength and self-sufficiency." Young men credited his exercise program for gains as diverse as overcoming the effects of polio and typhus, conquering alcoholism, and curing acne ("no more pimples, hardly") Even after his death, his offices continued to be flooded with grateful letters, many from very young men: "what kinds of cars have you lifted by the rear bumpers?" asked one; "I'm fourteen years old. After 10 days of exercising I trust you completely," wrote another. Barry, a lawyer who grew up in the mean streets of New York, sent away when he was fourteen for the complete Charles Atlas weight-training pro-gram as a deterrent to neighborhood toughs. A few women also purchased the thirty-dollar course, but representatives of the Atlas empire were quick to point out that "we don't cater to women; we never have."

Seymour, a retired clothing manufacturer who grew up on the Lower East Side of Manhattan in the early 1950s, recalls that just after he started high school, a new family moved into his modest, mostly Jewish neighborhood. They were Italian, and one of the sons, a little older than Seymour, was good-looking and lifted weights. Seymour was immediately attracted—not to the young man per se but to the possibilities held out by the weights. He felt "an immediate magnetic pull," a feeling he declares himself unable to explain; "I'm not going to try to come up with a bunch of psychobabble to tell how I felt; it was just magic." At age sixty-five, Seymour is still proud of the fact that he entered high school weighing 126 pounds and came out weighing 200 and hasn't stopped lifting weights since. All over the city, thousands of young men like himself, the children of working-class immigrant families, met in gyms or in basements three or four times a week to lift their way to a muscular ideal. Atlas's sand-kicking ads notwithstanding, this training regimen had nothing to do, Seymour claims, with attracting girls. For him, bodybuilding conveyed a feeling of being a mensch: "when you walked down the street, you were a man among men." Along with his largely working-class constituency, Atlas counted a number of celebrities among his converts, including Joe DiMaggio, Rocky Marciano, and Fred Allen. Atlas himself remained in fine shape until he died of a heart attack at age seventy-eight. In his later years, *Life* magazine reported, he kept trim by flexing his massive muscles all the way to the bank.[10]

Plastic Surgery after World War II

During World War I, as discussed earlier, plastic surgery had clearly demonstrated that an aesthetically improved appearance could have social and economic benefits, and the profession introduced new techniques that could be readily applied to conventional surgery. Yet in the aftermath of the war, old prejudices resurfaced. Throughout the 1920s, while passionately defending the positive effects of aesthetic surgery on mental health and general well-being when performed to eliminate serious deformities, the profession's leading practitioners trivialized its importance when performed merely to restore beauty and the appearance of youth. Dr. Charles Conrad Miller, self-proclaimed father of modern cosmetic surgery, betrayed his ambivalence toward his specialty by writing that physicians who gave "a few added seasons to an actress by helping her to counterfeit youth cannot seriously lay claim to rendering serious service to the community," thereby effectively denigrating both his patients and himself. Even Sir Harold Gillies admitted to feeling guilty about profiting from cosmetic surgery but justified his prosperity by emphasizing the happiness that cosmetic work could bring, describing it as "an ode to an ugly woman."

Surgical advances took another leap forward during World War II. Once again, techniques devised for the battlefield passed into general use. Dermabrasion technology used to remove shrapnel fragments, for example, was later applied to civilian life, where, among other things, it was used to remove tattoos. Once again, most beneficiaries of wartime plastic surgery would be men— with a conspicuous exception.

On August 6, 1945, the first atomic bomb was dropped on the city of Hiroshima. Of the thousands killed or maimed by the explosion and its radioactive aftermath, twenty-five young women would gain particular renown. All were within one mile of ground zero when the bomb struck. As with the majority of the victims, most of their burns were in two areas: faces and necks, which were upturned as they watched the blinding flash, and hands and arms, raised reflexively in self-defense. Afterward, when the gray ash covering them was peeled off, their underlying skin appeared shiny, hard, and lifeless; eyebrows, lashes, and hair were burned away. The schoolgirl Shigeko Niimoto, one of the most badly disfigured, suffered such intense exposure to the bomb's searing heat that the lower half of her face melted into her throat, leaving her chinless. Equally devastating was loss of function caused by the burns: riddled with the raised edges of keloid tumors, scar tissue on hands and arms healed unevenly and froze limbs into awkward positions that left hands gnarled and useless.

Though a Tokyo hospital struggled to help the girls, it was poorly supplied, often lacking even anesthesia, and the doctors' knowledge of plastic surgery was limited. Japanese surgeons eventually concluded that they were inflicting more trauma than the bomb and called a halt to their ineffectual cutting. In 1955, ten years after the bomb had been dropped, Norman Cousins, the editor of *The Saturday Review* and a long-term critic of America's decision to bomb Japan, launched a fund-raising program to bring the twenty-five young women, dubbed the Hiroshima maidens, to New York City's Mt. Sinai Hospital for state-of-the-art reconstructive surgery, which, it was hoped, would restore them to normalcy. The project attracted media attention, catapulting both the maidens and the profession of plastic surgery into the public spotlight.

Plastic surgery was intended to restore as much normalcy to the young women as possible, but the severity of their injuries precluded any possibility of restoring perfection. Seeing a group of them twenty-five years later, an American journalist observed that though at first glance they appeared normal, closer observation revealed "uneven or slightly smeared features, all heavily covered with makeup." Transplanted skin brought problems of its own: it ages differently from natural skin and is more sensitive to sunlight, infection, and injury. Nor could the surgeries prevent cancers and other manifestations of radiation exposure later in life. Nevertheless, the surgeons accomplished their objective: the Hiroshima maidens returned to Japan looking acceptably normal, if not altogether so.

Though the surgery was intended as a humanitarian effort and though it involved correction of functional as well as appearance-related damage, it's interesting that the chosen beneficiaries were women. There was no shortage of Japanese men suffering from the effects of the bomb. But as female patients, the Hiroshima maidens were typical: after World War II, plastic surgery, for all its advances, reverted to being the province of middle-aged matrons worried about crow's-feet and sagging chin lines. The surgeon Walter C. Alvarez noted that a few men might resort to face-lifting "to hold their places in the theater or on the concert stage." Elderly men married to much younger women were also potential candidates.

Even the pope weighed in with an opinion on cosmetic surgery. In 1958, Pope Pius XII warned surgeons about the immorality of operating on patients who wanted to "enhance the power of seduction, thus leading others more easily into sin," and on those who sought "to satisfy vanity or the caprice of fashion." Jewish law also took the matter under consideration but rendered a more liberal verdict: cosmetic surgery for men was permissible if there was economic justification—that is, if having surgery enabled a man to support his family better. Jewish women were given greater latitude: plastic surgery could enhance a single woman's chances for marriage and could improve a married woman's relations with her husband, both desirable ends that over-rode some of the stigma of vanity. Even in a religious context, a distinction was made between what was permissible for men and for women, but reactions to cosmetic surgery still reflected the general feeling of society that too much attention to one's looks was unseemly. Makeup and fashion were one thing; surgical body alteration was quite another.

The profession did take several steps toward greater legitimacy during and immediately after World War II. By 1941, the American Board of Plastic Surgery (ABPS) had been established, with the goal of defining the specialty's boundaries and implementing standards for "academic accreditation and professional recognition." Prior to such standardization, practitioners often divided their time between plastic surgery and vaguely related specialties ranging from dermatology to dentistry. Training and apprenticeship were so haphazard that many aspirants trained in Europe. Not surprisingly, these shortcomings did little to enhance the profession's reputation and contributed to a perception of quackery among its practitioners. It was this sort of perception that the ABPS was determined to reverse. The quest for professionalization was aided in 1946, when it began publishing its own journal, *Plastic and Reconstructive Surgery*. By the early 1950s, nearly three-quarters of America's top medical schools offered training in plastic surgery, and by the end of the decade the field had nearly tripled in size, and its journal was one of the most widely read in the medical field.

The average cosmetic surgery patient in the 1950s was a white, Anglo-Saxon, married woman of the upper middle class. In a "group portrait" of his patients, Dr. John Medelman described them as "desperate or daring" women, none of whom came from the "lower class." While his own "better" class of patients were forced to rely on the "camouflage" he was able to create for them with his scalpel, Medelman commended lower-class people for being less preoccupied with their looks and better able to relate to the world as "unadorned," real people. For most women, face-lifts were luxuries rather than necessities. Articles attempting to persuade them otherwise began to appear in popular magazines but tended to reinforce rather than undermine the idea of surgery as a prerogative of the well-to-do—suggesting, for example, that it didn't cost any more to get a face-lift than to buy a fur coat or take a trip around the world. This, too, would change: by the 1990s, the average cosmetic surgery patient earned less than twenty-five thousand dollars a year, as the greater emphasis on looking good made cost a secondary consideration to perceived need.[11]

"The Most Vexing Problems of Married Life": Coping with Frigidity

In 1959, writing about male-female relationships in America, Diana Trilling observed that no matter how much one believed in sexual equality, "we all of us operate on the premise that men are the more important sex, whose condition determines the fate of society." One had only "to consult the record of Western civilization," she went on, "to see that it is men who steer the main course." The secret shared by most intelligent women, Trilling revealed, was that wifely self-effacement brought the greatest rewards. By preserving her husband's self-esteem "at whatever sacrifice of her own claims to equal esteem," a woman would be rewarded by having her femininity flattered by her husband's gratitude and adoration. Alternatively, failure to stroke the male ego would bring about national disaster: the collapse of a man would necessarily bring down the woman with him, resulting in ruin for all.

This oddly archaic analysis contains significant indicators of 1950s society. First are the assumed power relations between the sexes and the importance attributed to each sex. Second is the implication that relations between men and women are between husbands and wives. Although Trilling's advice may sound ludicrous to readers today, it accurately reflects her society.

In the 1950s, marriage was the normal state and was expected to bring happiness and a rationale for striving for the good life. After the dislocations of the Great Depression and the war, the home held out the promise of security, abundance, and personal fulfillment. It was considered virtually impossible for single adults to be happy or well adjusted. Though spinsterhood was the most pitiable condition of all, bachelorhood was also out of step with society: it implied immaturity at best, homosexuality at worst. Sociologists and psychologists studied the harrowing conditions of single life, with particular interest in the single man—who, unlike the spinster, was assumed to have chosen his socially irresponsible lifestyle. Some went so far as to recommend psychotherapy for any unmarried man over the age of thirty. Unmarried men were documented as being unhealthier than married ones, at risk for a host of ailments ranging from influenza to cirrhosis of the liver, and more prone to an early demise: they were four times as likely to die in automobile accidents and five times as likely to commit suicide as their married counterparts. Some observers reluctantly concluded that there were some legitimate reasons for a man to remain single: if he was extremely unattractive, for instance, or if he worked in a hazardous profession that might condemn a wife to widowhood.

Along with its other benefits, marriage legitimized sexuality. While sexual intercourse among unmarried couples met with hearty disapproval, within the home, as the historian Elaine Tyler May points out, "sexuality could be safely unleashed by both men and women" and "would provide a positive force to enhance family life." A woman's role wasn't confined to motherhood and housework: she was also expected to be a sexual companion.

Considering the importance of marriage and sexual harmony, sexual inadequacy carried ominous social consequences. Inadequacy referred not to male impotence but to female frigidity, which was believed to be reaching epidemic proportions: according to the American Medical Association (AMA), three out of four American women were frigid and derived no pleasure from sex. Many of these, the AMA went on, found intercourse painful and even revolting. Frigidity wasn't just a sexual problem; it could force husbands to seek extramarital sexual satisfaction, bringing evils ranging from venereal disease to corrosive jealousy into the home and ultimately leading to its destruction. Small wonder, then, that Americans considered female sexual dysfunction a threat to the American way of life.[12]

A number of causes for frigidity were proposed, some of which showed sensitivity toward women rather than castigating them as failures. Female sexual unresponsiveness could, for instance, result from socially instilled feelings about sex as dirty or taboo, and a few therapists even dared suggest poor male sexual technique as a cause. But many simply explained frigidity in terms of female shortcomings. Aggressive, competitive women couldn't bear being dependent on a man, and orgasm was a sign of dependence. Narcissistic, self-centered ones weren't able to show affection to men. Or women might just be too modern for their own good and feel entitled to equal orgasms along with all their other equal rights. Dr. Alfred Kinsey pointed out that women were culturally conditioned against enjoying sex and as a result were often so slow to be aroused that it was "entirely unreasonable to expect the male to shoulder this burden by delaying his own orgasm for indefinite periods." It seemed that the worst aspect of frigidity wasn't its destructive impact on women but its undermining of male sexuality.

Although on the surface the 1950s seemed to be a haven for unchallenged masculinity, worries about impotence had already arisen and were tied to concerns about eroding male authority and control. Part of the problem was that with the double standard for premarital sexual relations, women fell into a pattern of regulating sexual contact (saying no to male advances)—a condition that had to be abruptly reversed after marriage, when the husband was expected to take charge of sexual relations. Unfortunately, this didn't always happen, leading some experts to observe that women were becoming too controlling. Even more insidiously, males were being instructed to concentrate less on their own pleasure than on satisfying their wives—some of whom, complained one doctor, were unwilling to accept compromises and expected satisfaction every time.

Treatment of sexual dysfunction was complicated because few people came into contact with therapeutic specialists: prior to the 1960s, therapy was largely the preserve of a small upper-middle-class urban population. For men in particular, being under psychiatric care was considered shameful, indicating lack of inner direction and inability to "take it like a man." Most people, if they sought therapeutic help at all, went to medical doctors, clergy, or family members, few of whom had any formal training in marital counseling, much less sexual matters. In 1950, one-quarter of the members of the American Association of Marriage Counselors weren't trained in psychological counseling; most were gynecologists and other medical specialists. As a consequence, marriage counselors were, on the whole, regarded as ineffective. When it came to sex therapy, the few "experts" were much more concerned about frigidity than impotence.

Women's magazines dealt with the delicate subject of impotence by providing their readers with case studies. Roger and Mary were a happily married young couple. After about five years together, both began to lose interest in sex. Roger had a legitimate reason: he was working his way up the career ladder. Mary then, apparently all on her own, had a baby, thereby adding to Roger's burdens as well as her own. Blame for their collapsing sex life was ultimately laid at Mary's feet: her unrealistic standards, which were never clearly set forth, forced Roger to work too hard. Mary was losing interest in sex because of her own shortcomings, and Roger was losing interest in sex because of Mary.

Don't raise your expectations by reading too many sex manuals, women were told, although men were advised to read them. Don't tell your husband he doesn't make enough money, and don't overburden him with too many cocktail parties or backyard barbecues. These missteps were demoralizing, exhausting, and harmful to the male libido. If, in spite of all these precautions, impotence did rear its ugly head, it was usually attributed to legitimate, even noble causes. Men were working too hard and worrying too much about important things. In contrast, the frigid wife was neurotic and even vengeful, selfishly withholding orgasms as retaliation against her husband.

To ensure that male libidos continued to function smoothly, wives were impressed with the absolute necessity of being emotionally supportive and uncritical; a woman's "secret weapon" against impotence was being encouraging and cheerful. The worst thing she could do was confront her husband about his shortcoming. In a study of 151 "frigid" women conducted in 1951, all of them expressed the belief that speaking frankly about their own desires or offering suggestions as to how their sex lives might be improved would provoke resentment.

Doctors and other experts who wrote about sex and sexual problems for lay readers often made it clear that expectations must be reasonable. Discussing frigidity and impotence in *Cosmopolitan,* one doctor explained that fewer than half of married couples were sexually compatible, and perhaps "not one marriage in ten has a completely satisfactory sexual relationship." The key was for couples to understand that disappointment and lack of perfect sexual harmony were *normal* and not set their sights too high.

By the end of the 1950s, doctors had begun questioning earlier assumptions about the prevalence of frigidity and reformulating their definition of it: if a woman enjoyed lovemaking, with or without orgasm, she wasn't frigid. Since the term "enjoyed" was vague, medical experts tried to quantify it: gynecologists suggested that if a woman was able to experience orgasm 50 percent of the time, she was sexually healthy. If this view represents some progress, it also raises the question as to whether a man who only experienced orgasm 50 percent of the time would view himself as sexually healthy.

In both boardroom and bedroom, the world of the 1950s was a man's world. As long as women could be convinced that they could achieve fulfillment through homemaking and child care, and could be effectively excluded from responsible positions in the workplace, they would pose little threat to male social and economic supremacy. In the 1990s, the psychologist Michael R. Solomon coined the term "the Onassis Effect" to explain why men had become so attuned to looking good. Simply put: as long as men had almost total control of economic resources, they had little reason to worry about how desirable they were personally; desirability existed quite independently of physical attractiveness. Men didn't know it yet, but the Onassis Effect was about to be turned on its head.[13]

3

"FINDING THE REAL ME"

MEN IN THE 1960s

I do my thing, and you do your thing.
　　　　　　　　—Fritz Perls, "Gestalt Prayer"

In 1968, *The New York Times* described the spectacle of a hippie jogging shoeless through Central Park. His long hair was flowing, his tie-dyed shirt fluttered behind him, and one hand gripped a flower while the other held on to love beads. This incongruous scene was presented as an example of people on the margins of society engaged in a fringe physical activity. After all, who jogged in the 1960s? And why would a hippie care about jogging anyway? Actually, it's a vision that evokes many of the decade's contradictions. Members of the counterculture were often the highly educated children of a prosperous and influential middle class; yet they turned their backs on affluence and conformity. With their attention focused on protest, social change, and discovering their inner beings, young men appeared to care little about fitness or body image. They didn't work out, they were fond of drugs, and many seemed unacquainted with the notion of a comb. On the other hand, they were likely to prize the length of their hair, wore interesting clothes, and made a great fuss over eating natural foods. The early years of the 1960s seemed, deceptively, to be a continuation of the 1950s, only with a dynamic new president at the helm. By the end of the decade, America was changed forever, and so were many of its notions about health, fitness, and the male body.

Young Americans became vocal in their criticism of a society perceived as unfair to women, minorities, and the poor and overstepping its bounds in world affairs. Revolted by bureaucratic alienation, the corporate greed of companies reaping profits from the devastation of Vietnam, and the dehumanizing technocracy of the war, young Americans threw aside efficiency and blind obedience to authority for an "intuitive, affectively centered self-awareness, an empathetic feeling for others, and a relaxed, non-analytical attention to the present situation." Or, put more simply, Be Here Now, Get in Touch with Yourself, and Do Your Own Thing.

Doing one's own thing had diverse interpretations. Betty Friedan initiated the modern women's movement by disputing the notion that women could find fulfillment only as homemakers and mothers, encouraging them to move into careers once reserved for men. Women's economic power was quickly joined to sexual power, as double standards of sexual behavior began to break down. The American work ethic and the belief in work as the determinant of personal meaning also came under assault. With layers of bureaucracy dividing the white-collar worker from his final product as completely as assembly-line piecework separated the blue-collar laborer from his, men were turning into cogs in impersonal machines. Advocating a retreat from corporate conformity and the corrosive moral effects of the profit motive, thousands of Americans abandoned work altogether, while others left the "defective goals" of corporate life for more "personally fulfilling" employment. A San Francisco copier salesman quit his twenty-thousand-dollar-a-year job because he disliked being forced to "manipulate" people, turning instead to making sand-mold candles, while a management trainee abandoned his "dehumanizing" job with Texaco to work for a struggling small magazine where there were no fixed hours and he could wear an undershirt to work.

De-emphasizing work wouldn't seem an altogether bad idea; after all, the workaholic (a word that first appeared in the 1960s) neglected his family and undermined his physical and emotional health. But since work had traditionally determined the meaning of life for men and defined their roles in society, its displacement would leave a void that needed to be filled. A viable alternative soon appeared. Disillusioned by social turmoil, the declining attractions of the workplace, and the growing complexity of everyday life, Americans began to turn their attentions inward.

"Getting in Touch with Myself": The Human Potential Movement and Body Image

In the 1960s, a new doctrine of introspection spread through the American middle class. Grounded in Carl Rogers's client-centered therapy, the core of the human potential movement was a belief that each person possessed both unlimited potential and the capacity to achieve happiness. Though the movement focused on social and sexual relationships, one of its earliest manifestations, the encounter group, was initially intended to improve relations in the workplace.

First devised in the 1940s to train social scientists in human-relations skills, encounter groups found their way into the 1960s workplace, where they were initially aimed at resocializing managers alienated by the impersonality of corporate life. Though legitimized by their self-proclaimed role as executive training tools and pathways to stress relief, encounter groups also placed individuals and their needs in a central position vis-à-vis the interests of the corporation.

Encounter groups and other consciousness-raising therapies operated on the principle that group pressure swept aside phony emotions, exposing honest self-expression. Excessive verbalization and rational thinking were subjugated to living in the moment; what mattered were feelings, which should be expressed with complete impunity, no matter how shocking or self-indulgent. A major problem with this rationale was that the feelings and emotions that mattered most were one's own, often to the detriment of everyone else.

Steven, an economist working for a California think tank in the mid-1960s, was introduced to encounter-group therapy when several researchers in his department invited him to join a group that met weekly under the guidance of a psychologist. The group, made up of a dozen men and women, rotated among the homes of its members rather than meeting in the doctor's office, a tactic intended to convey informality and induce relaxation. Informality aside, firm rules were in place regarding behavior: for instance, members were not to ask each other questions about marital status or what they did for a living but to operate strictly on emotional and visceral responses generated during the sessions.

Remembering his encounter-group experience twenty-five years later, Steven focuses on one incident. Exercises requiring nonverbal communication were de rigueur, and one evening, members were asked to sit on the floor in a circle and express their feelings about each other nonverbally. After a few moments, one woman rose, left the room, and went to the host's bathroom. She returned with a bar of soap and a bottle of shampoo, which she silently presented to a man sitting across from her—a clear reference to his physical appearance, and one that humiliated him. He never returned to the group, and after a few weeks, neither did Steven.

That this incident revolved around a body-image issue is significant. A vital corollary to the de-emphasis on verbal expression was a heightened emphasis on the physical self. Touching exercises and physical expression of emotions ranging from affection to hostility were encouraged, and freeing the body became a metaphor for freeing the mind. As a result, the body became much more central to how individuals were viewed and how they viewed themselves.

Encounter-group therapy soon moved outside corporate walls to places like Esalen, where middle-class Americans could set about discovering themselves in marathon sessions, primal-scream therapy, and nude workshops, surrounded by the beauty of Big Sur. Realistic therapy, adherents were told, depended on total honesty; as the marathon pioneer George R. Bach explained, you had to let others know "exactly what and who you are and what are your expectations." Total honesty got a boost from therapy administered in the nude, which ostensibly heightened the intensity of the encounter and stripped away all signs of pretense, at least physical ones, while, of course, placing the body in a central position. A further influence came from the Eastern philosophical-religious tradition, which became enormously popular among the young. Zen, yoga, and other metaphysical doctrines stressed developing physiological awareness and self-mastery, ideas that would eventually be taken to the gym and the jogging track.

Encouraging people to get in touch with their feelings ultimately brought about a widespread belief that the good of the individual lay in a process that Tom Wolfe satirically described as the "new alchemical dream [of] remaking, remodeling, elevating, and polishing one's very Self, and observing, studying, and doting on . . . Me!" In the 1960s, the alchemy would focus on the mind, but in the following decade it expanded to include body image. The luxury of such self contemplation, both mental and physical, was made possible by postwar prosperity and Americans' pursuit of self-fulfillment through consumerism. And one postwar creation aided in this effort through its celebration of both consumerism and body image—albeit not the body image of males.[1]

Playboy's Vision of the Good Life

First published in 1953, Playboy claimed one million subscribers and two million dollars in advertising revenue in 1960, along with an empire of key clubs and specialty merchandise. The magazine's message was that American men should plunge wholeheartedly into the "swinging life," including unmarried sex. But wasn't the message of the 1950s that sex was best confined to the marital bedroom, with all of its husbandly obligations? How could such an aberrant publication find favor in times like these? In her provocative 1983 book *The Hearts of Men,* the feminist author Barbara Ehrenreich came up with an explanation: at the time *Playboy* hit the newsstands, men were already balking at the burdens of breadwinning, especially in light of the threat of imminent death from stress and overwork. The issue is more complex, however, and has more to do with consumerism than with male mortality.

To begin with, *Playboy* wasn't really new. Its basic format came from *Esquire,* a revolutionary concept in men's magazines launched in 1933 with the motto "Man at His Best." Though introduced in the depths of the Depression and priced at fifty cents a copy when most major magazines cost a dime, *Esquire* immediately captured an enthusiastic audience for its sophisticated mix of articles on fashion, sports, and style. Magazines like *True* and *Argosy,* still popular in the 1950s, emphasized gritty male activities, including sports, especially fishing and hunting, and building, repairing, or tinkering. Magazines featuring nudes also existed but had limited appeal because of their crudeness and poor quality. *Esquire* targeted college-educated, middle- to upper-middle-class men, a previously neglected market. The *Esquire* man wasn't a playboy; he was "tall, distinguished, middle-aged . . . [and] well-positioned." In other respects, *Esquire* and *Playboy* were similar, especially in their middle-class orientation, but *Esquire* lacked the editorial fortitude to move more strongly into the realm of sexuality, believing— incorrectly—that such a foray would fail in the fearful 1950s. Like the publishers of *Esquire,* Hugh Hefner wanted to appeal to the tastes of sophisticated men; however, he advocated sexuality as natural and highly enjoyable. At the peak of its circulation in 1972, *Playboy* was promoting its vision of the good life to seven million readers.

Daring as its centerfolds may have been, *Playboy* was very much in tune with middle-class values. Though it trumped *Esquire* in its celebration of sexuality, *Playboy* essentially reinforced materialism. Any man could acquire the trappings of success—a terrific apartment, a sleek car, a state-of-the-art hi-fi system, a beautiful young woman on his arm—but only if he earned enough money and set aside the burdens of marriage and family, at least for the immediate future.

By promoting consumerism, Hefner was upholding rather than denigrating the work ethic; the difference, of course, was that wife and children fell out of the equation. The triumvirate of work-leisure-consumption that defined the male role remained intact in *Playboy*'s ethic. But instead of working to buy backyard barbecues and using their leisure time to mow the lawn, men were encouraged to work for their own ends. Only communists were opposed to the good life promoted by *Playboy,* Hefner stated, blatantly linking his magazine to capitalism and the American way.

In spite of *Playboy*'s success, Hefner wasn't able to transform men into hedonists or even perennial bachelors—precisely because, titillating and sophisticated as it tried to be, his magazine catered more to materialism than to real sexual liberation. By showing how to live in style, *Playboy* promoted the same images of the good life as General Motors and Listerine. Within its covers, men were portrayed much as they were in mainstream magazines: well-dressed, usually fully clothed, looking less sensual than successful, less vain about their bodies than about their clothing and cars. Men, according to *Playboy*'s philosophy, were irresistible to women, but less because of how they looked than because of their ability to live in style.

Through the first decade of *Playboy*'s publication, Hefner wasn't pushing as extreme or as antitraditional a message about marriage as was generally believed. At the magazine's inception he declared, "I want to make it clear from the very start, we aren't a family magazine." Subsequent statements, however, were less radical: "We are concerned," Hefner claimed, "with a period of life that is not really long enough, a period of play at the finish of education and before *taking the responsibility of having a family*" (italics mine). This comment suggests a breadwinning role deferred rather than abdicated. In another interview, Hefner claimed that "if [men] spend their early years doing what *Playboy* suggests, [they] wind up with a happier, more stable marriage." Rock Hudson and Doris Day perpetuated the same notion in films like *Pillow Talk,* in which the male hero is expected to sow his wild oats before marriage to ensure against postmarital infidelity. Unlike *Playboy's* heroines, Doris Day was expected to remain a virgin. Even Hefner, however, hadn't explicitly said by the mid-1960s whether or not he supported premarital sex or abortion. In the late 1960s, railing against feminist attacks on his magazine, Hefner indignantly proclaimed that "these chicks are our natural enemy . . . unalterably opposed to the *romantic boy-girl* society that *Playboy* promotes."

Hefner was never able to extricate his publication from what one critic referred to as its "prepubescent fantasies." Part of the problem was that although the "typical" *Playboy* reader was a twenty-nine-year-old urbanite who ostensibly drank, smoked, and traveled more than other Americans and earned more than ten thousand dollars annually in the early 1960s, many readers who wrote into the popular *Playboy* Advisor column "sound[ed] like sixteen-year-olds still worried about their complexion problems." The much-ballyhooed after-hours parties at the Playboy Mansion were described by many attendees as pretentious and dull, consisting of "bored people [with] nothing in common dancing and drinking and sitting around trying to make conversation, just so that they can brag . . . that they were there." Despite the magazine's raffish reputation, its parties sound strangely similar to suburban cocktail parties. Despite its claims on the hearts and minds of young men, its key clubs made many younger patrons feel more like they were "at a meeting of World War II veterans" than a palace of sex: in reality, many of the magazine's younger readers, the majority, didn't have the financial status that would allow them to become regulars at the upscale but fundamentally conservative clubs.

Ultimately, the appeal *Playboy* tried to gain among the truly sophisticated was undermined by awkward, bawdy jokes and advertising that ran the gamut from genuinely high-status products to imitation shrunken heads and Sweat perfume. Although editorials suggested inviting women over for an evening of mood music and "quiet discussion of Picasso [and] Nietzsche," the real message was that women were sex objects. It would take more than a glossy men's magazine to move men out of their suburban backyards.[2]

"Gleaming, Streaming, Flaxen, Waxen"—Hair!

When asked in the film *The Wild One* what he is rebelling against, Marlon Brando answers, "What have you got?" The 1950s rebel appeared as a role model, mostly among the young; whether rock idols like Elvis Presley or film stars like James Dean, rebels were usually identifiable by their cheeky or sullen attitudes and hair that was longer than the norm. The most radical backlash against 1950s conformity was expressed by the Beats, who distanced themselves from the dreariness of mainstream culture by growing their hair long and not bothering to comb it. But beatniks inspired few converts, possibly because of their association with infrequent bathing and sleeping on mattresses on the floor. For the most part, the young were relatively docile and conformist, like their parents. Not until the 1960s did long hair and rebellion join forces and become associated not only with fringe groups, celebrities, and rock stars but with millions of middle-class university students. "You can't tell if he's a boy or a girl" was a gibe directed at long-haired young men, who at times were physically attacked. Furious controversies, fistfights, strikes, court actions, and even interventions by the American Civil Liberties Union took place on behalf of, or in resistance to, long-haired American males.

For many, long hair represented a threat to American manhood by making men appear feminine. As television brought the increasingly unpopular Vietnam War into the living rooms of America, millions recoiled at its destruction and bloodshed. Many middle-class young men seemed to be doing all they could to distance themselves from it, not only by protesting and avoiding military service but by looking as unlike soldiers as possible. Returning veterans, casting about for explanations for their ill treatment at the hands of an ungrateful nation, blamed the growing feminization of society for negating their sacrifices on the battlefield. Masculinity seemed no longer to be valued or appreciated in a society where young men were walking around with flowers in their hair. Many civilians agreed: members of a Wayne State University fraternity met at a barbershop and had all their hair cut off to dramatize their rejection of the emasculinization of American men.

In 1964, *The New York Times* carried the first of a series of articles on the clash between longhairs and bastions of authority like school boards and athletic departments. The first round in the battle came when a Connecticut high school student was suspended after he grew Beatle-like bangs. His bangs were actually quite short, considerably above his eyebrows, while the rest of his hair was trimmed close to his head. Nevertheless, controversy raged for months, and numerous appeals were exhausted before the student was handed an expulsion order from the Connecticut school district. In Long Island, when five young men showed up at school with long hair, the school district isolated them, like plague carriers, in separate classrooms. School athletic departments took an especially jaundiced view of long hair on men, equating it with female passivity—a quality few coaches were looking for in their players. When boys on the tennis team of Haverford College in the Philadelphia suburbs refused to trim their long hair, the tennis coach resigned.

Not all the images conjured up by long male tresses were negative. Long-haired men weren't just rebels; they were *young* when the value of youth was escalating. Sexual freedom and blurring gender lines softened some of the stigma attached to feminization, real or imagined. In any case, it was all a matter of perception: hard hats might find long hair feminizing, but Mick Jagger thought it was sexy and scoffed at the notion that "being masculine means looking clean, cropped, and ugly." Jagger's proclamations were not to be taken lightly: in the 1960s, rock stars were superseding film stars in setting the agenda for male fashion and overall body image.

Eventually, extremely long hair faded away except among a smattering of aging hippies, but men continued to wear their hair much longer than in the 1950s, often augmenting it with sideburns and mustaches. A greater variety of styles developed, notably those reflecting pop-culture idols like the Beatles and John F. Kennedy. The greater attention to hair boosted the popularity of toupees, now called hairpieces. Instead of relying on "mail-order rugs," men consulted professional hairpiece makers like New York's Guy Greco, who, for an average fee of $350, provided clients with "a product as personalized as its natural predecessor," painstakingly custom-woven one strand at a time from hair purchased from Italian peasant women. For men unwilling to spend that much, conventional hairpiece makers like Taylor Topper and Squires for Men offered styles starting at $75, including the "youthful tousled," "modified Beatle," and "JFK." For the more adventuresome, a San Francisco entrepreneur provided hippie wigs for $45. At mid-decade, each of the three largest hairpiece manufacturers reported annual sales well in excess of one million dollars.

For the man who refused to wear a hairpiece but wanted to be in tune with the times, hair weaving was an alternative. Developed in Harlem as a remedy for black women whose own hair had been made brittle by straightening treatments, hair weaving attracted growing numbers of white men between the ages of twenty-five and forty, especially those who wanted to look like rock stars.

Weaving involves braiding the client's own hair into fine lengths of nylon thread attached to the scalp by foundation seams. As hair grows out, clients must return every six to eight weeks for a tightening of the threads. Not only did men dislike maintenance on this scale, but it wasn't long before hair weaving generated complaints about both safety and efficacy. Bacteria multiplied under weaves, and because woven hair was attached at the sides of the head rather than at the hairline, in windy weather it tended, as one disappointed wearer complained, to "rise up like the vinyl roofs of old cars moving down the highway."

As the civil rights movement moved black images into the white mainstream, African American styles also influenced men's adoption of perms. In an ironic turnabout, the crew cut lost its association with pinstriped conformity and became the style of choice for trendy gay men, while permed curls were embraced by those most manly of men, professional athletes (especially baseball players, more than one hundred of whom sported perms at the beginning of the 1970s). Though men claimed convenience was the main reason for their curls, many admitted to perming their hair because it made them look younger. What mattered most wasn't what an abundance of hair said about a man's politics—for example, a sympathy with the civil rights movement—but what it told the world about his youthfulness, sexuality, and power.[3]

Keeping Fit in the 1960s: IC, Bullworkers, and Vic Tanny

Men continued through the first half of the 1960s to adhere to the general exercise patterns of the 1950s. No-effort exercise gadgetry was, however, joined by a new approach to getting in shape. In the 1920s, laboratory experiments had shown that when one leg of a frog was tied down, that leg became stronger than the other one as a result of the frog's straining against its bonds. Ramifica-

Bodybuilding and men's health in the late nineteenth century: strength through healthy living (Courtesy of the private collection of David Chapman)

Charles Atlas shows off his physique. In the pre-Schwarzenegger days of body-building, emphasis was on strength, not just appearance (Courtesy of Corbis/Bettmann-UPI)

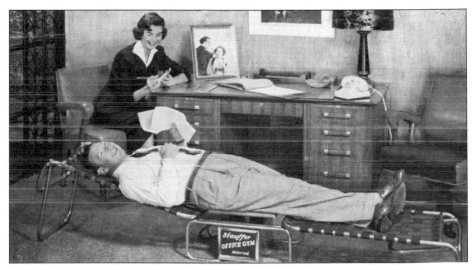

The original caption for this ad read "If your doctor says you must reduce without strain, here's how to lose that old-fashioned bay window . . . The Stauffer Office Gym is motorized to do your exercise for you by gently rhythmic motion. No discomfort"

MEN: DON'T DYE YOUR GRAY HAIR LIKE A WOMAN'S!
GROOM IN YOUTHFUL MASCULINE COLOR

Men who have dyed their gray hair wish they hadn't: *They're stuck with the tell-tale dye which slowly fades leaving their hair streaked like a woman's.*

Now you can groom your hair each morning in seconds, and before your unbelieving eyes your hair has become not only natural, gleaming, healthy —it has regained your own youthful color. That's exactly what happens! As you rub in ColorGroom—just as you have been doing with your favorite hair dressing—it imparts to your hair the natural-looking color that will take off years from your appearance. And you're not stuck with ColorGroom. ColorGroom will not rub off on your pillow, yet a shampoo removes the color any time you wish. It's just as simple as that: ColorGroom is rich in lanolin, is not sticky or greasy. And it is NOT A DYE!

If you are not absolutely satisfied, return ColorGroom and get every penny back. Mailed in plain wrapper.

COLORGROOM

Brian-Lloyd Co., Dept. C-2
11 East 47 Street, New York 17, N. Y.

Please send me a 30 day supply of Color-Groom in ☐ Black ☐ Brown ☐ Blond. I enclose $1.98. If I'm not satisfied that ColorGroom is all you say it is I may return it for full refund.

Name ....

Address ....

City .... Zone ... State ....

Magazine ad for hair coloring for men from the 1950s

Not everyone found "streaming, gleaming, flaxen, waxen" hair beautiful in the 1960s (Courtesy of Photothèque)

As Gerald Lloyd "Kookie" Kookson III, the parking-lot attendant turned private eye on 77 *Sunset Strip*, Edd Byrnes was the embodiment of male vanity in the 1950s (Courtesy of World Wide Photo)

The buffing up of G.I. Joe: the original G.I. Joe doll (1964), above, and an action figure introduced in the 1990s, opposite (Courtesy of Hasbro Industries)

Getting into shape without effort with Trim-Jeans

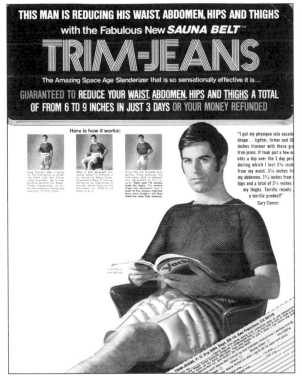

JFK links fitness to holding back the tide of communism in the early 1960s (Courtesy of *Esquire* magazine)

tions of this discovery languished until two German physicians applied them to the human body in 1953, thereby giving rise to the new "science" of isometric contraction, or IC. Isotonic exercise enlarges muscle by moving it, while isometric exercise pits muscle against an immovable object without moving the muscle itself. Adherents claimed that isometric movement stimulated 100 percent of muscle fibers compared with only 50 percent in isotonic exercise. Furthermore, there was no danger of strain, because static muscles were immune to damage no matter how great the pressure applied. While it couldn't reduce poundage and had no effect on stamina or endurance, IC was touted for its ability to trim waistlines by several inches through a few daily exercises that took only seconds.

By the 1960s, IC had become firmly established in athletics, used in professional football and other sports to build athletes' strength. The Green Bay Packers, one of the first teams to adopt the new miracle system, attributed their astoundingly successful 1961–1962 season to its benefits. IC was almost immediately found to be known to the Russians, making it all the more essential that Americans master it. IC held out the promise of transforming Americans, and especially out-of-shape executives, into powerful Samsons, but without a lot of unsightly bulging muscles.

Claims about the benefits of isometric exercise quickly escalated to the point where it was being touted as capable of adding "forty health-packed years" to one's life in just "a few fun-packed minutes each day." Best of all, since only fifteen seconds were required for an IC exercise session, the boredom of conventional workouts was avoided. Busy executives could simply place their hands underneath their desks while dictating memos to their secretaries, push for six seconds, and stay fit and strong. These miracles could be accomplished outside the office as well: "Think of all the time men spend waiting around for women," quipped advertisers, pointing out that such empty moments could be spent building strong abdominal walls.

From a manufacturer's standpoint, isometrics had one major drawback: once the instruction book describing the exercises was purchased, no further equipment was needed. Marketing savvy soon bridged this gap with the Bullworker, which was billed as a revolutionary exerciser based on isometrics. Though ostensibly used by professional athletes, including Muhammad Ali, the Bullworker's promotions sounded strangely like advertising for Sauna Belts and Trim-Jeans: its outstanding attribute was that to reap its benefits, the user barely had to move. Thin arms could be transformed into muscular pillars and flabby abdomens turned to steel, all with a few efficient exercises requiring only seconds. Before the Bullworker, anyone could do isometrics with no equipment; now the public was convinced it needed a product. The Bullworker served as a model for the American way of exercise, blending the "science" of isometrics with effortlessness, convenience, and consumerism.

Ultimately, isometrics ran afoul of medical scrutiny, not because it was ineffective, like spot reducing, but because it was harmful. Studies of weight lifters showed that severe isometric exercise radically increased blood pressure because the tension it engendered cut off blood flow. At greatest risk were those most likely to be using isometrics—flabby older men. One doctor's prescription: give up low-effort IC for high-effort jogging. But this wasn't a prescription many men were ready for—yet.[4]

Somewhere between overexertion and no exertion lay the prospect of going to the gym. The typical gym, however, was a low-rent, bare-bones smoke-and-sweat-saturated hangout for boxers and bodybuilders; few self-respecting middle-class men would venture inside one. Major cities also had health and athletic clubs, the latter generally by invitation only and serving the upper-middle and middle classes. Like the Golden Door Spa, health clubs were more like vacation resorts than exercise centers. Sunlamps and massage tables were more in evidence than barbells; instead of sweating with free weights, members lounged in steam rooms and chatted about the stock market. A typical "workout" might consist of a few minutes under the sunlamp and twenty minutes in the sauna, followed by a massage, a quick bite to eat, and a shave. The more ambitious might try a brief session of leg lifting and stretching. The few members who did serious workouts referred to the sunlamp-steam-massage contingent as "ghost members"; but these "ghosts" represented by far the largest segment of most health clubs. The general view was that exercise was a necessary evil, to be made as palatable as possible by reasonably pleasant surroundings and the congenial company of fellow sufferers. Then along came Vic Tanny.

Tanny, a onetime weight lifter who won a New York State championship in the 1930s, was passionately committed to exercise for cutting down weight and for its therapeutic benefits. In 1940, he opened a gym in Santa Monica, California, and twenty years later owned more than eighty health clubs, grossing over thirty million dollars annually. Tanny saw himself not only as a health guru but as a political savior. By spreading his gyms worldwide, he expected to bring about a major U.S. victory in the Cold War; all that Americans needed to prevail over Russia was regular workouts at Tanny facilities. Tanny even contemplated a massive demonstration of strength and fitness to be held at the Los Angeles Coliseum, a spectacle he was convinced would terrify the Russians. No less than that consummate cold warrior John F. Kennedy, Tanny believed that the fitness of a nation's people was inseparable from the power of the nation itself. But far more than his politics, Tanny's formula for fitness pushed the right middle-class buttons and made him the father of the modern American health club.

Instead of dreary inner-city hangouts, Tanny's establishments were temples of luxury and respectability. Charcoal grays and pinks predominated; lighting was flatteringly soft, carpets thick, exercise benches covered with white leather, and the deodorized air filled with Muzak. The clubs resembled nothing so much as middle-class living rooms, which made them perfectly attuned to their time and clientele.

Along with their aesthetic charms, Tanny's clubs offered an entirely new fitness experience. Workouts consisted of real routines, performed with gleaming chrome equipment. At the same time, the environment was one of restraint and decorum, where excessive grunting was frowned upon. Tanny's routines were moderate; much of the exercise consisted of stretching and use of light weights. It was a formula calculated to appeal to a middle class that appreciated the value of fitness but wanted to achieve it in pampered moderation. And it was especially appealing to men because it did not emphasize diet. Philosophically, Tanny was opposed to diets because nobody (especially men) stuck to them. His advertisements called for Americans to "take it off, build it up, make it firm"—a message that demanded physical effort, but not in unreasonable doses.

By the end of the 1960s, Tanny's empire had fallen into a shambles. Charges of fraudulent advertising and deceitful sales practices brought a rash of court judgments at the same time that enthusiasm about exercise was waning. Sales representatives used high-pressure tactics to induce clients to sign up, preferably for long-term contracts; they in turn were given no quarter from Tanny, who once sent out telemarketing instructions concluding with the admonition "If you fail to get an appointment, take a gun out of your desk and shoot yourself." Americans weren't ready for sustained, committed exercise; after a few weeks of working out, many tried to escape their expensive contracts. An explanation for Tanny's failure was offered by Rudy Smith, who a decade later launched the successful Holiday Spa chain of California health clubs. In the 1960s, Smith said, there wasn't much emphasis on muscles and good bodies; for a generation absorbed in war protests and social reform, "lousy bodies were a status thing."

There were two forms of exercise in tune with 1960s ideals. Women's magazines had begun to mention the benefits of yoga, touting it as an ancient beauty secret, and tai chi, incorrectly but enthusiastically described by *Vogue* as a form of calisthenics.

Initially, both were directed at women, and their appeal lay in their presumed effortlessness. The counterculture's romance with yoga spread to some men, who tended to view it as a means less of losing weight or firming up flab than of intensifying body awareness and joining the physical body more closely to the spiritual self. But few men over the age of thirty had much interest in yoga.

For many of these, the game of choice was golf. President Eisenhower had promoted the game's therapeutic benefits, and doctors applauded its effects on the respiratory system, as open-air exercise pumped oxygen into tired bloodstreams, as well as the salubrious effects of a smooth golf swing on aging hips and arms. Golf harked back to the nineteenth century, when sports were valued for instilling qualities like moral virtue and sportsmanship, and was credited with improving everything from concentration to a sense of fair play—not to mention patience.

In 1969, *Business Week* noted that while Americans' aversion to exercise was running as high as ever, "real" exercise was becoming legitimate. As doctors struggled to define what constituted adequate exercise, golf came under attack. Doctors dismissed it by pointing out that not only did it not burn off calories but it increased tension if not played well. Within only a few years, the venerable game was demoted to the level of bowling—a pastime for the torpid.

Virtually overnight, after years of overcaution about the dangers of excessive exercise, doctors switched gears and campaigned to undo physical neglect. The body of the typical American male, warned one physician in 1968, was so atrociously maintained that if his age were based on the condition of his circulatory system, he was middle-aged at twenty-five. The alarm had been sounded not by bodies that looked bad externally but by bodies that weren't functioning well internally. The link between stress, excess weight, and heart disease, already trumpeted in the 1950s, had prompted furious debate over the role of diet, exercise, and personality type—but few answers as to how much exercise was necessary or whether it was necessary at all. Typical of the confusion was a 1954 British study comparing sedentary bus drivers with conductors who spent their workdays running up and down stairs on London's double-deck buses. The study's findings that the conductors suffered less heart disease than the drivers were soon challenged, most notably on the question of whether the drivers' health was the result not of their activity level but of the higher responsibility and stress of their jobs.

Contradictions and confusion abounded, but men were sufficiently worried about their physical condition to respond eagerly to an emergent "fitness" industry whose products promised to bestow the "joy of elastic arteries" on short-winded, flabby males. In addition to buying effortless exercise equipment, Americans were spending fifty million dollars at the end of the decade on exercise machines like treadmills and stationary bicycles. "You can jump out of bed and start to work!" busy executives were told by the makers of Exercycle, which every self-respecting businessman was expected to have in his office, his bedroom, or both. But even as manufacturers exulted over exponential increases in sales, they remained fully aware that their products were "not likely to make perspiration popular"; significantly, the hottest seller in 1969 was a treadmill device called the *walker*-jogger. Amid ongoing ambivalence about how much sweat was necessary, a new health mentor emerged with a radical strategy for building good health through exercise. Dr. Kenneth Cooper, a former air-force surgeon and health researcher, introduced the gospel of aerobic exercise. Serious exercise was about to begin.[5]

Plastic Surgery and the Male Psyche

At the end of the 1940s, about 15,000 Americans every year had cosmetic surgery. By the end of the 1960s, this number had swelled to nearly 500,000, but female patients still outnumbered males by more than twenty to one. The surgery was attracting more patients because it continued to advance technically, offering not only face-lifts but body-sculpting procedures like breast augmentation and stomach tightening. The 1960s "no bra" look was blamed for sending women running to plastic surgeons' offices, where they could take advantage of new "Natural Feel" silicone implants in a variety of sizes. To explain their growing patient lists, plastic surgeons cited not only the popularity of bralessness but also the decade's "emphasis on youth and nudity."

Still, general attitudes about plastic surgery hadn't changed much. Surgeons and laymen alike continued to frown upon the idea of healthy people submitting to surgery to banish unwanted wrinkles or bulges. Some members of the medical profession argued that plastic surgery should be limited to patients with serious deformities resulting from birth defects or bad car accidents. To many critics, the desire to improve on nature was indicative of a "sick" society in which "the *Playboy* image of nubile youth" had triumphed. Cosmetic surgeons may not have agreed, but they were concerned about the psychological condition of potential patients.

The link between psychology and cosmetic surgery dates back to the beginning of the twentieth century, when psychoanalytic thought was dominant and analysts were trained to ferret out the reasons *why* a patient was worried about a particular physical defect. Alteration of the "symptom"—through a nose job, for example—without understanding the underlying motivation for having the surgery might cause the patient to refocus the unresolved problem onto some other body part, leading to an endless cycle of dissatisfaction with one's body no matter what cosmetic procedures were performed and no matter what their outcome. Even the most successful body changes, psychiatrists warned, could be followed by a period of maladjustment because people might not feel like themselves and might become psychologically disoriented.

Throughout the 1960s, surgeons used psychological testing to screen patients, rejecting as many as half of all applicants on this basis. Johns Hopkins Hospital subjected *every* prospective cosmetic surgery patient to a rigorous mental examination on the premise that the plastic surgeon's skill was irrelevant if he failed to analyze correctly his patients' psychological motivations. Psychiatrists offered tactics for identifying psychotics and misfits: schizoids could be recognized by their avoidance of eye contact and their tendency to squirm when asked why they wanted surgery, while obsessives were identifiable by their overly careful grooming. Plastic surgeons bemoaned the difficulty of deciding whether to perform cosmetic procedures because, as one explained, "if you're not careful, you can tip a neurotic into a really bad situation." Occasionally, mistakes were made, as in the case of a woman who appeared normal but, after having a face-lift, "ran amok," divorcing her husband and going off to Mexico, where she took a lover half her age.

If women, the more natural candidates for cosmetic surgery, could suffer such traumatic reactions, how much worse would be the impact on men? Of 117 patients who applied for cosmetic surgery at Johns Hopkins Hospital between 1957 and 1959, 20 were men—every one of whom was diagnosed by the hospital's psychiatric staff as "seriously disturbed"; more than a third were diagnosed as psychotic. Psychiatrists described male cosmetic surgery patients as having "sweeping" personality problems and designated them "a far sicker group psychologically" than their female counterparts.

Those outside the medical field held basically the same views about cosmetic surgery. The attorney David William Horan warned that whereas doctors defending themselves in malpractice suits were usually regarded sympathetically by juries, who wanted to believe in both their competence and good intentions, doctors facing a charge related to cosmetic procedures could not expect this advantage. The average juror didn't know anyone who had had elective cosmetic surgery and didn't understand why a man, in particular, would subject himself to an unnecessary operation.

Though the majority of cosmetic surgery patients were women, doctors had noticed a small but steady increase in the number of men requesting face-lifts by the end of the 1960s. The medical profession, however, continued to approach male surgery with caution and to recommend "careful pre-operative evaluation and possibly psychiatric evaluation" before committing to surgery. *Plastic and Reconstructive Surgery* berated the lay press for underplaying the potential problems associated with facial surgery and for implying that a man could trade in his old face "as easily as a second-hand car." Clearly, neither American men nor their doctors were ready to embrace cosmetic surgery as a path to male self-improvement.[6]

Sex in the 1960s: Fern Bars, One-Night Stands, and the Pill

In the 1950s, the "swinging single" vision had emerged from the pages of *Playboy*. According to the magazine, the ideal single was a handsome, financially successful bachelor. It was much harder to convince women that being single was desirable, especially since prior to the mid-1960s they generally did not go to bars unescorted or have casual sex with interchangeable partners. It was left to the entrepreneurial Helen Gurley Brown to create an image of the *Cosmopolitan* woman by equating singleness with sexiness and encouraging women to become proficient at sex and enjoy it uninhibitedly.

Brown's job was made easier by the sexual revolution and the human potential movement's emphasis on satisfying individual needs. Being single evolved almost overnight from a questionable state at best, and a pitiable one at worst, to a glamorous and desirable lifestyle. Legitimization of singlehood was boosted when the first singles bars opened on Manhattan's Upper East Side in the mid-1960s. Amid their fern-bedecked, Tiffany-lamp-lit ambience, a revolution in dating and sexual behavior would take place.

Both men and women flocked to the new temples of mating and dating with great expectations. But, as Barbara Ehrenreich points out, casual sex has always been *the* macho symbol; what if this male territory suddenly must be shared with women? And what if those women demand new standards of quantity *and* quality in their sexual encounters? To become swingers, women had to transform themselves from prey into predators, make themselves as available as the men who warily circled around them.

To disguise their predatory ambience, singles bars vied to offer the most luxurious accoutrements. Describing his lavish club, which featured overstuffed leather chairs and a mosaic dance floor lit to look like stained glass, a Denver entrepreneur explained that it wasn't really a bar but a sophisticated cocktail party for discriminating men and women turned off by the body-shop atmosphere of his competitors. Low lights added to the mystique, diminishing eye contact and enhancing and softening appearance. But no matter how low the lights or plush the decor, bars and clubs were hunting grounds.

Men spent hours grooming and primping before heading out for the evening. Once customers were ensconced among the ferns and low lights, their tactics included the "three-second stare rule," intense eye contact intended to evaluate looks and to establish interest. The stares often went both ways, with women scrutinizing male looks as closely as men scrutinized theirs. Many were openly critical of men who were overweight, badly dressed, or obviously trying to disguise a flaw—like wearing an ascot to hide a flabby neck or a cap to hide a bald head. Men were aware of this criticism; in studying a popular Manhattan singles bar, sociologists found that although men consistently expressed a preference for the best-looking women, few actually approached them, apparently fearful of rejection. Men also believed that women attached more importance to men's looks than they acknowledged. Even more dismaying was that the more attractive and financially well-off a woman was, the higher premium she placed on how a man looked.

While upping the ante on male looks, women didn't abandon their traditional interest in a man's career and financial status. Criticism of their occupations and incomes aroused resentment in many men, who considered it an unfair double standard: even successful women weren't willing to reverse financial roles and take responsibility for the economics of dating. The psychologist Warren Farrell, self-proclaimed liberated man and author of three best-selling books on contemporary masculinity, points out that a man would be very much aware that "the same woman who competes with him at his office, who may even be his economic equal or superior, still grades him on his wage earning." Recalling his Beverly Hills singles bar days, a lawyer admits that he and his friends invented a different occupation for every evening—always one better than the one they actually had. Ploys like these were hardly conducive to intimacy or honesty and, even if successful, might not be enough: if they spotted someone more attractive, women moved on. Resentful men often responded by refusing to pay for drinks or dinner.

By the end of the decade, the bicoastal singles industry that began with New York's bars and California's vast singles-only apartment complexes had permeated the entire country. Even in the suburbs, former havens of married-with-children couples, the singles population had nearly doubled. Single Americans weren't hesitant about spending their money, especially on luxury goods and leisure activities. Recognition of their discretionary spending power didn't go unnoticed by advertisers. Single women, for instance, spent twice as much annually on clothing as married ones, and 40 percent of the singles population went to the movies every week compared with only 16 percent of married couples.

In response, advertising glamorized and eroticized single life and heightened the importance of sex as a source of personal fulfillment and self-esteem. The problem with making sex so central to self-definition was that, like breadwinning, not all men were good at it. Nor did men's problems with the new sexual order come only from singles bars; the medical profession also added to the pressure for male performance.[7]

When the birth-control pill Enovid was introduced in May 1960, people anticipated that it would liberate sexual pleasure from the risk of pregnancy and "release pent-up womanly passion." Doctors and counselors predicted a plunge in the rate of marriage problems, only to discover by mid-decade that whatever its benefits for women, the pill had not-so-beneficial effects on many men.

Gynecologists and other medical professionals observed that trouble often began when "previously normal" wives suddenly experienced sharp increases in passion as a result of being freed from pregnancy fears. Instead of being delighted at this turn of events, many husbands were dismayed. Some claimed to prefer the unpredictability of sometimes being turned down, while others, who thought of themselves as sexually insatiable, were jarred when enthusiastic wives offered them the chance to prove it. For many men, when women assumed the dominant role in sexual relations or became "the least bit animalistic," both egos and erections were prone to collapse. Instead of ushering in an era of sexual enlightenment and marital bliss, the birth-control pill removed the biological basis for the double standard, turning women into what the sociologist David Riesman called "critical consumers of male performance." Small wonder that by the end of the 1960s, one doctor had called for a revival of the "shy Southern belle" as an appropriate model for American womanhood and a solution for the deteriorating American marriage.

In 1966, Dr. William Masters and Dr. Virginia Johnson's *Human Sexual Response* celebrated the inexhaustible ability of women to experience orgasms. Using a device resembling a plastic dildo connected to a camera to observe and photograph more than ten thousand female orgasms, the doctors concluded that not only were women capable of multiple orgasms but their orgasms could last as long as forty-three seconds, a physical performance impressive in itself and even more so in comparison to Kinsey's findings that men's entire sexual performance lasted, on average, no more than two minutes (requiring, Kinsey dutifully recorded, between forty and fifty thrusts to achieve). Masters and Johnson not only documented the prevalence of the female orgasm but took a far tougher stand than Kinsey on what constituted premature ejaculation: if a man couldn't control himself long enough to satisfy his partner at least 50 percent of the time, he was a failure.

The orgasm, thrust into public life by medical research and by the higher visibility of sexuality, promptly became, as *Esquire* announced shortly after publication of Masters and Johnson's opus, "*the* new female status symbol." Just as two decades later the ticking of biological clocks would raise female anxiety about childlessness, women who hadn't had an orgasm by the time they reached thirty were likely to panic, believing there was something dreadfully wrong with *them*. Old attitudes didn't die easily, and it wasn't immediately recognized that providing the female orgasm was a *male* responsibility. Frigidity continued, at least for a while, to be an obstacle for women to overcome; even Masters and Johnson designated "preoccupation and fatigue," not male incompetence, as the greatest deterrents to female sexual response. Advice columns cautioned women that happy marriages—that is, marriages with orgasms—weren't "field daisies" that could sprout anywhere; they had to be nurtured, like "fine hybrid rosebushes." As to who was to do the nurturing, women were told that both the likelihood and the intensity of orgasms could be enhanced if they strengthened their pelvic musculature and moved their bodies vigorously during intercourse, "as if your behind [is] loaded with ball bearings."

In 1970, the two doctors published *Human Sexual Inadequacy*, an overnight best-seller that dealt less with the joy of orgasm than with the agony of sexual failure. Claiming that the greatest cause of escalating divorce rates was sexual incompatibility, which they believed to afflict half of married couples, Masters and Johnson argued that sexual dysfunction had become so serious that it could no longer be left in the hands of psychologists and ministers and must be considered a full-fledged medical issue. Sexual incompatibility, the doctors made clear, wasn't just a female issue; historically, the single constant source of male sexual dysfunction had been "the level of cultural demand for effectiveness of male sexual performance." All a woman had to do to be potent, Masters concluded, was to lie still. If she didn't have an orgasm, however, it probably wasn't due to failure on her part.

At the end of the 1960s, women were being told that having orgasms was their right, and it was a man's obligation to provide them. Not surprisingly, men didn't always respond well to this burden. In response to statistics indicating that 60 percent of American women rarely or never climaxed, one unsympathetic man said that nevertheless they probably loved their husbands and "enjoyed their embraces"; why wasn't that enough? Was every woman in the world now entitled to frequent orgasms and every husband required to provide them?

As the 1960s drew to a close, utopian optimism and social activism waned, battered by a general backlash against the escalating violence of protest movements and the shrill demands of competing interest groups. Instead, Americans turned inward and became an intensely psychological people obsessed with thinking about themselves and examining the meaning of their lives. Described as a "therapeutic search for the self," the new introspection shaped the consciousness of what Tom Wolfe identified as the Me Generation, for whom self-awareness applied, by extension, to the physical and sexual self. Exercise, diet, vitamins, and cholesterol levels became national obsessions as Americans came to believe that improved personal appearance and good health could guarantee social success and lead to love and happiness.[8]

4

A CULTURE OF NARCISSISM

MEN IN THE 1970s

People who don't go to health clubs and aren't in the shape
they should be in either lack . . . intelligence or character.
—Rudy Smith, president, Holiday Spas

The psychologist and social researcher Daniel Yankelovich, reflecting on the "new rules" of personal conduct that followed in
the wake of the 1960s, was concerned that the old self-denial ethic
had been replaced by "the strange moral principle that 'I have a
duty to myself.' " Yankelovich was one of many social critics to
identify the distinguishing quality of the 1970s to be the ascendancy of a culture of narcissism. Rooted in the individualism and
self-actualization of the preceding decade, and combined with an
increasingly hedonistic consumerism, attention to the self offered
refuge from a world that was becoming darkly unpredictable.

The term "pathological narcissism" was coined by Sigmund
Freud at the turn of the century. Narcissism exists in everyone but
becomes pathological when associated with unrealistic expectations
and preoccupations. The American Psychiatric Association's
Diagnostic and Statistical Manual of Mental Disorders, fourth edition
(*DSM-IV*), identifies pathological narcissism as a "pervasive pattern

of grandiosity [and] need for admiration" that begins in early adult-hood. Characteristics of the narcissist include an exaggerated sense of self-importance, need for excessive admiration, lack of empathy for others, and the belief that one is "special and unique." Further-more, the *DSM* continues, narcissism typically involves "preoccupa-tion with fantasies of unlimited success, power, brilliance, *beauty*, and ideal love" (italics mine). Above all, it is concerned with self-esteem regulation; and as Americans have come to derive less comfort from conformity to social constructs like church and community, self-esteem has become more dependent on external events. In the case of men, as long as they were unchallenged in a patriarchal society, self-esteem was readily derived from their privileged positions. By the 1970s, this had ceased to be the case.

In 1979, in an attempt to explain some of the psychic disloca-tion of that difficult decade, the historian and cultural theorist Christopher Lasch published *The Culture of Narcissism,* a jeremiad against the self-absorption of modern society. Lasch saw narcissism less as a psychological malady than as a cultural one. Having aban-doned political protest and social reform, Americans were turning inward—but not toward the family and community, as in the 1950s. Instead, they were obsessed with finding what Lasch called "techniques of emotional self-management" in order to cope with self-doubt created by self-preoccupation. By this time, 1960s self-awareness therapies had expanded to include a mind-boggling array of guides, manuals, and methodologies promising self-transformation and personal liberation. Jerry Rubin, who had for-merly busied himself with political protest, spent the first five years of the 1970s experiencing "est, gestalt therapy, bioenergetics, rolf-ing, massage, jogging, health foods, tai chi, Esalen, hypnotism, modern dance, meditation, Silva Mind Control, Arica, acupunc-ture, sex therapy, and Reichian therapy." Yet no matter how much attention the new psychological man lavished on himself, he was plagued by anxiety, depression, and psychic emptiness and was dependent on the admiration of others for his own mental health. Narcissism, far from being a celebration of the self, was indicative of profound self-doubt, the result of which was an escalation of attention to one's personal feelings and one's looks.

Though Lasch's critique of hedonistic individualism and misplaced therapeutic impulses contains a great deal of truth, narcissism wasn't the only factor behind men's preoccupation with body image. Unprecedented developments in postwar American society were also factors: the decline of American power and prestige abroad, and economic stagnation and collapse at home. As grand expectations nurtured since the end of World War II collided with new limitations, Americans became disillusioned, fearful, and self-preoccupied. The convergence of these cultural and economic forces would have especially dire consequences for the most privileged group in America.

The Last Good Year

For more than a quarter century, Americans had enjoyed an economic boom of staggering proportions. Then came 1973, which economists darkly designated America's last good year. If a single turning point can be identified, it would be the 1973 OPEC oil crisis, which revealed that America no longer controlled its economic destiny. Under assault from intensified international competition, U.S. economic growth ground to a virtual standstill, with devastating effects on wages and incomes.

Flush with success in the rich postwar years, corporations had become "top heavy armies . . . full of unnecessary troops who were not equipped to face serious industrial warfare." Downsizing was a logical response, as was a process called vertical disintegration, in which old pyramidal structures were displaced by flat organizations, with no room for middle management. From the end of World War II until the end of the 1960s, men between the ages of forty and fifty could expect their earnings to increase by 30 percent over a ten-year period. From 1973 until the early 1980s, they would see a 14 percent decline in their ten-year earnings.

Worse yet, corporate belt-tightening, mergers and takeovers, and automation eliminated hundreds of thousands of jobs, especially well-paying ones. Automation alone had eliminated ten million industrial jobs by the end of the 1970s. In 1975, nine million people in America were unemployed.

Unemployment cut across all occupations, even the most prestigious. Although dramatic images of unemployed Rust Belt blue-collar workers and shuttered auto plants dominated the media, one in six displaced workers was a manager or professional, and one in five worked in a white-collar technical, sales, or administrative job. Computers and telecommunications cut a swath through the ranks of middle managers, replacing them as sources of information.

For a middle class unaccustomed to downward mobility, these changes had devastating psychological consequences. Income loss also meant losing many of the perks of middle-class status, like home ownership. The proportion of Americans who owned their homes fell for the first time ever. As baby boomers entered the workplace en masse, armed with the highest proportion of college degrees in the nation's history, they would overwhelm the sagging job market and turn the expected correlation between higher education and higher income on its head.

Expectations of personal fulfillment had been stimulated by 1960s idealism as well as by the rise of national affluence and increasing opportunities for previously disadvantaged Americans. But growing opportunities for one group meant decreasing opportunities for another. Much of the ensuing misery was attributable not only to social and psychological realities but to structural changes in the workplace.[1]

The Gamesman

In 1950, just over one-third of U.S. jobs were classified as white-collar. In 1979, just over half fell into this category. The shift to white-collar work underlined a parallel development: America had become a service economy. The problem with service jobs was that many of them paid less than the jobs they were replacing, especially in manufacturing. Service-sector growth also skewed unemployment statistics: many laid-off workers were able to find work, but usually at much lower salaries than their former jobs paid.

As the corporation changed, so did its employees. A 1960s survey of Fortune 500 companies indicated that the three traits most in demand for executives were decisiveness, intelligence, and the ability to inspire loyalty. Of these, the last was cited by more than 80 percent of respondents. Among companies with more than one billion dollars in annual sales, three-quarters of the CEOs had been in their jobs for more than twenty years and expected similar dedication from their successors.

A decade later, loyalty and conformity no longer guaranteed success or security, and corporate life required different styles of management and job performance. At the end of the 1960s, youthful entrants into the workplace were demanding meaningful work, openness in communication, and freedom to express individuality. But observers noted that while these idealistic young executives talked a great deal about the need to remedy the shortcomings of the corporate world, as well as those of society at large, few did much to bring this about— primarily because, as one "old" executive pointed out, "they are so absorbed . . . in their own personal development." Asked in 1979 how important he considered loyalty, a young manager responded, "Loyalty? That's kind of archaic."

If idealistic rhetoric about changing corporate culture was largely theoretical in the 1960s, the economic climate of the 1970s prompted real change. Corporate strategists called for "heroes" and "outlaws" to run beleaguered companies. The ideal leader was described as a "gamesman," an innovative risk taker exemplified by John F. Kennedy. He was bright, informal, flexible, and enthusiastic, in stark contrast to the outdated, paternalistic image typified by Dwight D. Eisenhower. Physically, any quality suggesting tiredness or aging raised questions about a man's competence and ability to stay the course.[2]

The workplace wasn't the only source of male insecurity; men had to cope with radical changes in their relationships with women as well. The growing importance of youth, the putative sexual revolution, and feminism had fused to force men to reexamine the old question "What do women want."

Body Image and the Single Life

In the mid-1970s, being single had become not only legitimate but desirable, even glamorous. Physical appearance became more important as it became likely that women and men would marry later, stay on the dating circuit longer, and have more sexual partners over the course of their lives. Of the many factors that created the growing cohort of single people, the escalating divorce rate is perhaps most evocative of the 1970s and the Me Generation's quest for happiness.

Once an indication of personal failure, fraught with humiliation and shame, divorce became a positive life choice in the 1970s; there was even a line of greeting cards to congratulate the recently divorced. A century earlier, divorce most often resulted from the failure of one partner, or both, to fulfill society's expectations of marital stability. Refusal to have children was just cause, as was unwillingness or inability to provide sexual companionship; more vaguely, divorce might be requested if one's partner was emotionally unstable or of bad character. America's divorce rate, though high compared with that of other countries, was still only 3.5 percent. By the mid-1970s, the divorce rate had reached 50 percent. The decade was also distinguished by the rapidity with which couples got divorced: in 1976, nearly one-third of divorces occurred after less than four years of marriage, and 40 percent of marriages collapsed after less than five years.

Rising divorce rates are often blamed on feminism. Nineteenth-century social critics were already complaining about the connection between divorce and female emancipation (rather speciously, since women didn't have the vote yet). Even then, not everyone saw divorce as negative: reformers and supporters of women's rights regarded it as a positive step for women victimized by bad marriages. By the 1970s, blame had once again been heaped on women's liberation. There is no denying that rising divorce rates and women's liberation were related: as women gained economic opportunity, unhappy marriages became easier to leave. It's still true that the marriage least likely to end in divorce is the one where a wife is totally dependent on her husband's earnings. But women's liberation wasn't the real problem.

Americans weren't inherently opposed to the idea of getting married, despite the high rate of divorce. What they were rebelling against was being married to the wrong person. Finding the right mate the second time around would be no easier: although four-fifths of divorced people remarried in the 1970s and 1980s, remarriages broke up at a higher rate than first marriages. Divorce was a logical outcome of the quest for self-fulfillment, because the more men and women became aware of needs that weren't being served, the less likely they were to stay in a situation that failed to contribute to their personal satisfaction.

Not only were more Americans exiting unsatisfactory marriages; continuing the trend that began in the 1960s, they were marrying later—in many cases, much later. Along with divorce, cohabitation, once frowned upon, became another means of lessening the intensity of commitment to another person and maintaining more personal freedom. At the end of the 1980s, looking back over a decade of research on marital disruption, Dr. Teresa Martin and Dr. Larry Bumpass concluded that the increasing divorce rate wasn't attributable to changes in the male-female power dynamic, or to female employment, or even to more liberal divorce laws. Rather, it was a result of "the increasing cultural emphasis on individualism."

The growing tendency among the middle and upper-middle classes to forgo having children also made divorce more practicable. In the 1950s, childlessness had been an aberration confined to a minority of couples made to feel socially embarrassed by their failure to reproduce. "Of all the accomplishments of the American woman," *Life* informed its readers in 1956, "the one she brings off with the most spectacular success is having babies." But men also rooted their identities in parenthood. Birthrates surged among all classes and ethnicities in the 1950s, and the sharpest increase of all occurred among the most educated women. But in the 1960s, college-educated women led the way to a new childless trend, choosing instead to pursue careers. Those who did opt for motherhood often chose to have only one child.

Critics promptly targeted feminism for causing women to value careers over children. Feminists countered by pointing to economic realities, which forced many women to work because a single breadwinner couldn't sustain a middle-class lifestyle. But just as parenthood had been valued by both women and men in the 1950s, the decision to remain childless was made by men as well as women. Desire among adults for freedom and self-fulfillment was a factor, as was biology. Medical progress in fertilization techniques made it possible for women to defer childbearing to a much later age.

In 1971, Ellen Peck published a best-selling primer on how to catch and keep a man by avoiding the trap of children. "For most of us," Peck wrote, "the addition of children means the subtraction of something else from life"—like trips to Switzerland and a firm body. "Sensual" and "maternal," she went on, were different types of femininity, and the wise woman would have little difficulty deciding which model to choose. Parenthood wasn't only hard physically and economically; it brought psychological change as well: the impulsive free-spirited girl would be insidiously replaced by a *mother*. Peck's sentiments were echoed by men, who complained that fatherhood demanded that they become more responsible and more mature. As a fifty-four-year-old college professor explained, he couldn't even think of having children because "I've got so much working on myself and nurturing myself and taking responsibility for myself, it's a full-time job for me." Besides, he added, he thought of himself as "thirtyish," and fatherhood would make a serious dent in this illusion.

In the mid-1970s, only 7 percent of American families belonged to a "typical" household made up of a working father, a stay-at-home mother, and two children, and at the end of the decade one-quarter of all households consisted of single people. Even if they didn't want to get married, most singles did want to be in some kind of a relationship. But relationships, in an age of individualism, were tricky things.

As the breadwinning role became less uniquely male, men placed more emphasis on personal and emotional needs. A Los Angeles attorney returning to the dating circuit was confounded to discover that "the most high-powered businessman talks about his relationships, not his job." But though they seemed to recognize the importance of interpersonal dealings, men—and women—didn't always find it easy to make the sacrifices necessary to sustain a relationship. For many, the relationship was seen as only temporary: when it ceased to satisfy, it could be disposed of. And the love object was likely to be selected on the basis of visual appeal.

Prior to the 1970s, men and women married when both had the advantage of youthful good looks. Thereafter, the mating-and-dating scene was made up of much older people. Men found themselves at risk for rejection on the basis of looks and age, especially when, as was often the case, they wanted to date younger women. As a fortyish Manhattan doctor discovered, "all of a sudden you reach an age where you look at a young woman and—click—you're not even under consideration." One thing that young women seemed to like was a full head of hair.[3]

New Options for the Follically Challenged

Though flowing tresses for men had fallen out of favor by the end of the 1960s, hair continued to play a central role in projecting positive masculine images. In 1970, Vidal Sassoon proclaimed hair the sex symbol of the coming decade, putting pressure on both sexes to have "good" hair and lots of it. (For Sassoon, the 1970s were apparently also the decade of facial surgery, which in 1972 he somewhat reluctantly admitted to having had.) Hair wasn't just sexy; it was part of the anatomy of the fit, healthy American male. In response, the pharmaceutical industry created a whole spectrum of hair products that promised not just to disguise baldness but to prevent it.

Toupees had sunk even further in prestige because of their artificiality, a quality at odds with sensibilities about naturalness stemming from the back-to-nature idealism of the 1960s. Young college-educated Americans combined their revulsion for modern technology with ecological consciousness. Humans were seen as out of touch with the natural environment, and distanced as well from that most natural and personal of all commodities, their bodies. The American marketplace was soon awash in natural foods and natural clothing fibers. In such a milieu, what could be worse than a detachable hairpiece? It was much better to regrow the hair one had lost.

The Helsinki formula, based on a corn derivative known as polysorbate 60, was a treatment developed and marketed to restore lost hair. Commonly used as a binding agent in prepared foods as well as an additive to cleaning solutions, polysorbate 60 was found to have another intriguing quality. While using it to clean the forty thousand mice that served as test subjects in experiments on skin cancer, Dr. Ilona Schreck-Purola of the University of Helsinki hospital noticed that the mice were growing patches of dense, coarse hair.

Schreck-Purola published her observations in an obscure British technical journal, but they failed to stir much interest in the scientific community. However, the findings caught the eye of an enterprising Californian, Bob Murphy, who used polysorbate 60 to develop a product he named New Generation. It quickly attracted imitators, and one of these, Pantron I, was soon outselling the original, thanks to infomercials starring the actor Robert Vaughn and the recruitment of Schreck-Purola as product endorser. Both New Generation and Pantron I claimed to use polysorbate 60 as their essential ingredient.

The ensuing court battle to determine the rightful owner of the formula need not concern us. By 1985, the Food and Drug Administration had banned nearly all over-the-counter baldness remedies, including the Helsinki formula, for failing to fulfill their promises to grow hair. Polysorbate 60's scientific importance lies in its contribution to the research that led to the discovery and marketing of Upjohn's minoxidil, the only product to date found to restore hair to balding men, although at substantial cost and with mixed and limited results. Both polysorbate 60 and minoxidil evolved from a growing understanding of the causes of baldness, as scientists gained new insights into the relationship between chemistry and heredity. They discovered that the aging process causes hair follicles to attract testosterone, which in turn causes hair to fall out. The theory behind polysorbate was that it washed away testosterone before follicles could be affected. Likewise, minoxidil was believed to block testosterone buildup while stimulating follicle growth. Before these two baldness treatments came on the market, most products for male hair loss were based on little more than hope and superstition. Now at last, science had entered the arena, enormously enhancing the credibility of the chemical hairgrowth business.

While the legal and scientific ramifications of polysorbate 60 are important, the attitude expressed by its discoverer is indicative of cultural differences in the perception of hair loss. Schreck-Purola admitted to complete mystification about the intensity of the Helsinki-formula wars and Americans' obsession with overcoming baldness. In Finland, she said, "we are not thinking all the time about hair loss." What American man, she asked, has ever died from male pattern baldness? Unless, she concluded, it was from suicide.

If a man couldn't regrow his own hair, he could follow other paths to make false hair a true body part, connected to his body not only psychically but physically. At first, manufacturers tried to create better attachment methods so that even if the product wasn't a body part it wouldn't fall off. The earliest, the Micro-Lock wig, was described as semipermanent, attached to what was left of the client's own hair with tiny aluminum compressor tubes. This process was called, reassuringly, bionic binding. The Micro-Lock wig also gave a boost to another popular product of the 1970s, the Water Pik toothbrush, which many men used to clean underneath their bionically bound hairpieces in lieu of expensive scalp brushes. Semipermanence still fell short of expectations, however, leading to the brief and ill-fated popularity of hair implantation.

Implantation was performed on at least ten thousand men over several years. Instead of using real hair, the process used acrylic fibers designed for the manufacture of carpets and imitation furs and often soaked in toxic dyes. Bacteria used the fibers as conduits into the scalp, causing scalp degeneration, irreversible hair loss, and severe infections that in some cases could only be controlled by antibiotics so virulent that they caused kidney damage. Complaints soon reached epidemic proportions, prompting warnings from the medical profession.

Harold, a Los Angeles businessman, was a typical implant victim. He hadn't given much thought to being bald until his mid-forties, when his wife died; reentering the dating world, he found himself worrying about his appearance. Uncomfortable about buying a hairpiece, Harold paid $1,250 for an artificial implant. He suffered through weeks of blinding headaches, bleeding, and severe pain before returning to his hairless state. By the end of the decade, men's romance with these innovative but flawed hair systems had ended, mainly because of the introduction of a miraculous breakthrough billed as "the only product guaranteed to grow hair."[4]

Exercising the Me Generation
and Running to Ecstasy

For many men, the 1970s brought disenchantment with the sexual revolution, the ruthlessness of singles bars, and their career prospects. Drugs weren't the answer, and going to Esalen didn't make their lives perfect, no matter how many encounter sessions they screamed through. For many, the body became a source of self-esteem and self-mastery. In a climate of uncertainty about the stability of jobs and relationships, taking control of one's body became tantamount to taking control of one's life.

In the early 1970s, aerobics was the driving force behind the explosion of interest in running and other physically intensive athletic activities. Dr. Kenneth Cooper's theory, set forth in his 1968 best-seller *Aerobics,* was that heart-pounding aerobic exercise warded off physical ailments, especially heart disease, and could also help reduce stress and stress related maladies like ulcers. The targets of Cooper's experiments, conducted in an exercise clinic housed in a colonial mansion on an eight-acre Dallas estate, were men, who were most at risk for these disorders.

The basis of Cooper's system was the measurement of how much oxygen in the circulatory system is taken in and used up in a given time (the more oxygen used before exhaustion, the better one's physical condition). Though not the first to argue for the benefits of aerobic exercise over, for instance, isometrics, Cooper was the most successful, in no small part because of his innovative aerobic point system. Points were assigned for various activities— an evening of bridge, no points; a one-mile jog, five points—and this goal-oriented, quantitative approach proved highly effective in ensuring male participation.

Avoidance of undue perspiration became passé, as men scrambled to extremes of sweating, panting physical exertion. Experts now agreed that the best exercises were consistent programs of walking, jogging, or running—a far cry from earlier advice that warned men over thirty to avoid anything more strenuous than gardening or playing golf. The new doctrine of aerobics turned corporate fitness into a national obsession. "We make colts out of old 45s," claimed the PepsiCo executive gym, one of dozens that sprang up all over corporate America. Not all exercise programs took place inside company walls; businessmen were encouraged to get aerobically fit on their own through jogging with community clubs or playing tennis, and some came up with innovative individualized programs. One advertising mogul got his daily workout by shelling on the Florida beaches near his home, claiming that he stooped to pick up shells an average of five hundred times a day.

Asked in 1973 whether he thought women should engage in strenuous exercise, a Philadelphia doctor answered that American women didn't want to exercise, adding, "we don't breed women to sweat." So it was mainly men who were targeted by the fitness industry, including manufacturers of exercise equipment. Though sales of home machines skyrocketed, the real action took place inside the new temples of fitness, where one could see and be seen. By mid-decade, a subtle shift in the rationale behind exercise had taken place: strenuous workouts didn't just make the body healthier; they also made it sexier, firmer, and more attractive.

In the 1960s, beautiful bodies hadn't been very important. Young Americans, and some not-so-young ones, relied on dramatic clothing and masses of hair more than perfect measurements to express individuality and sexuality. The youth revolution thundered unchecked into the 1970s, but with a different orientation: instead of being expressed through political activism and protest, youthfulness would be projected by the body—a body that was as sexy, fit, and lean as an eighteen-year-old's. Ironically, at the same time that cultural liberation was providing new models of beauty and shifting toward more ethnically inclusive ideals, the age at which beauty or handsomeness was ideal was becoming more narrow. For women, youth was best defined by slimness; for men, by leanness and muscularity. For single men and women, a worked-out body became an essential tool for mating and dating.

The rise of health clubs paralleled the rise of the singles population. For disillusioned patrons of singles bars and neighborhood taverns, clubs provided an attractive social alternative (although for many this meant getting up to work out at about the same time they used to get home from a night on the town). Just as in the singles bars, status was defined by a rating system. The difference was that health-club members were judged not by the stylishness of their clothing or the attractiveness of their faces but by the condition of their bodies.

All of a sudden there was nowhere to run and nowhere to hide. The journalist Martin Hochbaum, who began a lifetime routine of working out when he was in high school in the late 1950s, remembers the gym as a place where "you wore a white T-shirt or a gray sweatshirt, an old bathing suit, and combat boots." In the 1970s and 1980s, bodies were exercised not in floppy sweatsuits but in a rainbow array of revealing fashions that exalted the good body while cruelly exposing the bad one. Television, film, advertising, and city streets swarmed with taut bodies in skin-tight jeans, skimpy T-shirts, leotards, and high-cut jogging shorts. Although women were the primary victims of the emphasis on slenderness and youthfulness, men discovered that the protection once afforded by body-concealing business suits was fast slipping away.

Working out also promised to heighten sexual allure: exercise increased not only muscularity but testosterone levels, enhancing both internal and external masculinity. Even if a man wasn't especially witty or intelligent, men's magazines advised, a woman would be less likely to kick him out of bed if he had a good body. Asked how long he intended to keep up his daily 5 to 7 a.m. workout sessions, one young man answered, "Until I get a date."

For many women, men who refused to work out were of questionable virtue; if nothing else, they were probably lazy. A conversation between women in a West Hollywood health club suggests how meaningful fitness had become as an indicator of male character: "he has just about everything—money, looks, a great job"—commented one woman, but "he will not work out." Asked if she planned to "let him go," she responded, "Do I have a choice?" Another young woman, asked what she thought about men who didn't belong to health clubs, shook her head and said she found them "strange." Women liked meeting men in the gym because, as one New Yorker explained, you could see what you were getting without the camouflage of clothes. "It's a more efficient social setting than bars," said one health-club member, because "it makes the selection process easier." At the gym, a man could quickly be disqualified as a potential mate purely on the basis of his body, whereas "under other circumstances you might take an interest in his mind . . . or fall under the spell of his humor" before discovering flab, fat, or other physical horrors.

Surveying the members of upscale clubs, one could wonder why anyone bothered to be there, since everyone seemed to be in perfect physical condition already. Some prestigious clubs claimed their members joined only after getting in shape at lesser clubs; "we have no fat people here," the manager of Manhattan's prestigious Vertical Club announced proudly, making clear that the point of belonging to his club was to *stay* in shape, not to get in shape. New York's Definitions gym was established for people who already belonged to other clubs but were willing to spend six hundred dollars a month for individualized workouts tailored to their body goals. Upscale locker rooms were redolent of "sport" perfumes and lined with floor-to-ceiling mirrors that allowed patrons to see how they looked in their $350 exercise outfits before heading for Nautilus machines and aerobics classes.

"You can't afford to let yourself go" was the mantra of the exercise set; doing so would lead to psychic and physical bankruptcy. According to Rudy Smith, the president of the Holiday Spa health-club chain, working out was a means of unlocking potential, "like being entrepreneurial." If you were an executive and couldn't make the decision to keep your body in shape, how could you be trusted with other important decisions? The rhetoric of goals and decision making was especially effective in pushing men into exercise routines, which, as one man explained, provided "a sense of achievement that cannot be measured as clearly in our work or personal relationships." With all the potential benefits attributed to working out, it's hardly surprising that at the end of the 1970s nearly half of adult Americans claimed to exercise regularly. There was one form of exercise that didn't require a health-club membership and demanded virtually no equipment. For the Me Generation, running was the perfect sport.[5]

In 1970, the running population consisted largely of middle-aged, overweight executives and politicians literally running for their lives to combat sedentary lifestyles, bad diets, smoking, and stress. The news media were especially fond of tracking the jogging routes of Senators Strom Thurmond and William Proxmire around the Potomac Basin. Initially, running to fend off death from inactivity was the only acceptable reason to do it; the idea of running for pure pleasure was inconceivable. When the evangelist Billy Graham started a fitness program that incorporated several miles of jogging, he found that the hardest part of his routine was coping with the stares of onlookers.

In 1969, there were fewer than forty marathon races in the entire country; by the mid-1970s, that number had skyrocketed to nearly two hundred. The New York City Marathon, which had 126 starters in 1970, had over 16,000 entrants in 1980. Prior to the 1970s, most people who ran marathons were serious runners competing for a top place. At the end of the decade, twenty-five million Americans were transformed into runners for whom the sport wasn't just an athletic undertaking but a psychological and even spiritual one.

In 1972, Frank Shorter won the marathon at the Olympics—the first American to do so in sixty-four years—and gave a great boost to the general public's interest in running. Two years later, the California pathologist Thomas J. Bassler came up with the Marathon Hypothesis. Bassler advocated supervised marathon running for cardiac patients, based on his observation that not a single death from heart disease had been documented among marathon finishers of any age. That Bassler and his associates were extrapolating from a select group of fit, young, and highly trained runners to an entire population somehow was lost in the clamor of enthusiasm over the miraculous preventive effects of long-distance running. Running was credited by corporate executives not only with helping their hearts but with helping them stop smoking, preventing jet lag, and curing everything from hangovers to alcoholism to the common cold. Before long, books on running dominated best-seller lists, *The Runner* magazine became an instant success, and running had become a sport for Everyman—or at least for a great number of white, middle-class men.

Since running requires so little expenditure on equipment and offers so much time flexibility, it might be expected to have broad class appeal. But while white-collar men gasped on treadmills and jogging tracks, and were soon joined by growing numbers of women, blue-collar Americans showed little interest in running or in any other aerobic sports. The average marathon runner was described as "a male, 34 years old, college-educated, physically fit and well-off."

One could reason that working-class indifference to exercise was due to the physical exertion required for many blue-collar jobs; in this context, jogging might seem a second job. Blue-collar men were confounded by the popularity of running because it lacked the macho component commonly associated with sports.

Football was macho, a sport in which you inflicted pain on someone else, not yourself; forcing oneself to run twenty miles sounded more like masochism than sport.

If working-class men didn't grasp the joys of running, runners were only too anxious to explain its appeal, which often had little to do with pure exercise. Some saw running as a panacea for the lack of spiritual fulfillment that seemed to permeate society, even for men who were financially secure and successful. Others believed that the successful men who formed the core of the jogging movement ran to reclaim their once-secure world, now undermined by civil unrest, the aftermath of Vietnam, and a general retreat from belief in American power and virtue. In the opinion of a former 1960s radical, jogging and the fitness movement were nothing more than ways for the affluent symbolically to reject the comforts of their privileged lives by punishing their bodies.

Running also incorporated the middle-class virtue of deferred gratification by demanding long-term effort to bring about rewards. The psychiatry professor Michael Sacks saw the masochism of urban athletes as puritanism turned inward: the strenuous self-punishment had the ultimate objective of self-perfection, thereby legitimizing the suffering. It was true that pain seemed an integral, even desirable part of running. Mike Frankfurt, a New York attorney who ran ten miles a day every day no matter what the weather, described the experience as one of jarring pain; he never knew, he proclaimed almost joyously, what part of his body would hurt when he got out of bed in the morning.

In this most psychologically oriented of decades, legitimate positive links were identified between running and mental health. Running was believed to abolish linear thought and allow for increased creativity, evoking comparisons with meditation. When psychiatrists at the University of Wisconsin prescribed an experimental routine of jogging for severely depressed patients, those patients did as well as or better than those treated in conventional therapy. Psychiatrists even jogged alongside their patients to break down communication barriers and prescribed jogging routines instead of pills.

Even for men not suffering from any particular disorder, running promised a path to spiritual transcendence closely attuned to its times. "After a good run, you feel sort of holy," Jim Fixx, the author of the jogger's bible, *The Complete Book of Running,* confided to his legions of fans, advancing the popular belief in the potential for achieving personal perfection. A Los Angeles jogger marveled that with each movement and each inhalation he could feel "the whole world, its hopes, aspirations, dreams, sorrows, disasters," while Michael Spino, the director of the Esalen Sports Center, described running as a spiritual experience that made him want to kill his "old" self while he ran to make room for a "new, integrated Me."[6]

If these benefits weren't enough, running's ultimate claim was sexual enhancement. When the University of California at San Diego compared sexual responses of runners with men who walked for exercise, runners reported significantly higher arousal and sexual performance. On a less positive note, the solitary and occasionally all-consuming nature of running could prove sexually inhibiting. In response to a survey conducted by *The Runner,* nearly half of men claimed to spend more time thinking about running than about sex, and one-quarter said that if forced to choose between the two, they would give up sex.

Physiological reasons for the psychological benefits of jogging aren't altogether clear. The best-known gratification associated with running is runner's high. Descriptions of runner's high attest to the influence of 1970s cultural phenomena ranging from mystical self-awareness to the drug culture. Some described runner's high as a Zen-like experience, while others said it had a hallucinogenic effect, complete with changes in visual perception, colors, and patterns. Dr. Bernard Gutin, a professor of applied psychology at Columbia University, attributed runner's high to stimulation of alpha brain waves but was unclear as to how this occurred, while other doctors believe that running has a positive psychological effect because it changes the body's chemical composition. Skeptics dismiss it as hypoxia, or lack of oxygen to the brain.

The new fitness revolution had a very different character from that of the late nineteenth century: instead of team effort, most paths to fitness would be either contests between two opponents, like racquetball and tennis, or solitary pastimes like running and bodybuilding. If long-distance running did little to prepare an athlete for getting along with others, it certainly bestowed a satisfying sense of control. Runners don't have to worry about teammates. Accompanied by and competing with no one but himself, the runner was the exemplary athlete for the Me Decade. Knowing that their bodies were firm and healthy was also comforting for baby boomers passing thirty: for many of these, the importance of running lay in its ability not to fend off heart attacks but to postpone the effects of aging.

Like health clubs, running had begun as a venue for good health, but the importance of lowered cholesterol readings and improved aerobic performance would be superseded by what it could do for physical appearance. Asked about the current boom in health clubs in his city, a Chicago club owner expressed skepticism about the role of personal health. Chicagoans, he said, hadn't "cast aside their cigarettes to avoid emphysema [or] shed twenty pounds to decrease their high blood pressure." They were doing those things "so their shirts don't open on basketball-sized bellies." As for runners, they were running marathons "because all the best-looking broads are running marathons."

Fitness had clearly switched gears from the 1950s. Group calisthenics and national goals had been supplanted by a quest for individual perfection. Explaining the mania for running, sociologists cited motives like health benefits, longevity, and weight control but added that the sport's solitary nature and focus on personal achievement contributed to a "culture of the Self." Unkind critics pointed out that with both running and masturbation "there are no teammates, and the activities of one's opponents are far less significant than one's own state." As one heart specialist commented wryly, perhaps the greatest benefit derived from running was "the sense of superiority runners feel over everyone else." Even the T-shirts given to marathon participants were an advertisement for their wearers' moral supremacy, declaring, in essence, "I am healthy and care about my body."[7]

Plastic Surgery: The Dawning of Respectability

As it had in the preceding decade, plastic surgery continued to make great technological strides, but its lack of prestige within the medical profession persisted. At Bellevue Hospital in New York City, plastic surgeons were encouraged to perform their operations at other, less prestigious hospitals and leave Bellevue's operating rooms free for "real" surgeries. The head of Bellevue's plastic surgery department refused to schedule more than two cosmetic procedures a day for fear of making his department appear frivolous. Doctors were chastised for referring to rhytidectomies as face-lifts or to rhinoplasties as nose jobs and told to use the proper Latin terminology because this sounded more dignified. By the 1970s, cosmetic surgeons, tired of bad press and second-class status, had mounted a spirited counterattack.

In 1971, Dr. John Lewis, the president of the American Society for Aesthetic Plastic Surgery, devoted much of his annual address to urging his colleagues not to be ashamed of their craft. In a 1980 editorial for *Plastic and Reconstructive Surgery*, Dr. Eugene Courtiss argued that vanity could only be considered excessive if it went beyond what was considered normal. Since normalcy was what most patients expected from cosmetic surgery, they could hardly be accused of narcissism. Before long, plastic surgeons were claiming that they were making the normal *better* than normal.

The new campaign soon paid off in terms of how plastic surgeons felt about themselves: "We have a happy specialty," a Manhattan cosmetic surgeon said proudly, "one that is not fraught with tragedy and death." Asked if he felt his profession was maligned, another New York surgeon answered yes, some discrimination did remain, especially among older general surgeons. But, he said, brightening, "at a cocktail party, you're a hit . . . socially, this is an accepted thing and people are delighted to have a plastic surgeon at one of their parties."

Making vanity acceptable was of key importance in attracting men to cosmetic surgery. "Self-neglect is out," men were told in the 1970s, and "vanity is in." By the early 1970s, practitioners had noted an upward spiral of inquiries from men, mostly upper-middle-income professionals between the ages of forty-five and sixty. Doctors claimed that as larger numbers of men sought surgery, "male patients of normal psyche are the norm rather than patients with psychological problems, as in the past." One suspects that as the popularity of cosmetic surgery increased and vanity was culturally transformed into a positive trait, psychological evaluation of patients in all but extreme cases was quietly abandoned. "It is only natural," doctors proclaimed, "for people to wish to *look* as vibrant and healthy as they feel." Looking healthy wasn't the only consideration, of course; people wanted to look young.

Getting older hasn't always been greeted with dread, but in the twentieth century came a series of insidious shifts in the valuation of aging. In 1979, a study of ninety-five primarily industrial societies found that the second most important reason stated for negative stereotyping of the elderly was the decline in their physical appearance. As for men in the workplace, *The New York Times* neatly summed up the consequences of aging by pointing out that corporate shrinkage was also shrinking the ranks of "the C.E.O. belly, the wizened Walter Cronkite face of experience . . . and the furrowed brow of the thinking man." Dr. Alfred Kinsey's studies of human sexuality went a step further by linking changes in physiology to sexuality, with particularly unpleasant consequences for men. For the male, the single most important determinant of what Kinsey dryly referred to as "frequency of outlet" was age. Loss of potency became age-relative, with middle age the time of decline. Growing older took on ever grimmer connotations as sexuality became increasingly important to self-esteem. Men now had something even more dire to worry about: a malaise known as the New Impotence.[8]

The New Impotence

When asked in the early 1960s what effects the rumblings of feminism might bring about, a professor at New York University dismissed the subject with breezy aplomb. Women's new "sexual bravado," he predicted, would be short-lived even among the most sophisticated. "Men," he said, "are interested in sex, but women are interested in curtains and babies." As it turned out, they were also interested in orgasms and sexual proficiency.

In 1972, three psychiatrists published an article titled "The New Impotence." Noting that more young men were complaining of impotence and more young women were complaining about sexual inadequacy in their boyfriends, the psychiatrists suggested that social attitudes toward premarital sex, especially among women, were instrumental. A complaint common to all cases cited in the article centered on women's demands for competent male sexual performance. Their female partners' excessive demands drove subjects to inhibition, social and academic deterioration, and inability to have normal heterosexual sex. One young man was described as having been perfectly content with petting and necking, but his girlfriend found these activities immature and unfulfilling and asked that they move on to intercourse. When the couple tried to have sex, the young man ejaculated prematurely and suffered so much damage to his self-esteem that he became impotent. The study's conclusions had less to do with psychological and physical conditions than social ones: "Women," the authors stated, "seek and expect orgiastic release. Virginity is largely irrelevant." The "put-upon" Victorian woman had evolved into the "put-upon" 1970s man.

There was widespread agreement among doctors that as women became more aggressive, impotence was bound to increase. The urologist B. Lyman Stuart accused the women's liberation movement of launching a power struggle between the sexes that would intensify the stresses of modern life, especially for men. In combination with the birth-control pill, which had given women control over their reproductive lives, female aggressiveness was blamed for transforming sex into a command performance detrimental to men's "natural" sexual dominance as well as their pleasure. The predatory excesses of liberated women had created disequilibrium, pressuring men to demonstrate their potency while simultaneously making it harder for them to do so by undermining their confidence and self-esteem. One therapist claimed that casual sex was responsible for an impotence rate of 80 percent on "first encounters" because of performance anxiety. In reality, the causes of the new impotence "epidemic" were more complex and far-reaching.

Before women's liberation, explained a twenty-one-year-old college co-ed in 1972, women were not expected to initiate sex; since men only made advances when they felt like having sex, there wasn't much of a potency problem. Now, she went on, "it's stupid to be cute, passive, and subordinate. I have just as much right as he to be aggressive." For most men, it wasn't the greater availability of sex but the balance of power that was unnerving. Initiation of sexual contact by women became a recurrent complaint. It seemed that immoderate female demands were pressuring men to demonstrate their potency while simultaneously making them less able to do so: suddenly men were confronted with demands not only for sex but for *better* sex.

Worse yet, feminists and sexologists made it clear that women not only could enjoy sex but could do so without a penis. The 1970 publication of the feminist Anne Koedt's article "The Myth of the Vaginal Orgasm" set forth the proposition that it was the clitoris, not the vagina, on which female sexuality and orgasm were centered. Women's attempts to fit their experience to a male-defined sexual norm, Koedt argued, not only denied them orgasm but led most women to fake vaginal orgasm simply to satisfy their mates. Germaine Greer joined the clamor by taking aim at the missionary position, pointing out that it not only loaded a woman down with a man's weight but failed to place the clitoris in an advantageous position for stimulation and offered little more than "the shattering impact of pubic bone on pubic bone."

A few years later, Shere Hite's nationwide study of female sexuality offered a similar indictment of the assumption that women should automatically be able to achieve orgasm from vaginal intercourse. While many women preferred orgasm achieved by intercourse because they liked the intimacy, the overwhelming consensus was that penile-initiated orgasm was less intense and less satisfying. Hite concluded that female sexuality, in all its complexity and uniqueness, was being undermined because it was defined and judged in terms of its response to male sexuality. While some women may have welcomed the discovery that they could exercise better control over their sex lives, without reliance on male partners, men were less pleased by this turn of events. The psychologist Leslie H. Farber pointed out that the new laboratory-inspired autoerotism was a surefire way of avoiding "the messiness that attends most human affairs" because it "interferes not a whit with the . . . *rights and desires of others*" (italics mine).

But focusing on self-gratifying orgasms over intimacy also placed love and companionship in secondary positions. Both men and women had been led to expect perfect potency and perfect orgasms; but for many critics of the new sexual order, the ones most at fault for stirring up the cauldron of resentment and disappointment were women, whose demands for sexual fulfillment had made them more sexually accessible but also more sexually threatening. Yet it was clearly unrealistic to blame the entire impotence epidemic on liberated women. Lifestyle played a role as well.

At the very time that female sexual satisfaction was evolving into a right rather than a privilege, the growing rate of divorce and singlehood was increasing the chances of women having sex without orgasm. Social scientists studying American sexual behavior found that the likelihood of a woman having orgasm during partnered sex was strongly correlated to whether or not she was married. Among married women, the rate of usually or always having orgasms was 75 percent, versus only 62 percent for unmarried women; the rate of never having orgasms was also lower—only 2 percent versus 11 percent. These data were similar across ethnic, religious, racial, and educational, as well as age, lines. Supporting these findings, a positive correlation was found between sexual dysfunction and marital status among adult Americans, with married couples experiencing a lower incidence of sexual problems.

The study's authors concluded that the myth of single people "flit[ting] from partner to partner and . . . having a sex life that is satisfying beyond most people's dreams [is] . . . mostly a media creation," as was the impression that everyone who was having sex, especially good sex, was young and beautiful. Even among married people, all was not perfect in the sexual realm: in one survey, 43 percent of women and 31 percent of men reported having difficulties ranging from lack of interest in sex to inability to experience orgasm. Ironically, the sexual revolution had intensified the importance of physical appearance while making it harder to achieve one of the main objectives of looking good: having good sex. The assumption that good sex was there for the asking proved stubbornly persistent, however, and those who fell short of the mark were likely to have a sense of personal failure. For many, recreational drug use held out the promise of raising sexual encounters to new heights.[9]

Drug use in the 1950s had prompted shudders among the middle class, who looked at it as a problem of the inner-city poor, but in the 1960s widespread middle-class drug use became part of the ethos of self-discovery. It took on a youthful, daring cachet, and psychedelic drugs in particular reinforced feelings of communality, spiritual intensity, and knowledge of the inner self—and enhanced one's sense of sexual power. In reality, in marked contrast to their perceived benefits, drugs had negative consequences for potency.

Marijuana and LSD were the drugs of choice for a generation searching more for enhanced mental and spiritual connections than enhanced bodies, although the effects of these drugs had a decided sexual component, whether real or imagined. Marijuana was commonly believed to have aphrodisiac qualities, a belief particularly prevalent among people who had never used it. Harry Anslinger, former commissioner of the U.S. Bureau of Narcotics, described a case where a young man and his girlfriend, after smoking a single marijuana cigarette, engaged in such passionate behavior in full public view that horrified neighbors had them hauled off to jail.

A hallucinogenic that acts on the central nervous system, marijuana actually has varying effects on sexuality. Though reputed to increase sexual desire and pleasurability in the short term, marijuana can cause users progressively to lose interest in sex over longer periods. Male researchers who smoked marijuana daily for nine weeks experienced a one-third reduction of testosterone levels. THC, marijuana's active ingredient, suppresses testosterone production, causes temporary impotence, and decreases sperm count; in women, marijuana has been found to disrupt the menstrual cycle.

Users of LSD also touted its sexual-enhancement qualities. Timothy Leary thought that women were particular beneficiaries, since LSD made it possible for them to have hundreds of orgasms at a time; among men, Leary claimed the drug could prevent homosexuality. At one point, he credited LSD with being the greatest aphrodisiac of all time. He later claimed he had been misquoted and said that LSD had nothing to do with sexuality but rather aroused an all-embracing love for one's fellow man. The media vastly preferred Leary's first description, further promoting LSD's image as a sexual drug. Users, however, described their sexual activity as having a detached quality, more "interesting" than "exciting." Medical experts claim that no specific sexual function has been found for LSD.

Downers like heroin, used by many men to last longer during sex, inhibit both desire and performance by depressing the central nervous system. Heroin creates a condition of dissociation from reality, a state of virtual nirvana in total opposition to sexuality. In the 1970s and 1980s, psychedelics were largely displaced by cocaine. When coca was first introduced into industrialized society in the nineteenth century, it was considered a potentially valuable stimulant for making the laboring classes work harder and provided a popular form of recreation for the new, fast-track urbanized society. Coca's negative qualities didn't take long to surface, and by 1930 the drug had been outlawed in the United States. When it roared back into popularity as cocaine, it became especially popular among middle- and upper-middle-class Americans looking for a boost on the sexual and social fast track. Cocaine suited the 1970s generation, for whom striving in an anxious and restive society had replaced passive surrender to hallucinogenic imagery.

Cocaine was unapologetically sexual and promised heightened vitality and power, the same benefits conferred by the health club: but cocaine conferred its benefits instantly. Known as the "pimp's drug" for its sexual-enhancement effects, cocaine typically has a more pronounced sexual effect on men and allows prolonged duration of intercourse. Despite its priapic reputation, however, cocaine eventually contributes to sexual dysfunction by damaging neurotransmitters essential to sexual activity. Long-term use is addictive and eventually causes declining sexual desire accompanied by increased nervousness and paranoia; heavy users ultimately lose interest in sex. Amphetamines are also credited with increasing sexual desire but often make orgasm difficult or even impossible, especially for men, and prolonged erections can result in painful episodes of temporary priapism.

Alcohol also plays a role in impotence. Shakespeare's warning that alcohol "provokes the desire, but . . . takes away the performance" is quite correct: alcohol is a brain depressant with anesthetizing effects on both cognitive and sexual functions in large doses. The primary function of alcohol in nearly every society is reduction of anxiety, with concomitant relaxation of culturally imposed inhibitions. This latter quality has prompted the widespread belief in alcohol's aphrodisiac qualities, but excessive use actually has the opposite effect. Erectile failure, especially among middle-aged men, is common with alcohol abuse, although doctors observe that men rarely acknowledge alcohol as the cause of their sexual failures. Physiologically, alcohol seriously impairs testosterone production with negative consequences for potency; it is also toxic to the testes and therefore to sperm production. Alcohol damage to the liver alters hormones, especially estrogen, which in heavy users concentrates in excessive amounts and undermines sexual drive.

Even ordinary drugs can cause impotence. Over two hundred prescription drugs, especially many commonly prescribed for high blood pressure or depression, can interfere with the erectile process. Over-the-counter medications, including painkillers, eyedrops, and cold and allergy preparations, as well as Valium and other drugs intended to calm the central nervous system, can produce impotence. So can Tagamet, widely prescribed for ulcers, and hypertension drugs like beta-blockers. One of the worst over-the-counter culprits is cigarette smoking, which causes vascular abnormality and interferes with the liver's metabolism of sex hormones. Anabolic steroids cause sexual dysfunction and shriveling of the testicles. Overall, drug-related impotence, whether from legal or illegal drugs, is estimated to account for one-quarter of the outpatient population of impotence treatment centers. As the population continues to age, with an accompanying increase in health problems that require long-term medication, this trend can be expected to continue.[10]

Though drug use became widespread, it wasn't an everyday activity for the majority of men. Work continued to be an essential part of the male agenda. Work equaled power, which equaled potency, which was equated with sex. Wrenching though unemployment was for all its victims, managers and professionals, more accustomed by the nature of their jobs to autonomy and to feeling responsible for their successes and failures, were especially hard-hit. Skidding downward from their privileged positions was as devastating as it was unprecedented and was viewed by many men as a form of castration.

Work itself could be a source of impotence-provoking stress. Blaming male sexual dysfunction on the pressures of work wasn't a new idea: Hippocrates had blamed impotence on "preoccupation with male affairs" (as well as on having an unattractive wife). Even doctors who heaped most of the blame for rising male impotence on aggressive women suggested that overwork fostered sexual dysfunction. The work ethic and its emphasis on getting the job done were often carried into the bedroom, where a quick sexual encounter, rather than an intimate or nurturing one, could be viewed as a task accomplished, a goal fulfilled.

While admitting that hard statistics were impossible to come by, medical doctors and clinical psychologists singled out executives as likely victims of sexual dysfunction because their competitiveness and need to prove themselves made any failure traumatic. In this view, sexual failure resulted less from male-female tensions than from workplace pressures. In 1981, a Washington, D.C., business executive founded Impotents Anonymous, a self-help organization modeled on Alcoholics Anonymous.

For many working couples, sex simply became more work. Even the remedies could be problematic: couples who turned to sex therapy were likely to get homework assignments, and sex manuals contained a barrage of instructions—still aimed more at men than women—hammering home the importance of technique. Gearing sexual instruction to men put sex into a context familiar to many: a job to be well done. Unfortunately, this could transform lust into stress.[11]

The end of the 1970s brought no diminution of America's economic problems. Middle-income Americans continued to slide into lower-income categories as corporations reorganized. The term "temp" no longer referred to secretaries, as companies began hiring many employees, especially managers, on short-term contracts. Those members of the labor force who had traditionally been most favored—white men—now began to see their status and self-esteem erode. For many, the solution to this problem would lie in developing the physical attributes of masculinity to new extremes and turning to the scalpel to carve out the appearance of youth and vitality.

5

BINGEING AND BUFFING UP

MEN IN THE 1980s

> The clang of Olympic plates being tossed onto the ends of
> bars on the various racks around me was a crazy orchestra of
> primeval percussion. It sounded so Stone Age, so anciently
> *human* there . . . I mean, the place pulsed.
> —Bodybuilder describing ambience
> of Washington, D.C., gym

"I have always meant to be a better-looking person," declared
forty-five-year-old Remar Sutton in 1985. His insecurities about
his looks, Sutton confessed, had ruled his life. To rectify this situation, he embarked on a curious quest: he decided to become a
handsome man. A former advertising executive, Sutton had been a
heavy smoker and drinker much of his life; Kenneth Cooper, after
giving him a physical examination, declared him to have a biological age ten years higher than his chronological age. Though fitness
and health were part of his goal, Sutton was more interested in
becoming *handsome*. He devoted an entire obsessive year, at a cost
of $100,000, to "achieving hunkdom," a project he chronicled in a
book and a series of articles published in major national newspapers. After a year of jogging, weight lifting, dieting, and other

appropriate behaviors, Sutton's biological age was five years younger than his chronological age—but more importantly, his *exterior* body was now ten years younger, a triumph Sutton measured by calculating how many young women eyed him when he strolled down the beach. "My inward rating of how I feel about my body every day," Sutton stated, "is way up."

For an otherwise unremarkable, middle-aged professional man to undertake such a project would have been unthinkable in the 1950s—or at any other time in American history. But the 1980s weren't just any time; they were an era that gave new meaning to the idea of self-indulgence and self-absorption. The Me Generation metamorphosed into the yuppie, or young urban professional. Believed to originate during the 1984 presidential campaign, the term was loosely applied to urban baby boomers with white-collar jobs; more specifically, it referred to the high end of this demographic group, an estimated four million young Americans who, with their M.B.A.'s, BMWs, and IPOs, became models of selfishness, consumerism, and obsessive ambition. The yuppie was defined, above all else, by his *lifestyle*; one became a yuppie on the basis not of what he produced but of what he consumed.

Though in reality not everyone with a high-end lifestyle lived in the city, the true yuppie *had* to be there because, as one young man explained, "there are no health clubs in the country." The city was also the likeliest place to find Bloomingdale's stores, and the yuppie's defining quality was his ability to express his individuality by what he could buy. In addition to health clubs, chic department stores became ideal meeting places for singles, allowing prospective mates to demonstrate their taste and spending power.

The yuppie may appear to be light-years away from the more sensitive and introspective man of the counterculture. But the seeds of individualism sown in the 1960s were responsible for creating yuppies, who were baby boomers obsessed with self-identity and self-determination. Geoffrey, a lawyer who had been active in liberal demonstrations in the early 1970s, even getting teargassed in the process, explained his metamorphosis into a far-less-activist, $200,000-a-year urban professional by declaring, "I will always be a community-minded person; it's just that the shape of my concern may change." In many cases, the shape of that concern didn't extend far beyond one's own body, bank account, and trendy neighborhood.

Yuppies were responding to the realities of the economy: well aware that they were unlikely to be offered secure jobs or guaranteed advancement due to company loyalty, they did the only sensible thing. They became entrepreneurial and self-interested, obsessed with, as the title of a best-selling book put it, looking out for number one.

With its glitzy excess and widening gulf between haves and have-nots, the 1980s are comparable to the Roaring Twenties. Many Americans, baffled and disturbed by the nation's changing moral climate, yearned for simpler days and called for a resurgence of family values. The defeat of the Equal Rights Amendment in 1982 and escalating antiabortion violence sent a message that women were overstepping their bounds and needed to return to "natural," traditional feminine roles as wives and mothers.

Some things didn't change: wages and salaries, as well as job security, continued to decline, leaving working people, especially men, searching for alternative sources of self-validation. Social and economic turmoil didn't reduce expectations of personal fulfillment but made it necessary to find it in nontraditional places, heightening the importance of image. Indeed, carefully crafted self-presentation was a touchstone of one of the most visible and powerful men in America.

Ronald Reagan's presidency defined the decade politically and was a masterpiece of staging and theatrics in which image played a central role. The journalist Haynes Johnson wrote that "Reagan and television fitted into American society like a plug into a socket," producing a "parade of pleasing images" that not only entertained and informed but promoted and reinforced affluence and celebrity. Reagan created a powerful image of himself as leader—one based largely on illusion, because nearly everything he said in his television appearances was scripted. But as Neal Gabler pointed out in his analysis of the intersection of celebrity and real life, Reagan's smooth and successful presidential "performance" upped the ante for every subsequent political aspirant. Reagan was careful as well to script his physical image to fit the times—times that would have been uncomfortable with a president who looked old (even if he was). His lack of gray hair even in his seventies, his photo opportunities on horseback at his Santa Barbara ranch, all conveyed an image of dynamic, youthful leadership.

The Reagan years were marked by massive deregulation in the television industry, paving the way for cable TV, satellite dishes, and VCRs. These increased the amount of time Americans spent watching images on their televisions, as well as the variety of images available. Programs were intended not just to entertain but to sell images, identities, and lifestyles, making it possible for Everyman to emulate the rich and famous.

Ironically, the escalating importance of being "somebody" coincided with an economic climate that was anything but conducive to self-esteem and success. For many, the 1980s were a time of stagnation and decline. Demographically, too, the pressure was still on: the fastest-growing segment of the population continued to be single people.

Undermined by disillusionment and AIDS, the appeal of singles bars was in decline. As an alternative, millions of men and women turned to courtship via personal advertising. Personals weren't new but in previous years had been considered disreputable and were generally relegated to the back pages of underground newspapers or sex magazines. In the 1980s, personals cropped up everywhere and avoided the racy, insinuating copy of their predecessors. Advertisers emphasized their desire for long-term relationships, not one-night stands. Nevertheless, as in singles bars, ads were essentially concerned with the bargaining and exchange of commodities.

Psychologists, intrigued by this new method of mate selection, were quick to analyze its underlying motivations and strategies. Not surprisingly, they concluded that people tried to make themselves appear as desirable as possible in order to attract responses. Men were looking for physical attractiveness while women looked for financial security.

A review of personal advertising, however, presents a different picture. From January 1982 to the end of the 1980s, *Los Angeles* magazine, a glossy upscale monthly, published personal ads from 3,370 women "in search of" men. Though they were most likely to emphasize qualities like "professional," "educated," and "financially secure," nearly one-third specified *physical* characteristics. Key words included "tall" and "handsome" but also "fit," "trim," and "muscular." Women could be unkind, demanding "no beer bellies," "must have hair," and "no big guts." A popular code word was "VGL"—for "very good looking." Considering the qualities that women in the 1950s claimed to be looking for, women's emphasis on body image is striking. In response, an array of new products offered to heighten and perfect everything masculine, if only a man had the time, money, and will to pursue them.[1]

New Horizons in Hair

In 1980, a thirty-eight-year-old dialysis patient taking medication for high blood pressure began to sprout random hair on his nose, forehead, and other body parts. This wasn't the first time a link had been noted between medication and hair—or plumage: when male hormones were experimentally injected into mynah birds in the 1950s, their feathers fell out. When injections were discontinued, the birds stopped shedding and regrew their plumage. The problem with hormonal treatments was their undesirable and potentially dangerous side effects. Clearly, a manufacturer who could produce a viable hair-regrowth lotion without side effects would have the discovery of the century. This was precisely what pharmaceutical giant Upjohn set out to do.

In 1983, Upjohn began testing minoxidil's predecessor, a blood-pressure drug called Loniten. The company spent over $100 million developing a safe, topical form of the drug, practicing on a rare form of macaque monkeys, which bald in patterns similar to humans. Encouraged by experimental results, Upjohn called for human volunteers to participate in tests at twenty-eight medical centers. Enthusiastic males called from all over the country, jamming the phone lines so other patients couldn't get through for months.

In spite of this ebullience, results weren't overwhelming. About half of the test subjects did grow hair, but less than half of these were able to raise more than a fuzz. Results varied slightly in subsequent testing, but overall, no more than 15 percent of the men grew hair that could be classified as dense. Still, evidently convinced that being able to grow some hair on some men some of the time was good enough, Upjohn launched Rogaine in 1988.

American men had spent $200 million a year on hair restoration and preservation remedies before Rogaine; Upjohn apparently expected that this entire amount would be transferred to its coffers, which isn't quite what happened. Initially, the company targeted the medical community. When Rogaine earned barely a third of its goal in its first year, marketing switched to an aggressive pursuit of general consumers, with equally dismal results.

If having a handsome head of hair was so important, why didn't men embrace Rogaine? The drug was too expensive, required too many applications over too long a period of time, and had too small a success rate to attract the following Upjohn had anticipated. Average monthly cost was sixty dollars, and it had to be applied twice daily for at least a year before results (if any) could be seen. Rogaine did hold the line against balding, but only if used religiously—and forever; if applications stopped, new hair fell out within months. Rogaine worked best on younger men and better on less-bald than very bald men. It only stimulated follicles on the top of the head, providing little help for receding hairlines. As in the laboratory tests, Rogaine produced real hair in less than one-third of users. And Rogaine had a troublesome psychological component: its required daily applications gave it the feminizing aura of a cosmetic product.

This isn't to say that Upjohn's miracle drug was a failure; as of 1990, more than two million men worldwide had used it, and sales in that year, though short of original hopes, topped $140 million. In 1993, Upjohn asked the Food and Drug Administration (FDA) to allow nonprescription sales, but the request was rejected because of doubts about the drug's effectiveness. Three years later, the FDA allowed over-the-counter sales, and Rogaine's customer base soared from 400,000 to more than 2.5 million. Analyzing the agency's change of heart, the *Los Angeles Times* concluded that "in a society that places much emphasis on looks, the effectiveness question no longer appears to trouble the FDA."

Rogaine soon had competition from Merck's Propecia, the first prescription pill for treating male baldness—although Merck's savvy marketers, mindful of the dangers of raising unrealistic expectations, emphasized that their product prevented or retarded hair loss, not that it grew hair. Some enthusiastic Wall Street analysts projected sales of two billion dollars a year—but like Rogaine's, Propecia's results were less than stellar. On average, patients who took the drug for a full year gained between eighty and ninety hairs in a one-inch circle on the tops of their heads, hardly a lush crop. And if taking a pill seemed more user-friendly than rubbing a chemical solution into the scalp, it still had to be done every day. For many men, wary of chemicals and bored by daily routines, the answer would lie in the surgeon's office.[2]

An apocryphal story claims that, centuries ago, Japanese women were the first to transplant hair. Because virginal brides were expected to have adequate pubic hair, girls lacking natural endowments had hair transplanted from their heads. Whether this story has any merit, it is true that moving small plugs of hair with a sharp punching instrument from hair-bearing parts of the scalp to bald areas was first performed—on a man—by a Japanese doctor in 1939. Hair transplantation was first performed in the United States in 1959 by the New York dermatologist Norman Orentreich, using the Japanese punch-graft method. By the 1980s, hair transplantation had become the cutting edge of hair-replacement technology and promised to be the answer to many men's prayers.

Hair transplantation followed a course similar to hairpiece purchases: initially, most clients were in the entertainment business, and most were older. In 1980, the average age of a patient at the world's largest hair-transplantation center, the Bosley Medical Group of Beverly Hills, was thirty-seven; by 1989, the average age had fallen to thirty-one, and men in their late twenties were coming in for preventive procedures. Most clients were businessmen and professionals, but nearly 20 percent had blue-collar jobs; about 65 percent were single. About a quarter of Bosley's patients were women, who are more difficult to treat. Because women's hair-loss patterns typically differ from men's, their donor areas are unpredictable, and transplanted hair may fall out. The cost of restoring hair density for the average balding man is twelve thousand dollars, though tabs upward of thirty thousand dollars are not uncommon. When asked why so many young men of moderate means were willing to pay these prices, a Bosley representative blithely suggested that it could be looked at as the price of a new car.

For many men, the greatest deterrent to hair transplantation was detectability. Large plugs of hair moved around in early transplant procedures looked artificial and even bizarre, more like toothbrush bristles than hair. Instead of moving clumps of hair, doctors began to use mini- and micro-grafts consisting of only a few hairs, or even single hairs inserted at the hairline.

Three basic methods were common. The most popular, based

on Orentreich's punch-graft method, frees a graft of hair with its roots attached from one area and relocates it to a bald place, much like transplanting a bulb. In the flap, or pedicle, method, a flap of hair-bearing skin is rotated or draped over the bald scalp. Tissue-bearing healthy hair remains attached by a stalk of skin, called a pedicle, that nourishes blood vessels in hair roots and shafts. In the strip method, an entire line of hair is moved rather than multiple punches. Risk of rejection increases with size (entire strips may be rejected), and the more hair is moved, the more scarring will be visible. Also, strip grafting offers little assurance that relocated hair will grow in the same direction as surrounding hair.

More sophisticated transplantation methods require more office visits and more money. Good marketing techniques are also necessary to persuade patients that the high price of adequately covering their bare heads is worth it. Since men tend to underestimate how bald they are, surgeons photograph the tops of potential clients' heads, using Polaroid cameras and bright lighting to high light bald scalps in all their shocking vastness. If patients still balk at the expense, or don't have enough donor hair to move, why not reduce the size of their scalps? Trying to cover broad expanses of bald scalp with insufficient donor hair was, as one surgeon explained, tantamount to "putting a 6-by-12 rug in a 9-by-12 room; no matter how you rearrange it, it'll never cover the whole floor." Unfortunately, scalp reduction, a process in which the scalp is sliced open and a sizable strip of skin removed, not only presents scarring problems but disrupts hair-growth patterns. In Los Angeles, attorneys placed ads in local papers encouraging men whose heads resembled those in the accompanying photographs to call for legal counseling: photos showed the back of a man's head with a jagged, shiny scar running down the center of the crown, his hair falling in random clumps on either side.

None of these disappointing results deterred the forward march of technology. In 1984, Dr. Richard Anderson gave a presentation to a gathering of dermatologists and cosmetic surgeons in which he showed slides of African tribal women whose lips and ears had been enormously distended by inserting various materials. Their skin, Anderson explained, wasn't just stretched; the tissue itself had expanded. Scalp skin is very elastic and will expand easily, and this principle led to the tissue-expansion method of hair replacement. In tissue expansion, inflatable silicone bags are implanted below the scalp surface and injected every two weeks with saline, causing the surrounding area to expand. After two to four months, the balloons are removed, the bald areas cut away, and the enlarged hairy portion pulled over. Though faster than other methods and likely to provide a more even spread of hair, tissue expansion proved impractical for men unwilling to walk around for months with balloons in their heads.[3]

In view of the physical pain and varied success rate of hair transplantation, why are men willing to undergo it? Until recently, little research had been done on the psychosocial effects of hair loss. In 1987, the psychologist Thomas F. Cash conducted a study to determine attitudes and assumptions about men with visible hair loss. His findings confirmed negative stereotypes about baldness. Balding men were seen as less confident, less interesting, and even less friendly than men who had full heads of hair. The greater the hair loss, the more negative the impression.

Cash concluded that contrary to macho stereotyping, three-fourths of American men had "a significant psychological investment in their physical appearance," with one-fourth reporting general dissatisfaction with their looks. Hair loss represented a crucial area of discontent; 92 percent of men interviewed said they would be concerned if they began to lose their hair. In extreme cases, men might even become suicidal, feeling they had lost their identity along with their hair. In the economically turbulent 1980s, psychologists suggested that losing hair symbolized losing control, and businessmen, especially if they were out of work, became major customers for hair-replacement centers. Among men who were single and not dating, especially younger men, hair loss had disturbing social consequences. Women consistently rated bald men as less attractive than men with hair.

Though men may start balding when young, hair loss increases statistically with age. In a society obsessed with looking young, balding carried serious social penalties. Even plastic surgeons recognized the connection: Dr. Felipe Coiffman, a pioneer in hair transplantation, touted the benefits of his specialty by observing that correcting baldness produced a more youthful appearance than eliminating wrinkles.

Many men took years off their ages with over-the-counter potions that coated the hair surface, though not always convincingly, to disguise gray. Professional hair dyeing for men became widespread, including sophisticated techniques like highlighting. If they were found out, men usually claimed to color their hair to gain an edge in the workplace. Hair was a power accessory, its styling as important to the bank president as to the young single man trying to attract a mate. As the president of a major executive search firm put it, image is a packaged good, and "you don't want to put your cereal into a gray box." By the end of the 1980s, more than a third of executives had opted for some type of hair coloring.

While an abundance of hair on the head indicates youthfulness, a hairless male body has traditionally indicated the same thing. Ancient Egyptians shaved their bodies with pumice and razors, and Julius Caesar, while fretting over going bald, carefully removed facial hair with tweezers and shaved his entire body.

The ancient Greeks found nothing more beautiful than the adolescent boy, with his smooth limbs and virtually hairless body; it's an image that has resurfaced among male models who are as sleek and beautiful as Michelangelo's statue of that perpetual adolescent David. For modern men, pressure against hirsuteness came from varied sources: women who found hairy chests and backs repellent, and the sleek hairless look of male fashion models. Sleek bodies, of course, must be free not only of hair but of excess fat.[4]

Male Eating Disorders

As women have become more outspoken about men's bodies, they have expressed preferences for specific body types. Most continue to favor the mesomorphic ideal identified by William H. Sheldon. Men with broad arms and heavy upper bodies are viewed more favorably than thin men, and many women consider a well-developed chest the most sexually stimulating part of the male body. Muscularity is one thing, however; being muscle-bound is quite another. Many women consider extremely muscular men, like bodybuilders, vain and disgusting and find it annoying that men work so hard to cultivate this body type even though they know women don't like it. The more educated and sexually liberated a woman is, the less likely she is to find the Atlas physique attractive—perhaps because she feels less of a need to be protected by a strong male!

Women express particular fondness for small male buttocks and universally dislike large ones. The least popular body of all is the pear-shaped "Alfred Hitchcock" look, with its small shoulders and wide hips. The negativity aroused by this body type transcends physical considerations: fat men give the impression of being negligent and careless, their lives out of control—a common perception about overweight people of either sex. They also seem to be flaunting a double standard at odds with gender equality: women no longer accept the notion that they're the only ones who need to be lean. They argue that since men, with their lower body-fat levels, are less prone to weight gain and store fat less readily, their inability, or refusal, to shed excess pounds indicates laziness and irresponsibility, if not arrogance.

Women's views in the 1980s were reflected in the business world. While overweight men might be hired fairly routinely for lower executive positions, very few men in top corporate positions were overweight. A 1987 study of 850 male M.B.A. graduates showed that overweight males in managerial and professional positions paid an estimated thousand-dollar penalty in annual salary for every extra pound they carried. Only men were included in the study because of the almost complete absence of overweight women in upper management. Disparities like these did little to assuage women's hostility toward overweight men.

Unlike women, men worry more about body shape than about excess poundage. Even if a man doesn't play football anymore, he wants to look as if he does. Men tend to be repelled more by flab than by heft because flab interferes with achieving classic muscularity and the athletic V shape both sexes admire. For some men, concerns about body shape and weight manifested themselves in male eating disorders.

"I am a normal, everyday kid, a 17-year-old who lives with anorexia every day," begins an article for *ANAD*, the newsletter of the National Association of Anorexia Nervosa and Associated Disorders. "My parents have always pushed me to do my best. Trying always to be a perfect kid, I decided to go on a diet and take off five or ten pounds." Three meals a day, the author goes on, declined to two, then to "a bite every once in a while," and, finally, to nothing at all. "It felt great! I decided maybe five or ten more pounds . . ."

For anyone who knows the symptoms of anorexia and the characteristics of the typical anorectic, this story is familiar. Anorexia nervosa is a severe psychological disorder characterized by the pursuit of a thin body to the point of emaciation. It is accompanied by an unrealistic dread of weight gain and severe body-image distortion. The typical victim is a young, white, high-achieving middle-class woman. The anorectic cited above meets all of these criteria but one: he is a young man.

In the early 1970s, anorexia was still considered rare. Ten years later, it was estimated that one in every 200–250 women suffered from it. Anorexia afflicts seven million adolescent girls and young women in America, and patterns of bingeing and purging are reported among girls younger than ten. Karen Carpenter is one of the best-known victims, dying from starvation in the midst of fame and fortune. Even the fitness advocate Jane Fonda admitted to years of bingeing and purging. Women's special susceptibility is a direct result of society's idealization of thinness; their striving to conform to this ideal creates a perceptual gap between the actual and the ideal body, while magnifying the importance of every inch and pound of that gap. In other words, women are far more likely than men to believe they are fat when they aren't.

The first diagnosed case of anorexia nervosa, though not known by that name at the time, was reported in 1694, and its victim was a sixteen-year-old male. A number of accounts were subsequently published of self-starvation in young males. Dr. Robert Willan, who gained renown as the father of English dermatology, was called on in 1790 to treat a fourteen-year-old boy who had refused to eat for seventy-eight days. Despite Willan's efforts, his patient died. Today, along with seven million female sufferers, one million American males are believed to have eating disorders, a figure considered understated because males tend to be underdiagnosed. Men resist seeking treatment for emotional problems, no matter how severe their physical manifestations; and they don't want to be diagnosed with a woman's disorder.

Even symptoms and behavior that would immediately arouse suspicion about a woman often escape notice in a man. Patrick, a New York banker, was never asked why he appeared to be wasting away before the eyes of family and co-workers. Nobody became curious about his long absences from his desk, which he spent doing calisthenics in the bathroom or running up and down twelve flights of stairs to work off lunch. The ninth-grader Gary Grahl woke up at 3:30 every morning to do hundreds of sit-ups and push-ups, bicycle ten miles, run ten miles, and lift weights. He cut out all sweets and snacks from his diet and stopped going out socially, because it cut into his exercise routine. During all these years, his parents thought his weight loss was just a sign of excessive workouts. Both men were able to carry off their bizarre behavior because of cultural preconceptions: Patrick's obsessive stair climbing and Gary's nocturnal exercises could be rationalized as healthy male activities.

Ten percent of diagnosed bulimia patients are men, a figure that goes up among college populations. Bulimia has the same objective as anorexia, but instead of dieting, bulimics rely on bingeing and purging, which, repulsive as they may be, are more appropriate behaviors for males than self-starvation is. For men, overeating is much less socially stigmatized than for women; a male bulimic who stuffed himself for hours at a time at restaurant buffets remembers that nobody seemed to notice, although he thought, correctly, that "a woman going back and filling plate after plate of food would . . . be talked about." When Gary confided to his parents that he thought he might be anorectic, "they laughed and said, 'You're not a teenage girl, dear.'" So persistent was their belief that their son could not be suffering from a "female" ailment that they continued, over the next four years, to attribute his severe weight loss to "training too hard" for school sports; finally, at the age of twenty-one, Grahl checked himself into a hospital.

The psychiatrist Arnold E. Andersen, the leading authority on male eating disorders, divides at-risk men into four groups. The first includes men who suffered from childhood obesity and were teased and excluded from sports. A second category consists of gay men trying to improve their body image, but Andersen cautions against assuming that every male with an eating disorder is gay. In the third group are men whose fathers suffered from ill health, especially heart disease, because they were overweight; many may have died from heart attacks, leaving their sons terrified of becoming fat. Fourth and most prevalent are men and boys whose weight obsessions are related to sports and athletics. Dr. Cynthia Adams, a professor of mental health, has proposed a fifth category of men at risk: the male who dreads the onset of aging; along with his "little red sports car and young wife," this specimen rates thinness as a major indicator of youthfulness.

For male athletes like wrestlers, bingeing and purging to maintain weights has become virtually institutionalized, so commonly practiced that it has lost much of its stigma. One man said he never traveled without paper bags in his car; another admitted his eating habits were out of control when his chest cavity weakened after years of vomiting a half-dozen times a day. Athletes at risk for eating disorders include middle-aged male runners, who, in their obsession with dieting and body weight, are comparable to women who have anorexia. Obsessive male runners usually come from middle-class backgrounds, are highly goal oriented, and have a tendency toward depression. Like anorectics, they demonstrate "increased narcissistic investment of the body" and become preoccupied with weight loss well beyond that resulting naturally from exercise.

Not surprisingly, career considerations also play a role. Men admit to bingeing and purging to control weight after being passed over for promotion in favor of more slender men. In some treatment centers, the ratio of men to women has changed over the past ten years from nearly all women to 50:50, with most male patients citing "career disadvantages" as the driving force behind their need to lose weight. Looking like "the Pillsbury doughboy," explains Dr. Robert Flanery, the director of a major eating-disorders program, won't help a man move up the career ladder.[5]

Despite the growing rate of male eating disorders, most men continued to look askance at dieting as contrary to their muscular ideal. Many middle-class males turned their attention to a very different means of reshaping their bodies. Weight lifting became the second most popular American recreational sport next to running, and bodybuilding, formerly a fringe activity associated with the lower classes, became solidly upscale.

Making Muscles Respectable; or, "No Pecs, No Sex"

In the mid-1970s, sports fans ranked bodybuilding thirty-fifth in popularity—just behind tractor pulling. Bodybuilding was seen as purposeless muscular development; unlike "real" athletes, bodybuilders didn't seem to do anything (although one defender of the activity, Mike Katz, former offensive guard for the New York Jets, pointed out that bodybuilding demanded far more work and dedication than football—six to seven hours a day versus an hour and a half). The common perception of bodybuilders was that they were stupid, uncoordinated, and even menacing in their musclebound massiveness.

Ten years later, everything had changed. Purses of fifty thousand dollars for bodybuilding competitions had become common, and spectators paid hundreds of dollars for a single ticket. Joe Weider, who had scraped together seven dollars in 1940, at the age of eighteen, to begin publishing a twelve-page magazine called *Your Physique,* owned an empire of fitness magazines and products, and his *Muscle & Fitness* magazine sold more than 400,000 copies a month. Gold's Gym had blossomed from a single shabby room into more than four hundred franchises worldwide. What had happened can be summed up in two words: Arnold Schwarzenegger.

Charles Gaines, credited with "discovering" Arnold, brushes this off by saying, "Arnold is like the Matterhorn—we didn't discover him, we just noticed him." When the bodybuilding documentary *Pumping Iron* was released in 1977, the whole world noticed Arnold, who became an immediate celebrity, not only because of his spectacular body but because he didn't look like a behemoth, was heterosexual, and was quick-witted and articulate. He was, in a word, normal. Schwarzenegger was able to laugh at his sport, claiming, in spite of his enormous success, not to take it seriously. He recognized the theatricality inherent in posing and flexing and capitalized on it, to the benefit both of himself and of the sport. Arnold may have been theatrical, and the self-obsessed posturing of bodybuilding may have been absurd, but his relative normalcy and personal charm had an enormously positive effect on what had been looked down on as a pastime of lumbering muscleheads. In the 1980s, bodybuilding became respectable.

Arnold wisely stressed the health and fitness benefits of bodybuilding at a time when these were at the forefront of American consciousness, along with a widespread belief that having a good body was a path to personal happiness. With Schwarzenegger's help, the Me Generation adopted bodybuilding as a form of self-help that promised personal transformation through physical alteration.

When the world's first bodybuilding contest was held in 1901, both muscular form and the nutritional and fitness aspects of the sport were emphasized. Charles Atlas had promoted muscles as a means of getting the girl and as a route to self-confidence and healthy strength; implicit in Atlas's message was that bodybuilding was transformative—by changing his body, a man could change his life. The sport also held out the elusive but seductive promise of not only physical improvement but absolute perfection. Ironically, in the course of molding their bodies, bodybuilders of the Schwarzenegger era also subjected them to stresses and workouts that were anything but healthy or sane.

Serious bodybuilding demands such a relentless routine that devotees are virtually unable to work full-time; most content themselves with part-time work as bouncers, bodyguards, and bill collectors. A few do modeling, and some heterosexual men—estimates range from 30 to 80 percent among West Coast bodybuilders—turn to hustling.

Schwarzenegger saw bodybuilding as both a competitive sport and one by which the general public could stay fit. The problem, as with running, was in drawing that fine line between exercise and obsession, even among so-called amateurs. A bodybuilder needs almost ten years to get himself into championship condition. He has to work out more than three hundred days a year, two hours per session, twice daily. Schwarzenegger's routine consisted of "forty tons a day, six days a week."

If runners are likely candidates for anorexia, bodybuilders are likely candidates for a disorder called reverse anorexia nervosa—or, among the gym set, "biggerexia." Men with this condition continue to see themselves as small and puny, no matter how huge they get. This type of body fixation makes bodybuilding similar to running in that the pursuit of good health and fitness can be taken to unhealthy extremes. When Sam Fussell, the middle-class son of two New York academics, became fanatically devoted to bodybuilding in the 1980s, he described the sport's effects on his body with brutal clarity: his hands raw from lifting, so weakened by steroids and dieting that he "couldn't run twenty yards without gasping for air," his buttocks aching from steroid injections, and his skin pimpled from tanning lotions, Fussell was far from anyone's conception of physical perfection.[6]

Diet, geared toward minimizing body fat, is a major culprit in undermining bodybuilders' health. To develop "cut" or "ripped" muscles, bodybuilders must take in only about fourteen hundred calories daily, eliminating all fat and eating only salads and high-protein food like broiled chicken, tuna, or egg whites. The high-protein diet probably originated among the ancient Greeks: in the classical period, wrestlers ate as much as ten pounds of lamb per day to enhance their performances at Olympia. The ultimate effect on Greek athletes hasn't been passed down to us, but nutritionists agree that even average Americans consume twice as much protein as they need; bodybuilders take in twenty to thirty times too much, and high protein intake can drastically shorten life span. The nutrition and kidney specialist Dr. Barry Brenner of Harvard Medical School has predicted an epidemic of kidney failure among bodybuilders, based on experiments linking excessive protein intake to adverse kidney function. Dieting is often supplemented by bingeing, purging, and using diuretics. Sam Fussell described fellow bodybuilders whose skin was so transparent from injecting diuretics that veins, arteries, and even capillaries were visible; their body fat was so low that muscle fibers could be seen moving under the skin.

Surgeries for overstrained body parts are common, as are degenerative ailments ranging from arthritis to hypertension. Weight-lifting equipment carries its own dangers: in a single year, a list of weight-equipment injuries compiled by the National Injury Information Clearinghouse included more than 4,800 contusions and abrasions, 236 concussions, 3,700 fractures, 681 amputations, and 344 avulsions (the "tearing away of a body part"). Schwarzenegger has described regularly passing out and vomiting while performing his routines; it's virtually mandatory to reach this state of physical overload, for only then does the bodybuilder know he's worked hard enough. The bodybuilder David Porter explains that making any sort of significant change in the body's appearance requires willingness to endure "heavy doses of pain," not, Porter emphasizes, the mild pain associated with overly vigorous exercise but "pain of significant stature . . . a way down deep burning . . . that spreads through the chest, arms, shoulders, and back muscles." According to recent medical estimates, the average professional bodybuilder has a life span of fifty-five years.

The physical dangers of bodybuilding go hand in hand with emotional ones. Emotional connections of all kinds are often forced to take a backseat to the demands of the sport; for instance, Schwarzenegger refused to return to Austria for his father's funeral because it would have meant breaking training. Because it requires such total self-focus, bodybuilding tends to be isolating and solitary even in the middle of a crowded gym. Wives, if they exist, are referred to in the trade as "bodybuilding widows"; intimacy and sexuality are undermined by sheer exhaustion. Sexual nirvana comes from other sources, which often have little or nothing to do with another person. Bodybuilders attribute a sexual rush to the phenomenon called the pump—the moment when a great flow of oxygenated blood rushes into the muscle, making it visibly larger.

To some, the pump is even better than sex. Schwarzenegger described the experience of lifting weights as orgasmic, and in an article for a bodybuilding magazine titled "My First Time," a young man rhapsodizes about the first time he loaded up to 205 pounds of weight.

Even dating can be problematic, assuming one has the energy for it. Since most women dislike the overpumped physiques and self-absorbed lifestyles of bodybuilders, Sam Fussell dated a woman bodybuilder—only to find that "there was barely room for our lips to meet over our swollen, pumped-up chests."

"No Pecs, No Sex": this quotation appeared in an advertisement for the upscale David Barton Gym in Manhattan, and it succinctly expresses what bodybuilding is all about. It isn't body*building* but body *image* that really matters; this is less a sport than a physical display. The same can be said to some degree about other professional sports, but most professional athletes must maintain performance standards; they must be able to do something, not just look as if they can do it. And while few American men can aspire to duplicate the athletic skills of major sports stars, presumably anyone, with enough determination and spare time, can acquire a perfect body.

An undeniable influence on the popularity of bodybuilding and display of the muscled body has been the increased visibility of homosexual culture. Blending of gay and straight style began in the early 1970s, with the advent of the gay liberation movement in the wake of the Stonewall riots in Greenwich Village. Masculinization of gay culture, although it began as early as the 1940s, intensified after Stonewall with a tough, virile new look defined by jeans, T-shirts, and construction boots, making many gay men look more macho than their straight counterparts. An equally important rebuttal of stereotypes was the explosion of interest among gay men in bodybuilding in the late 1970s. It was impossible to categorize cultivating of muscularity as a gay activity because it so clearly articulated classic masculine physical attributes, and the hard torsos of gay men evoked as much admiration among heterosexuals as among gays. Not only bodybuilding but clothing designed to show off those carefully crafted hard bodies crossed over into the heterosexual marketplace. In 1975, Calvin Klein had premiered his new clothing line at the Flamingo Club, a gay disco whose handsome young men inspired his print and TV ads—ads aimed not just at gay men but also at straight ones. By 1980, Klein had installed a gym in his office and worked with a personal trainer every day, no matter how hungover he was from the previous night's excesses. As concerns about body image and fashion have become more prevalent among men, strategies for keeping bodies youthful and hard have transcended sexual-preference as well as class barriers.

If bodybuilding is all about image, what is the image supposed to express? Does cultivating a powerful body send a message that in spite of having to share the workplace with women, men are still stronger and physically superior? Maybe—but there's an irksome irony here: muscles may be symbolic of masculinity, but bodybuilding, with its self-conscious posing and self-display, is oddly reminiscent of stereotypically feminine activities. Like beauty-pageant candidates, bodybuilders are judged on the basis of measurements, their identities reduced to sets of numbers. Contestants in bodybuilding competitions shave off their body hair and pose covered in makeup to enhance their physical charms; their preening, measuring, and dieting is more typical of female, not male, behavior. Even the process of competition is feminine: wearing the tiniest, most revealing briefs, the bodybuilder stands on a little podium and displays his most valuable asset. For the bodybuilder, none of this matters: bodybuilding is about self-control and self-mastery, as muscles confer self-esteem and a sense of accomplishment. Buffed and toned bodies can be seen as the ultimate expression of self-commodification, with washboard stomachs and bulging pectorals being the 1980s version of the 1950s house in the suburbs or a new station wagon. After he abandoned body-building, Sam Fussell lamented that if muscles were considered property, "I had regressed from a land baron to a serf."

What if Arnold had come along in the 1950s instead of the 1980s? It's scarcely conceivable that he would have had the same impact on middle-class men. Remembering his weight-lifting days in the family garage when he was sixteen, Michael, a businessman, describes lifting as an act of sheer vanity he and his friends did because they wanted to look good but adds that "none of us would admit that's why we were doing it. Not in 1952." Even in films, actors were rarely muscle-bound unless cast in historical costume epics. When it comes to male bodies in film, audiences have consistently preferred the lean and hungry look to that of Hercules; bulging muscles were fine for gladiators but not for ordinary men. Actors like Victor Mature, for example, rarely gained the female following of stars who had lanky, tall, and relatively unostentatious bodies. These trends prevailed even during the heyday of Schwarzenegger and Sylvester Stallone, whose major appeal would be to male audiences.

There are 656 muscles in the human body. To increase its strength, a muscle has to pull at least 50 percent of its capacity, a process that increases the size of protein filaments with the aid of testosterone (whose importance in muscle building explains why it's so much harder for women to develop muscles). For the serious bodybuilder, muscle building involves isometric, isotonic, and isokinetic muscle contractions precisely performed. Even if muscularity develops, styles may change and render all this effort obsolete, as when the "cut" look of the 1980s, with its prominent veins and chiseled definition, replaced the smoother, sleeker look of earlier bodybuilders. In the 1980s, the worst thing one could say about a bodybuilder, shuddered a Gold's Gym habitué, was that he looked "smooth."[7]

The Male Face as Business Accessory

As the economy continued to worsen, eleven million workers—10 percent of the workforce—were displaced from their jobs in the 1980s. In middle management, 600,000 employees, most of them male, were squeezed out of work in a single year. At the end of the decade, the numbers of white- and blue-collar workers who had lost their jobs were almost equal, something that had never happened before. For middle-aged men, the risk of job loss was especially high. Executive rank had traditionally corresponded to the onset of middle age, generally regarded as the peak time of a man's life. Prior to the 1980s, men between the ages of forty-five and fifty-four were at less risk of losing their jobs than workers overall. Now this ratio shifted, making men in this age-group among the most vulnerable.

Turning fifty has always been hard on managers, because it's the age at which most reach a professional plateau. In less turbulent times, aging employees could count on easing comfortably into retirement, but in the 1980s their condition was better illustrated by the case of the fifty-four-year-old middle manager Chris Toal. The victim of two layoffs in high-tech industry before landing a management position, Toal found himself far from plateauing. "You'd think that with gray hair and wisdom there [comes] some kind of respect," Toal lamented; instead, he found himself scrambling to learn new technologies while recognizing he had peaked in his career and would move no higher.

Of course, not every job created after the 1970s was downwardly mobile or service-oriented. One of the fastest growing sectors was the computer industry, which offers a sobering example of changing corporate culture and its consequences. In the 1950s, computers were synonymous with IBM, a company noted for its conservatism even when conservatism was the norm. IBM had a very traditional management code: loyalty was rewarded by a virtual guarantee of permanent employment and upward mobility.

Thirty years later, computer culture was defined by small, fast-track entrepreneurial companies whose typical employee was likely to be young and to wear blue jeans and a T-shirt rather than a suit. To keep pace with hot new competitors, IBM shrank its workforce from 400,000 to 220,000 between 1980 and 1995; in a single layoff, 40,000 people lost their jobs.

For managers, statistics skewed reality. While employment of factory and other blue-collar workers continued to plunge in the 1980s, the percentage of workers classified as managers actually *rose*. A closer look, however, shows that many of these jobs—in fast-food restaurants, travel agencies, and small bank branches—bore little resemblance to what is customarily considered management-level work. *The Wall Street Journal* observed that the long hours, minimal autonomy, and oppressive routines typical of such positions made many so-called managers feel as if "they are in a factory by another name." People laid off from old-style management positions, like those in the hard-hit aerospace industry, took drastic cuts in pay as well as in prestige because they had no other choice. Corporations were likely to view even the best-qualified prospective employee with suspicion if he had gray hair—as if his mere presence "would cause the organization's arteries to harden."

With the insecurity and stress, millions of men became aware that even to keep running, they had to look as if they could keep up the pace. Experience and seniority, once valuable, became liabilities likely to keep older, higher-paid employees in the unemployment line for longer periods. In the boardroom of the 1980s, it was no longer enough to be qualified for the job; a man had to *look* qualified, and this meant looking vigorous, dynamic, and young.[8]

Both women and men turned to plastic surgery to enhance their appearance. A major development for the profession, *Newsweek* reported, was "the change in the nature and function of the American face," which was no longer just ornamental but had become "a mobile billboard for its owner's brilliance, energy, and savvy." At a workshop sponsored by the American Academy of Facial Plastic and Reconstructive Surgery, the "80s Face" for men was described as having "a little heavier eyebrow, a little stronger nose with a little higher bridge and a more natural-looking tip, higher cheekbones, stronger chin." For the man who didn't have it naturally, the 80s Face was available through the surgeon's artistry. Women moving up the corporate ladder saw cosmetic surgery not as a luxury but as an economic necessity that enabled them to compete in a marketplace that valued youth. A New York surgeon claimed that women were demanding a more serious, less sexy look—the look of someone "on the floor of the stock exchange." Eye surgery for women began to shift away from the traditional wide-eyed girlish look to an "assertive, athletic" eyelid, while Dr. Jack Anderson of New Orleans offered corporate women "aggressive" noses instead of traditionally cute, uptilted ones. The bad news for men was that many of these women with assertive, aggressive faces were competing for the same jobs as they were.

Even men who felt confident about their experience and skills believed that, among candidates with equal qualifications, the best-looking was most likely to get the job or the promotion. When sixty-five-year-old Edward, a topflight salesman for thirty-five years, was relegated to working part-time, he blamed his declining fortunes on his face. "It's cruel," he lamented, but "no matter how good you are, your face can hold you back." Clients liked the way he looked after a face-lift, reported another man, and "trust[ed] his judgment more," which in turn made him feel more powerful and in control.

Changes in health-care management played a significant role in the fortunes of plastic surgery. During the 1980s, many doctors, frustrated by mounting red tape, price controls, and the intrusive supervision of HMOs, would move into lucrative elective fields like cosmetic surgery where patients were willing to pay whether or not the procedure was insured. In a reversal of long-standing assumptions that physicians could charge more for procedures covered by insurance, surgeons found themselves able to charge fees for elective procedures that were often far higher than what HMOs would pay. An example was the Seattle plastic surgeon Phillip Haeck, who spent half of his professional time reconstructing breasts for cancer patients. When insurance price-cutting reduced his income from these surgeries by 30 percent, Haeck switched to cosmetic breast-enlargement procedures that paid approximately $3,800 each, compared with only $1,980 for reconstructive work. Dermatologists, ophthalmologists, dentists, and ear, nose, and throat specialists flocked to cosmetic surgery because, as Haeck explained, by concentrating on elective procedures, doctors were no longer held "fiscal and emotional hostage" by HMOs.

Additional impetus came from a 1979 federal ruling allowing doctors to advertise, which had greater impact on cosmetic surgery than on any other medical specialty. The advertising blitz attracted thousands of patients who otherwise might not have considered plastic surgery. As demand for aesthetic procedures increased in response to successful marketing campaigns, new doctors flocked to the specialty, creating an oversupply.

Doctors responded with an even greater avalanche of advertising, set up monthly payment plans for patients, extended office hours, and began to accept credit cards. Aggressive promoters hired public-relations firms and organized free public symposia to provide information on the latest cosmetic opportunities. Though much of this publicity was aimed at women, it would only be a matter of time before some enterprising doctors recognized that men, too, were likely targets. Clearly, however, surgeons would have to overcome deeply entrenched male resistance.

To combat men's fears of feminization, the cosmetic surgery industry used fears of economic and sexual inadequacy. "In business today," runs a typical advertisement for aesthetic surgery, "a man wears his resumé on his face." A face ravaged by age or too many lunchtime martinis couldn't project the vitality and youthfulness that in the 1980s were determinants of executive ability.

Especially vulnerable were the unemployed: a San Francisco surgeon claimed that his fastest-growing patient category by the 1990s was out-of-work men. Even men who didn't fear losing their jobs often felt that looking younger would enhance their chances of moving up. As a result, cosmetic surgery became associated less with vanity than with economic survival.

Strikingly handsome or good-looking men consistently earn more than average-looking ones, who in turn earn more than homely ones. Studies of business-school graduates in the 1970s and 1980s that used a five-point scale to measure facial attractiveness found that males got higher starting salaries and continued to earn more money over time if they were handsome. Good-looking men were viewed as more masculine and more "motivated . . . and decisive" than unattractive ones. (Interestingly, this isn't necessarily true for women: while attractive women do fare better in the job market, extremely good-looking ones are often overlooked for promotion, apparently on the assumption that brains and beauty together are rare.) Even employees who don't interact with the public are viewed more favorably if they are physically attractive, and their work seems better.

In the 1990s, as a result of the stock-market boom, there has been a sixfold increase in cosmetic surgery among New York stockbrokers. A thirty-year-old broker explained that having a nose job made him feel "100% correct" when dealing with clients, and he credited his surgery with a 40 percent increase in income over the previous year. According to the marketing executive Kenneth Tong, when he started out in the corporate world thirty years ago, "the more weathered and wrinkled you were, the more character you had." In his mid-fifties, Tong decided he had enough character and got a face-lift.

For some men, blepharoplasty, or eyelid lifting, promised to restore a look of youth and vigor by banishing puffiness around aging male eyes. The earliest known blepharoplasty is credited to a Swiss surgeon who, in 1583, tried to restore a youthful appearance to a male patient by clamping excess upper-eyelid skin to his brow with screw clamps—a grotesque procedure that necrotized both eyelids and the surrounding skin. Modern blepharoplasties are considerably more sophisticated, although, despite their popularity and apparent noninvasiveness, they are far from simple: excess skin must be excised from muscle fibers, lumps of fat prodded out, and great care taken not to remove so much eyelid skin that the eye can't be closed completely—and all of this within millimeters of the cornea.

Blepharoplasties can't correct sagging jowls, drooping necks, or furrowed foreheads. For this, men must turn to the artistry of face-lifting. Initially, face-lifts for men and women differed little. As more men became patients, surgeons became more subtle—taking care, for example, to avoid giving them a wide-eyed feminine look by pulling the brows up too sharply. Aesthetically, a distinct space between eyelashes and eyebrows is considered attractive in women but not in men: lower eyebrows project a much more masculine look. Beards pose additional problems. Not only must each follicle maintain its delicate blood supply; placement is critical. To achieve a natural look, surgeons must leave a strip of skin between the ear and the beard area. The inexperienced surgeon who pulls facial skin back to the ear area will leave his patient with beard hairs sprouting on his neck and out of his ears. Not surprisingly, men don't want to look as if they have had surgery. The actor Robert Blake is said to have warned his surgeon, prior to having a face-lift, not to make him "look like a lizard, like everybody else."

A classic story among cosmetic surgeons described an overweight, middle-aged woman who entered a surgeon's office with a photograph of Jackie Kennedy, slapped it down on his desk, and announced, "That's what I want to look like." In the 1980s, men brought photographs from magazines and even drawings and diagrams to show surgeons precisely the result they expected. Clearly, cosmetic surgery was moving into the realm of pure male vanity.[9]

Medicalizing Impotence

Writing in 1954, Dr. David Stafford-Clark had laid down the standard ratio for organic versus psychogenic impotence: 90 percent, he declared, was psychogenic. This dictate went virtually unchallenged for thirty years and served to deter men from getting help because of their reluctance to admit to emotional problems, no matter how physical the consequences.

The work of William Masters and Virginia Johnson in the late 1960s, and of Dr. Helen Singer Kaplan in the 1970s, revolutionized impotence treatment by abandoning attempts to ferret out subconscious thoughts and instead focusing on the emotions and behavior of couples. The core of Masters and Johnson's therapy was sensate focus—allowing each partner to take turns giving and receiving pleasure, making fears and desires known to the other. But in a medical field becoming overcrowded with specialists, urologists would take an altogether different view of male sexuality. As the urology profession tried to bring more treatment areas under its control, male sexual dysfunction would be declared a disease rather than a psychological disorder.

In 1978, the first urology-sexology clinic was founded at the University of San Francisco School of Medicine. Within the next ten years, there was a 900 percent increase in the number of articles about impotence published in the journal *Urology*. Virtually overnight, psychogenic conditions were downgraded to contributing factors, if they were recognized at all. Even when psychogenic dysfunction was acknowledged, urologists recommended bypassing psychologists and blending "the organic with the emotional" through therapy offered in their own offices. One enterprising doctor suggested that nurses be trained to carry out patient counseling. Animosity quickly developed between doctors and psychologists: while urologists sneered at therapists as ineffectual hand-holders, the psychological community portrayed doctors as greedy usurpers.

Transforming impotence into a medical ailment was beneficial not only to physicians but to pharmaceutical companies, penile-implant manufacturers, and hospitals. Medicalized articles and advertising made information about impotence more acceptable to the mass media by treating it as a scientific issue. Most significantly, medicalization of impotence made men more accepting of it, both because of the centrality of erections to their self-esteem and because modern urology seemed to offer a near-magical technological fix—a pill, a shot, a magic medical potion, not a long session of psychoanalysis. Medical approaches seemed action-oriented: doctors were doing something about impotence, not just talking about it.

Dr. Karl Menninger had identified male patients' propensity for being reassured by active treatment in the mid-1930s, when urologists commonly treated impotence by administering rectal massages. The doctors were aware that massage was useless as a cure, but patients were reassured; something was being *done*. In addition, in the 1980s, as health-care cutbacks and the proliferation of HMOs eliminated coverage for therapeutic counseling, genuine medical problems were more likely to be covered by insurance. And treating the condition as a medical problem made it more palatable to men by absolving them of blame and failure.

The board of directors of the Impotence Institute of America, founded as a not-for-profit agency dedicated to dispensing information about overcoming impotence, was entirely made up of urologists. Urological clinics with names like Potency Plus blanketed the national media with advertising that told impotent men they had a physical ailment that should be treated medically. "Ten Million Men Suffer from Impotence; 95% Don't Need To," read a typical ad. Critics argued that this type of advertising was a ploy to fill hospital beds in a competitive health-care industry; others warned that such clinics were creating fertile ground for phonies and incompetents.

In response to urologists' accusations that psychological treatment of impotence prevented men from finding medical solutions, psychologists countered that impotence clinics were a long way from offering the quick fix men were hoping for. Clinics might require weeks and even months of expensive testing to rule out medical causes. Patient workups included extensive medical histories, meticulous physical examinations (including rectal and genital exams, penile blood pressure, and testing of reflexes), chemical analyses of blood and urine, hormonal studies to determine testosterone levels, and perhaps even erection-producing drugs to check for penile circulatory problems. Dynamic infusion cavernosometry and cavernosography, or DICC, tested blood inflow and venal occlusion in the penis; prostate-specific antigen (PSA) monitoring checked antigen levels in the prostate; bladder scans (expensive *and* painful) checked bladder control and "general urodynamics." Aside from attacking the expense of these procedures, critics posed a more subtle critique: the fear that many organically intact men were being offered surgical or pharmacological solutions to psychogenic sexual problems. They pointed out that some men were undergoing radical procedures like penile implants in order to avoid psychologically based therapies that might require "embarrassing self-disclosure."

Even the basic method used to differentiate between psychogenic and physiological impotence came under attack from urologists. Medical clinics commonly used a process called nocturnal penile tumescence (NPT), based on the principle that all healthy males between the ages of three and seventy-nine experience erections during a normal night's sleep. Erections occur four or five times in twenty- to forty-minute episodes. Psychological influences affecting potency are believed to be dormant during sleep, allowing erection to take place. If NPT testing showed erection occurring, which happened in the majority of cases, impotence was considered psychogenic. Urologists challenged NPT-based diagnoses by arguing that erection alone didn't indicate whether there was *enough* vascular volume to make effective intercourse possible—in other words, stiffness didn't necessarily indicate potency, and cases being diagnosed as psychogenic were in fact organic and the province of urologists, not psychologists.

Medicalizing impotence lures men into believing there is a standard for erections to which they must adhere. By quantifying the normal erection—it has to be hard enough to achieve penetration and last long enough to achieve ejaculation—medicalization forces men to conform to its specifications for masculinity. The results are twofold: first, men, like women, have their sexuality and desirability linked to physical parameters; second, emotion, sexual technique, and the role of one's partner are rendered insignificant. By making the erection the man, science isn't enhancing male sexuality but sabotaging it.

The success of medicalization can be attributed to good marketing but was also boosted by new scientific advances. Before Viagra, these fell into two major categories: penile implants and injection therapy. Penile prostheses are intended for men who are totally impotent due to disease or injury—not psychological problems—and the primary clientele is men in their late fifties and older. Early models appeared in the 1930s, when pieces of human rib cartilage were used as stiffening agents—with embarrassingly rigid and conspicuous results that were prone to infection. By the 1960s, plastic rods offered a more refined but nevertheless permanent erection. Not until the 1970s did realistic alternatives emerge in the form of the Finney Flexi-rod, which featured a silicone hinge that allowed the penis to hang at a relatively normal angle, and the Jonas Silicone Silver device made of twisted wires, embedded in silicone, which patients could twist manually to suit their erectile needs. When the wires showed a tendency to splinter and fracture, Teflon coating was added. By the end of the 1980s, prostheses had become fairly sophisticated, as inflatable designs allowed the penis to look and even feel normal in a flaccid state; erections were produced by squeezing a bulb located in the scrotum.

A major advance in understanding the physiology of impotence came with the development of pharmacological agents that could determine contraction or relaxation of smooth muscles in the two interior penile chambers known as the corpora cavernosa. The intricate hydraulics of the corpora are controlled by nerve centers in the spinal cord and brain that respond to intracavernosal injections of drugs that relax arterial muscles and allow blood to flow into the penis. Initially the injections were done by doctors but soon were turned over to patients to do at home.

Early versions of this drug therapy produced erections that lasted up to an hour but had side effects like scarring. Improved drug technology extended erection time to several hours and also reduced side effects. Injection therapy appeared to be a sexual success story—but enthusiasm was premature. In spite of a success rate of over 80 percent, only half of eligible males continued to use this method. Doctors suggested this was because men were fearful of self-injection and penile pain, but on closer examination, they found that injection therapy had a number of objectionable aspects.

When Paul, a fifty-three-year-old California businessman, began to experience erectile difficulties, he was persuaded by his doctor to try auto-injection. After a half-dozen tries he abandoned it because he wasn't able to find the precise dosage necessary and, as a result, had only partial erections. With persistence, he would have become more adept at administering the correct dosages but was embarrassed by his failures before reaching that point. He had tried to have sex with two women, neither of whom was a long-term companion with whom he had established mutual trust or with whom he felt comfortable discussing his therapy. Injections also had to be timed carefully, which led to an off-putting lack of spontaneity.

Subsequent technologies like Medicated Urethral Suppositories for Erection (MUSE), soft pellets inserted directly in the urethra, spared men the use of needles but evoked their own squeamishness. As the New York sex therapist Karen Martin explains, these therapies are nothing more than quick fixes that fail to address intimacy issues likely to be at the root of sexual dysfunction. Psychologists recommended that all medicalized methods be administered in conjunction with sex therapy—which, of course, held little appeal for men.

The vogue for medicalization made male sexual confidence purchasable in the form of implants and drugs. Though expensive, these purchases promised self-esteem with a minimum investment of effort or emotional commitment. In 1986, in the heyday of the medicalization frenzy, three U.S. pharmacologists were honored with the Nobel Prize for their research on the effects of nitric oxide in the bloodstream—research that would lead to the development of a wonder drug for the new millennium and cause one observer to comment that "the highest honor in Western Civilization was applied to a topic normally limited to locker room conversation."[10]

6

"NO MAN EVER NEEDS TO FEEL INADEQUATE AGAIN"

MEN IN THE 1990s

My motto isn't to be healthy. It's to look better naked.
—Owner of Manhattan's trendy David Barton Gym, 1994

Self-interest continued its upward trajectory in the 1990s, not only in the workplace but also in personal relations. Divorce levels had peaked in the 1970s, but commitment to another person, once demonstrated by marriage, had shifted to the more flexible ideal of the relationship. Relationships tended to be looked at from the standpoint of "What will it do for me?" Asked why she chose not to marry her boyfriend, a financial consultant explained that marriage would compromise her lifestyle and force her to give up an environment that expressed her individuality: "I have my apartment fixed up just the way I want." A young male stockbroker expressed similar sentiments about moving in with his girlfriend, whose work schedule and job demands might conflict with his trips and vacations.

Men had something else to worry about when it came to relationships. Women were tending to look for male partners younger than themselves, reversing the long-standing older-man-younger-woman equation. Nearly 25 percent of American brides married younger men in the mid-1990s, a figure that jumped to more than 40 percent for women between the ages of thirty-five and forty-four. Although women's greater longevity and later sexual peak are sound biological reasons for this, changing times are also important.

Younger men are appealing because they tend to be more adaptable to changing social roles than men over the age of forty-five. They are also more likely to have been raised by "liberated" mothers, making them more open in relationships. Older men, the historian Margaret Morganroth Gullette reported in 1992, were losing their traditional "easy access" to young women, many of whom weren't willing to put up with "deafness, bossiness, and psychological dependence."

Equally important, in the wake of the feminist movement the financially independent woman has no need to marry an older man for security. Educated young women are less likely to marry men substantially older than themselves for money because they believe they can make it on their own. "You would see these attractive young women," Gloria Steinem pointed out in 1994, "going out with potbellied men who were thirty years older than they were, just because they had money. The old men thought they were irresistible." Steinem's comment makes it clear that old male bodies aren't as desirable as younger ones. Fortunately for men of all ages, technology to improve the male body continued to advance on all fronts.[1]

Hope Sprouts Eternal

Hair transplantation became so popular in the 1990s that it began to attract doctors lacking both surgical and aesthetic skills. Lured by potentially huge profits, even psychiatrists and pathologists tried their hand at transplant surgery. At worst, some hair-transplant "surgeons" didn't have state medical licenses. Grotesque outcomes were often impossible to hide and hard to correct. Potential clients might be dissuaded by observing their own doctors, as in the case of a man who noticed that his doctor's front hair was pulled forward oddly, as if he was trying to hide something. What he was covering was a hairline that looked like "a little hedge or stalks of celery." Doctors also issued warnings about scalp reduction. Because the procedure was comparable to having a face-lift on top of the head, the scalp was subject to sagging back into its original position over time.

Dissatisfied patients established Web sites to air their grievances, complaining of having spent large sums of money for meager results. Many claimed to have suffered scarring or severe thinning of their hair as a result of grafting. One man who demanded a refund when his transplants produced very little growth was offered a new transplant session instead; the second session knocked out the few hairs remaining from the first, and the new crop raised no hair at all. The doctor refused to give him a refund. At prestigious centers like the Bosley Medical Group, patients who wanted Dr. Bosley himself were charged three times as much as the fee quoted on the group's price list. "These hair transplant factories," a disappointed client complained, "are . . . experts at selling the illusion of a youthful appearance through a full head of hair."

As a branch of cosmetic surgery, hair transplantation has many of the same risks as aesthetic procedures. Two-fifths of the work at the Bosley Medical Group consists of reworking botched jobs, whereas general cosmetic surgery has a one-third redo rate. In severe cases, hair-transplant operations can cause internal bleeding, nerve severance, nose malformation, and partial facial paralysis. Surgeries are long and tedious; implanting micrografts one by one requires hours and often an entire day as surgeons, accompanied by technicians, count out the number of spots in a patient's head—five hundred, one thousand, even eighteen hundred at a time—and gouge each with a tiny sharp instrument to make a bedding ground for the hairs. Cuts are only skin-deep, but scalp vascularity results in heavy bleeding, and the sensitive scalp area requires constant reinjection of anesthesia while patients wince, squirm, and occasionally faint. Nor does the aftermath inspire a sense of immediate gratification, because swelling spreads over the facial area and the grafts become encrusted with congealing blood. Nevertheless, in the late 1990s, balding men were spending nearly $800 million annually on hair transplants.

In the busy office of Dr. Randall Sword, rooms contain patients lying in chairs like those in a dentist's office. Little metal trays are heaped with soft drinks and snacks, because most patients will be in the chairs for a long time. In the first room, sixty-five-year-old Abe is having five hundred grafts placed in the front of his hairline. Sword has outlined a space a quarter of an inch wide and ten inches long on the back of Abe's head—the donor area from which living hair follicles will be harvested. Abe is stretched out in his chair watching one of four hundred videos stocked for patients' amusement, his head studded with large plastic hair clips that keep his wiry gray strands out of harm's way. He doesn't feel a thing when the doctor scores the penciled area with a stainless-steel blade and neatly slices out the strip with a scalpel.

As the cutting begins, blood pours down the back of Abe's head and streams onto the crisp blue paper towels clipped to his neck and shoulders. Abe, engrossed in his video, is unaware of the carnage. As Sword smoothly stitches up the gaping donor area with black surgical thread, a technician lays the pale, glistening donor strip on a saline-soaked gauze pad. Using a small ruler and a razor blade, she divides it into a jumble of grayish specks like tiny rice grains, each containing a living hair root and a few minuscule hairs. These must be aligned precisely, with the hair facing in the right direction, so that patients don't end up with swatches of hair growing in different directions. Great care must be taken not to break the fragile follicles or to overexpose the grafts to burning surgical lights. The work is exacting, but the technician isn't bored; "every head is different," she confides, and compares her work to crocheting—repetitious, but with a rewarding end product.

In the next room, Steve is having one thousand grafts inserted over his entire scalp, a process that will take eight hours. This is Steve's sixth and last visit, but the pleasant-faced, slightly heavyset forty-nine-year-old businessman has been having things done to his hair since he was twenty-three. Asked if he's doing this to attract women, Steve answers that he can't recall any woman overtly rejecting him because of his baldness but always felt that women were turned off by it. It doesn't matter, he says, whether women care about baldness or not; what matters is if a man thinks they do. As for his dating success since he's been adding hair, Steve believes he's now attracting "better" women.

In the third room, fifty-five-year-old Bernie, an aerospace engineer, is having his third transplantation procedure. Like Steve, Bernie has a long history of coping with baldness. He had implants installed in the early 1980s and kept them for thirteen years, a possible record. He had constant scalp infections, and his wife complained about open sores that never completely healed. To minimize the possibility of wires being pulled out of his scalp during sleep, Bernie slept for thirteen years with his pillow folded in half so his head wouldn't touch the bed. Even so, his sutures tore loose regularly.

Several years after he got his implants, Bernie was approached by an attorney and asked to participate in a class-action suit against the implantation industry. He refused; if the companies went out of business, who would take care of his hair? At that point, he was trekking twenty-two miles across town to the lone remaining practitioner. When the implantation business finally went under, leaving him without maintenance, Bernie surrendered to the inevitable. By this time, the wires had fused together with masses of scar tissue and grown into the bones of his skull, requiring surgical removal in a series of painful operations that left his head indented with scarring. This otherwise rational man managed to hide his baldness so well that neither his wife nor his five children had ever seen him without hair.

In 1996, the Houston cosmetic surgeon Anthony Pignataro came up with the newest addition to the arsenal of weapons aimed at baldness, one reminiscent of the ill-fated implants of the 1970s. In this procedure, based on a technique called implantology, in which artificial body parts like noses and ears are anchored to snaps embedded in patients' bones, titanium sockets are planted in the skull and allowed to fuse with the bone. About twelve weeks later, when fusion is complete, gold snaps are screwed into the sockets and artificial hairpieces attached to the snaps. Despite its science-fiction aura and a four-thousand-dollar price tag, the process attracted a following. A thirty-year-old customer who bought two snap-on hairpieces explained his decision in terms of a preference for dating younger women, who "like guys with a full head of hair." The future of the procedure is unclear: in June 1999, Pignataro pleaded guilty to criminally negligent homicide after a woman on whom he was performing breast-enlargement surgery died of asphyxiation while under anesthesia. By then, implants had staged a comeback under the auspices of a company called Ivari Centre International Capillaire. Since the procedure wasn't legal in the United States, clients had to go to France for implantation. The price tag: sixty thousand dollars.[2]

Better Bodies through Chemistry: The Steroid Epidemic

In the early 1990s, an estimated eighty-five million Americans were engaged in some form of weight training. Serious bodybuilders and professional competitors still came predominantly from less-educated blue-collar backgrounds, but the sport's popularity among middle- and upper-middle-class men made the muscle industry one of America's fastest growing. Even Ronald Reagan had posed for pre-briefing photos pumping up his biceps with light weights, and body-building took on a familial aspect, as the television game show *Family Feud* pitted Gold's Gym bodybuilders against an ordinary family.

Paralleling the popularity of bodybuilding was a growing recognition of its darker side. As long as bodybuilding was seen as an offbeat activity, worries about its effects on health and self-image were muted. By the 1990s, psychologists had begun to voice concern about the effects on boys of an obsession with muscularity. The psychiatrist Katharine Phillips is a specialist in body dysmorphic disorder, which she describes as "a psychiatric illness in which patients become obsessively preoccupied with perceived flaws in their appearance." Phillips observes that the disorder is becoming common among young males—with an average onset age of fifteen. Young men become convinced that they're puny and underdeveloped, no matter what the state of their bodies. These body-image misconceptions don't just come out of the gym; they come straight from popular culture.

Barbie dolls had already come under fire for creating unrealistic and even dangerous body-image ideals among girls; if Barbie were enlarged to human proportions, she wouldn't be able to walk upright. American males of all ages were made aware of the desirability of the hypermuscular, "cut" body when Hasbro Industries, maker of the G.I. Joe action figure, introduced G.I. Joe Extreme, complete with bulging biceps larger than his waist. If the original G.I. Joe doll had been life-size, he would have had a thirty-two-inch waist, forty-four-inch chest, and twelve-inch biceps, his successor would flaunt thirty-two-inch biceps, dimensions that even Arnold Schwarzenegger wouldn't be able to attain. Just as Barbie grew less like ordinary women, G.I. Joe, with his enhanced muscularity and definition, has become less like ordinary men. The greatest danger in this change, warns the psychiatrist Harrison Pope, is that it creates "a template for a he-man's body that cannot be obtained without engaging in obsessive behaviors." Among the worst of these is the use of steroid drugs.

In 1988, the world was shocked by the revelation that the sprinter Ben Johnson had used steroids to set the world record in the hundred-meter dash. Suddenly America became aware that athletes from Olympians to high school boys were taking steroids in record numbers. Ironically, the popularity of bodybuilding was most responsible for the surge in steroid use: as the fame and fortune associated with the sport grew, so did the demand to win—and the only way to do that was to be bigger than everyone else.

This wasn't the first time drugs had been used to enhance athletic performance. Athletes in ancient Greece took strychnine and hallucinogenic mushrooms to "psych up" for the original Olympic Games, and long-distance runners chewed on sesame seeds to heighten endurance. The first athlete known to have died from using performance-enhancing drugs was a French cyclist who collapsed from a combination of cocaine and heroin in 1886. Doctors boosted male athletic performance with monkey-testicle injections in the 1920s, and in the 1940s, testosterone therapy for older men improved their reflexes and endurance. Testosterone therapy was referred to as "sexual TNT," and it wasn't well received in the medical community, which could see no real benefit to it because it didn't cure a disease.

At the 1956 World Games, an American doctor, John B. Ziegler, observed that Russian athletes were using testosterone. Concerned that the Russians might be gaining an advantage over U.S. athletes, Ziegler came back to America and produced a testosterone synthesis. The drug, christened Dianabol, was administered in five-milligram doses to U.S. athletes. Within a few years, clearly pleased with the drug's effects, bodybuilders were sporting T-shirts reading DIANABOL, BREAKFAST OF CHAMPIONS. (More prophetically, a later version of the T-shirts proclaimed, DIE YOUNG, DIE STRONG, DIANABOL.) Doctors responded to Dianabol, which many users were taking in excessive dosages, by denying it could enhance athletic ability (despite clear evidence to the contrary) and labeling it a "killer drug," a charge not yet justified by hard evidence. Skeptical athletes dismissed these medical claims as spurious.

Steroids were in widespread use among athletes in the 1960s, along with a pharmacopoeia of other drugs, legal and illegal. Although their use hadn't been declared illegal, athletes were generally secretive. The greatest concern was reserved for "hard" drugs like heroin and amphetamines. In the 1968 Olympic Games, the only real testing of athletes was a chromosome check to verify that women competitors, many of whom had begun training with weights, often gaining a masculinized appearance in the process, were, in fact, women (the Polish sprinter Eva Klubokowska failed the test).

Initially, media attention to steroid use focused almost exclusively on Olympic athletes and other professionals, and there was little recognition of abuse among ordinary men. But college and professional athletes, especially in strength sports like weight lifting, were using steroids in the 1960s and 1970s (as was Arnold Schwarzenegger, though he didn't admit this until after he retired from bodybuilding). Before they became illegal, steroids were commonly used among bodybuilders, often under medical supervision and in comparatively minuscule doses. Usage surged after 1969, and in 1984, drug testing was initiated at the Olympic trials.

Anabolic steroids work by stimulating cellular activities that build muscle, increasing lean body mass and strength. They are derived from naturally occurring testosterone but are typically used by bodybuilders in doses one hundred times greater than normal body amounts. Side effects include stunted growth, breast enlargement, rectal bleeding, often-irreversible testicular shrinkage, and impotence; sperm counts can drop by nearly 75 percent in only two months of use. High doses cause clumping of platelets in the heart, triggering strokes and heart attacks. The most dramatic side effect is "'roid rage," unpredictable and explosive outbursts of aggressiveness caused when steroids bind with brain receptors. The most ironic side effects, considering that steroids are intended to build better bodies, are cosmetic: users lose their hair, break out in acne, and develop painful, ugly knots and scars from injections with massive syringes.

Considered more addictive than cocaine, steroids cause both physiological and psychological dependence, arising from users' obsession with body image. When steroid use stops, so does muscle development—along with feelings of power and self-esteem. Users can become so obsessive about maintaining their "perfect" bodies that, as one former user says, "they don't even care about death, only how they look in the coffin." As for bodybuilders as paragons of fitness, an observer at a Mr. Olympia contest dismissed them as a "mass of chemicals disguised in the form of a body."

An especially nasty drug is human growth hormone (HGH), a steroid derivative extracted from the pituitary glands of cadavers. The popularity of HGH began after drug testing was initiated at the Olympics: because it was naturally manufactured by the pituitary gland rather than synthetically produced, it was not detectable. This was the drug used by the former football star Lyle Alzado in his attempted NFL comeback; he later blamed his cancer on years of hard-core steroid use. Medically, HGH is used mainly for treatment of human dwarfism. Despite its exorbitant cost—as much as three thousand dollars per month—and its potential to cause acromegaly, an irreversible disease that distorts the growth of face, hands, feet, and even genitals before killing, 5 percent of tenth-grade boys in Chicago, according to a survey, bought it. HGH was also widely used by bodybuilding champions prior to contests.

Most of the U.S. steroid supply comes out of Mexico; the road between Tijuana and Rosarito is referred to as 'Roid Corridor. Once in the United States, steroids are most commonly found in gyms, which offer not only supplies of the drugs but role models, especially for the young. An estimated half million high school boys use steroids, and though most claim to take them to improve athletic performance, one out of four admits doing so for enhanced appearance. A seventeen-year-old described his group's role model as "this older guy, the biggest guy at the gym . . . not a nice guy, but he weighs 290 pounds without an ounce of fat. That's our goal." "First you're inspired by the hulks," commented another young interviewee; then "you inspire others."

A half million adult men also take the drugs, and among professional bodybuilders, the rate is generally accepted to be 100 percent. Anabolic steroid sales of $1 million were reported at the beginning of the 1990s, but estimated black-market sales were close to $400 million, even though steroid distribution was a federal offense punishable by five years in prison. Heavy users spend hundreds each month, often "stacking" different types of steroids simultaneously. One champion reputedly spent thirty thousand dollars a year on his steroid habit.

In the deceptively health-oriented ambience of the modern gym, bodybuilders regard steroids as just another training aid. They're especially popular among firefighters, police officers, and other men whose job performance can benefit from a synthetic boost. Steroid dealers claim to sell 90 percent of their products not to hard-core bodybuilders but to "yuppies in tights and tank tops" looking for a shortcut to the "ripped" look of extreme muscular definition that became popular in the late 1980s. Not everybody was lured by the siren call of steroids; sixty-five-year-old Seymour, who has lifted weights all his life, shakes his head when asked if he ever considered using drugs. "I got my muscles the hard way," he answers, pointing out that if the younger men working out around him in a crowded Los Angeles gym were to stop popping pills, they would look like punctured air bags in a matter of weeks.

By the 1990s, baby boomers were discovering unexpected—and unpleasant—limitations to the benefits of working out. No amount of jogging could indefinitely fend off the effects of aging; getting lean and muscular became harder with each passing year. Even exercise had a negative aspect: as flabby businessmen shed excess pounds sweating in health clubs, sudden weight loss left lean bodies festooned with loose, sagging skin and toned torsos at odds with tired, aging faces. "What bothers me the most," complained the plastic surgeon Ted Lockwood, "is instructors at gyms who tell people to keep exercising to lose fat." The most grueling workouts can leave parts of the body—especially the face—thin and gaunt while making no impact on what Lockwood calls "deep fat"— love handles, paunches—the fat most people really *want* to lose!

Many health-club habitués were men in their forties, fifties, and sixties, and one-fifth of competitive amateur bodybuilders were over forty. In 1996, the largest amateur bodybuilding contest in the East, the Southern States Body Building and Fitness Championship, added a sixty-five-and-older category. Though older competitors were able to keep their weight down, they were prone to more serious health consequences than young bodybuilders and were often unable to attain adequate muscularity. Even among younger men, diet and exercise were limited in their ability to work magic with body contours. For many, working out conflicted with the realities of modern life: the ninety-hour workweeks of fast-track entrepreneurs were incompatible with a meaningful workout schedule. Liposuction, however, promised to eliminate unwanted fat in a mere three hours, and translucent muscle-shaped silicone implants inserted through small incisions could surgically enhance recalcitrant muscular areas like calves and chests.[3]

Building It Up and Trimming It Down

With the widespread acceptability of self-improvement, caveats about the potential dementia of male cosmetic surgery patients virtually disappeared. In fact, attitudes about beautifying the body did a complete turnabout: far from being psychotic, the man who cared about his body was engaging in a healthy pursuit of self-fulfillment. "People get a terrific psychological boost out of aesthetic surgery in general," observed Ronald Iverson, a Palo Alto surgeon. "In today's society, a good-looking body is very important. It's not that a person is doing this to himself; society as a whole is trying to make you look better, look younger." While admitting that for the truly narcissistic individual, "you won't ever be able to do enough," doctors were inclined to agree that it wasn't dangerous or bad to *try*.

Men's hesitations about cosmetic surgery also seemed to evaporate. In 1983, men made up less than 10 percent of the practice of Harold Clavin, a successful Santa Monica plastic surgeon. Most were over forty-five, and the most commonly requested procedure was rhinoplasty, generally to correct breathing problems rather than for cosmetic reasons. By 1993, 25 percent of Clavin's patients were men, and their average age had fallen to forty. Instead of corrective nose jobs, they were getting eye-lifts and liposuction. Obviously, men were far less furtive about having surgery.

Male cosmetic surgery had become so popular by the mid-1990s that *Fortune* magazine recommended hot new stock issues directly related to the beautification of male faces and bodies. Among these were Laser Industries, a small firm specializing in cosmetic laser techniques for removing imperfections ranging from tattoos and nasal hair to wrinkles, and a venture-capital offering for a manufacturer of abdominal implants guaranteed to create the illusion of alligator abs. In surgical meccas like Los Angeles and New York, some surgeons claimed to have as many male patients as female.

As of the late 1990s, one-quarter of cosmetic surgery patients are men. Liposuction and rhinoplasty, the two most popular procedures, accounted for more than one-third of the $500 million spent on cosmetic surgery in 1996. An additional $55 million was spent on eye-lifts. Men also overcame their resistance to face-lifting, spending nearly $34 million on it. Laser surgery, in which skin imperfections are burned off, became so popular that some surgeons claimed that men made up one-third of their patients.

Men have become willing to experiment with a growing menu of aesthetic options in facial surgery. Instead of just getting rid of bags and wrinkles, they want to re-form their facial structure into a masculine ideal: they want lean, athletic, powerful faces to match buffed and toned bodies. At the same time, they want to look sensual, which accounts for the popularity of a procedure known as V-Y plasty. V-Y offers permanent lip augmentation, instead of temporary collagen and lumpy fat injections. Small V-shaped cuts are made in the inner lip, and stitches are placed behind them to push tissue forward, essentially turning the lips inside out. Lip augmentation, enthuses a San Francisco surgeon who often performs it as an adjunct to face-lifts, is excellent for men because it sends "subconscious signals of youthfulness without feminizing." If all this sounds otherworldly, there are also cutting-edge technologies that alter the skeletal contours of the face by moving bones.

Men most admire the muscular, athletic bodies typified by ancient Greek statues, but for ideal facial images they turn to twentieth-century icons, including comic-book heroes like Superman and Dick Tracy. Facial alterations to conform to these types carry an aura of respectability because they are intended not so much to beautify as to project strength and ruggedness. To reach these manly ends, malar (jaw) bones may be enlarged by bone grafts, while silicone implants can reshape chins and cheekbones. Surgeons can even create a cleft chin for men, commonly referred to as the Kirk Douglas look. To do this, the surgeon creates scar tissue that adheres to the chinbone as the incision heals, giving the appearance of a cleft—but, because it can't shift with changing facial expressions, it has a strangely artificial appearance. Artificial or not, the prospect of looking perfect and having a face that's in style has evidently captivated the imaginations of some men, and the plastic surgery profession has been quick to capitalize on their enthusiasm.

"Make the right decision—one that can boost your confidence, one that can impact the way you feel about yourself," urges a glossy framed ad for liposuction on the wall of a Beverly Hills plastic surgeon's office. Pictured is a lean, handsome man lounging

Marky Mark shows off his Calvin Kleins. The man of the 1980s no longer has his wife pick out his underwear (Courtesy of Corbis Images)

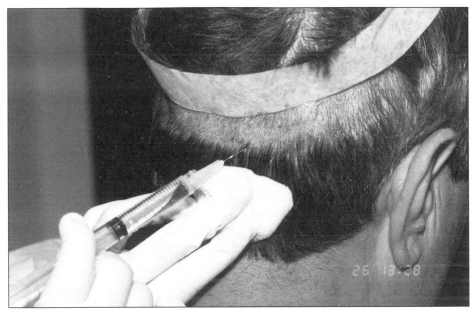

Numbing patient with injection of anesthesia before cutting out donor strip (Courtesy of Elliott & True Hair Centers)

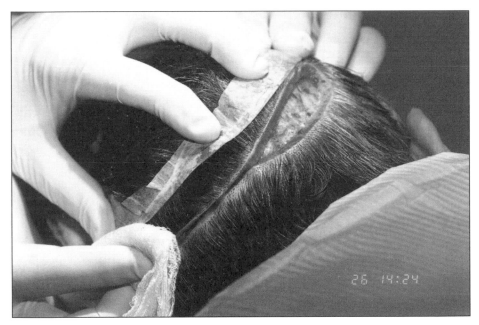

Incision made for donor strip (Courtesy of Elliott & True Hair Centers)

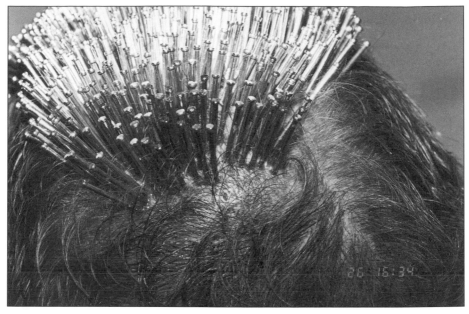

Patient's scalp scored with needles to keep incisions open for insertion of mini-grafts (Courtesy of Elliott & True Hair Centers)

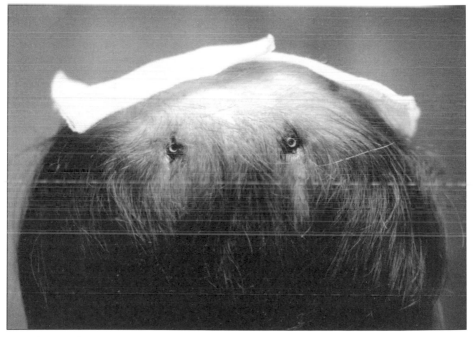

Based on techniques developed by surgeons to anchor artificial eyes, ears, and noses to human bodies, hair implantology uses snaps embedded in titanium sockets drilled into men's heads to anchor hairpieces (Courtesy of the *Buffalo News*)

One of the great accomplishments of the 1990s: inducting the penis into public discourse

"All this talk of Viagra and penile implants reminds me of a charming story about my own penis."

Viagra offered new sources of humor, here seen intertwined not only with medicine and human relations but with politics (By Joel Pett. Courtesy of the *Lexington Herald-Leader*)

Overcoming stereotypes and pulling in the other half of the potential customer base: a 1999 advertisement aimed at the male cosmetic surgery patient (Courtesy of Norton Rubble & Mertz on behalf of American Society of Plastic and Reconstructive Surgeons)

55 Minutes Can Change Your Life Forever!

- **PENILE LENGTHENING**
- **PENILE ENLARGEMENT**

Cosmetic Surgery International (CSI) consists of highly experienced cosmetic surgeons and urologists, bringing you the latest advancements in the medical field. Cosmetic Surgery International has performed over 10,000 procedures worldwide. Most patients achieve an average 1½ to 2 inches in length and up to 50% increase in circumference. It's no coincidence that 3 out of 4 men who choose penile enlargement choose *Cosmetic Surgery International.*

No man ever needs to feel inadequate again! Phalloplasticians hold out the promise of penile perfection
(Courtesy of Cosmetic Surgery International)

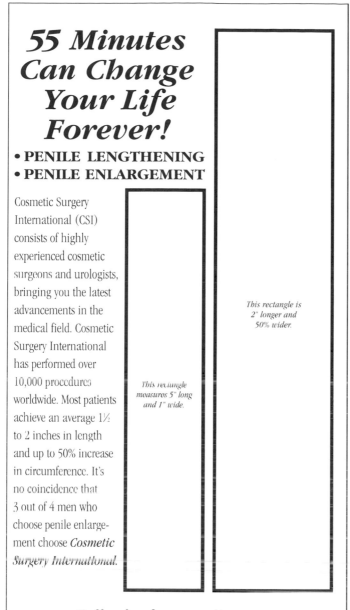

This rectangle is 2" longer and 50% wider.

This rectangle measures 5" long and 1" wide.

Call today for a complimentary consultation on penile surgery, or request our 35 minute informational video.

1-800-336-9996

COSMETIC SURGERY INTERNATIONAL

http://www.cosmeticsurgeryint.com

The new classic nude: Sylvester Stallone updates Eugen Sandow, who also did classical poses in the nude (Courtesy of Annie Liebowitz)

against the railing of a penthouse balcony and gazing out over the city skyline. His pajamas are unbuttoned to the navel, revealing a perfectly contoured, muscular body—one created, the ad implies, by the miracles of liposuction.

Liposuction was first performed in the early 1960s in Cologne, Germany, but it was initially hampered by a lack of specifically designed instruments and by a high rate of infection caused by the accumulation of debris during the procedure. Surgeons learned to employ irrigation to remove loose fragments, making the operation much safer and less traumatic—although "less" is a relative term. Liposuction involves an all-out assault on a host of body structures. It literally tears the skin away from attached tissues, indiscriminately removing blood and tissue along with fat cells. Both fat and blood clots travel through the body and may lodge in vital organs, where they can cause strokes or even death.

Because liposuction is intended to remove excess body fat, it was initially oriented toward women, who naturally have more fat cells. But body-contouring surgeries, especially of the abdominal area, became popular with men for whom strenuous workouts failed to eliminate love handles. Patients who undergo the procedure and believe they've been given carte blanche to overeat soon find that remaining fat cells expand to fill the gaps left by their liposuctioned brethren. The human body produces what endocrinologists call a "metabolic defense of fat"—meaning that no matter how much fat is taken out, it tends to come back, as anyone who has ever gone on a diet knows. Reputable doctors also explain that liposuction can't restore firmness: patients come out of the operating room with less bulk but with looser skin and increased dimpling. This tends to be less of a problem for men, who have less body fat and firmer skin and are largely immune to cellulite. But no matter how much fat it removes, liposuction can't create a hard body. For this, men are finding other solutions.

Certain parts of the body, especially calves and pectorals, can be difficult to develop. Technology and bodybuilders have joined forces to create the impression, if not the reality, of muscular development through the use of pectoral and calf implants. Originally developed to correct deformities resulting from birth defects and trauma, implants were initially used cosmetically by transsexuals who wanted more feminine bodies. In the 1990s, they were used to make men look athletic and powerful, increasing their sex appeal and self-esteem.

Many implant procedures are performed on bodybuilders, even though implants are banned by the International Federation of Body Builders, which uses X rays to detect them. Men also use implants to attract women. As women have become more outspoken about male bodies, their attention has centered on the buttocks. Buttock size can be reduced with liposuction, but this won't work for soft, sagging rears, which require surgical excision of loose skin—a buttock-lift. Undersized buttocks can be augmented with hard, disc-shaped silicone implants, a technology that has superseded earlier gel prostheses, which often ruptured.

Surgeons caution that *no* implants have been tested enough to be considered safe. Pectoral implants may cause irritation because of the constant stress on surrounding muscles and can even erode underlying bone. The case of Dermott offers an example of the pitfalls. A thirty-one-year-old aspiring actor, Dermott wasn't very tall but had a muscular, solid body that looked even more powerful because of his compact size. He worked out daily at Gold's Gym, a showplace for professional bodybuilders and serious weight lifters, but he was frustrated by his failure to match the bodies of the men he saw there every day, so Dermott treated himself to a set of pectoral implants. Several months later, one of the implants slipped out of place, a painful and frightening occurrence that required surgical repositioning. Dr. Brian Novack, a specialist in implantation surgery, points out that some doctors use mass-produced calf implants, three at a time, as pectoral implants: since they can't be precisely matched to a patient's chest configuration, they are likely to slip and slide around unless corrected by additional surgery. Calf implants are even more problematic because they exert pressure on weight-bearing calf muscles, causing them to deteriorate over time. Buttocks implants are the riskiest of all, since buttocks are constantly being sat upon.

Dr. Melvin Bircoll, designer of the chest implant, predicts that the biggest potential client base for his invention is aging male baby boomers no longer able to fend off flabbiness. Implants offer psychological satisfaction by creating an image of power. Calf and pectoral implants serve no functional purpose. Although they may make a man's body look more athletic, they are likely to hamper athletic performance. In view of the potential problems, surgeons suggest that the best candidate for implants—or at least the safest— is the relatively inactive man who just wants to *look* strong.[4]

Private Parts, Private Fantasies

In the late 1960s, while interviewing an eminent New York plastic surgeon for a book on the American culture of beauty, Kathrin Perutz jokingly inquired whether there was a surgery for enlarging the penis. She was told that such a procedure didn't exist, but that if it did, "some fellow [could] make a couple of billion dollars."

In the first six months of 1994, Dr. Melvyn Rosenstein of Culver City, California, didn't make a couple of billion dollars performing penis-enlargement operations, but he did gross $6.6 million. In the following year, American men spent twenty-four million dollars on penis surgery, and the American Academy of Phalloplastic Surgeons was formed by a dozen doctors, who confidently predicted a future membership boom. To help men learn about this new medical miracle, dozens of Web sites sprang up, offering information on penis surgery in a half-dozen languages. Later, Internet support groups would be formed for disgruntled patients.

Despite the centrality of the penis to masculine identity, it has traditionally been hidden in Judeo-Christian cultures. New openness about matters previously considered private and personal has changed this. Self-help books and movements encourage discussion of once-private feelings and behavior; advertising has abandoned its circumspection with regard to personal items like feminine-hygiene products; sexually transmitted diseases, menopause, breast implants, and personal sexual habits have become stock fodder for public discourse. In the wake of the insatiable need for new and controversial material, men's bodies could hardly remain immune. Whether suggestive exposure of the male body is considered enticing or simply outrageous, this increased visibility has placed a higher premium on penis size while concurrently increasing male anxiety about measuring up. But how large is large enough? And to whom does size matter?

In the preface to the 1949 edition of his book *Human Sexual Anatomy,* Dr. Robert L. Dickinson stated that "very exact measurements on 1,500 American white males . . . yield an average penis length of 6¼ inches." Most manuals published since have agreed that "average" penises measure from five and seven inches. The largest penis documented measured fourteen inches in length, but only one man in a hundred has a penis longer than nine inches. At the other end of the spectrum, Dr. Kinsey found that fewer than 5 percent of men have penises less than three and a half inches in length. William Masters and Virginia Johnson found that there is substantially more variation among penises in a flaccid state than when erect; many that are quite small will enlarge to satisfying proportion with an erection. Still, American men have become obsessed with penis size, presumably because they believe women are.

Dr. Joyce Brothers was told by urologists in the 1980s that virtually every one of their male patients wanted to know if his penis "measured up." In popular fiction, adjectives commonly used to describe the penis are "massive" and "huge." Most of these books are written by male authors, and men create most contemporary pornography. In reality most women aren't especially concerned about or critical of penis size—within reason, of course. For that matter, many women aren't overly interested in the penis as paradigm of male physicality, a lesson *Playgirl* magazine would learn to the tune of shrinking circulation and plunging revenues after the initial titillating shock value of its full-frontal displays of male nudity wore off. As Germaine Greer points out, men have posed for pinup shots for as long as women have, but this imagery is intended to "gratify the voyeuristic requirements of other males." Asked by *Esquire* magazine to critique male bodies, women pointedly responded that their minds "were not filled with dreams of extra-large penises." Instead, they talked about the smooth curve of men's shoulders and the soft crook of elbows—body parts less sexual than comforting and strong. "What is it with men and their measuring tapes?" one woman asked.

Psychologists suggest that concerns about penis size are grounded in social expectations about a man's ability to compete and achieve. These expectations are holdovers from a time when size and power were directly related to survival. As a result, penis size is still bound up—in the male mind, at least—with power. Many male sexual fantasies revolve around exerting control over weaker subjects, often by dominating them sexually. A more Freudian explanation suggests that men never fully recover from the emotional shock of first seeing the disparity in size between their own penises and those of their much larger fathers.

Male worries about falling short of the mark have been intensified by greater visibility of all the intimate details of personal life. A Texas urologist, expressing his belief that any man who was in the market for penis augmentation needed psychotherapy more than surgery, marveled that anyone would resort to such extreme methods to add an inch or two to an organ that spent most of its time "lurking out of sight." But these days, the penis isn't always out of sight.

Recalling his high school days in the mid-1950s, the comedian Bill Cosby related the lengths he went to in biology lab to find pictures of male anatomy. Stacking up translucent anatomy plates in hopes of getting a glimpse of male reproductive organs, Cosby admitted that he was "check[ing] out the penis department to see if I was OK, and there was nothing." He would have had far less trouble twenty years later: with throngs of men of all ages circulating between workout rooms, showers, and lockers, the health club provides safety in numbers and is the only socially acceptable place for heterosexual men to compare penis size.

Most patients suffer from a phenomenon doctors call "locker-room syndrome," meaning they want larger flaccid penises, rather than larger erect ones, to give themselves greater self-confidence among men. Like muscularity, penis size becomes a symbol of superiority, a competitive edge. Men are constantly exposed, through advertising and other media, to images of perfect male bodies with which they are obliged to compare themselves. The marketing of one of the most prosaic items of men's attire—underwear—underscores this fact.

It is perhaps no coincidence that phalloplasty began to attract a clientele at about the same time Calvin Klein was revolutionizing advertising for men's underwear. In the 1950s, underwear manufacturers and advertisers emphasized features like wash-and-wearability calculated to appeal to the person—usually a woman—likely to be doing the washing and ironing. Benefits like "seat room" and perspiration absorption stressed not sex appeal but functionality. Live models were rarely used; ads relied on pristine line drawings and color sketches in which men wore modest briefs *and* undershirts, as if to separate the half-clad male body as completely as possible from the product. Klein's moody, revealing displays of muscle-bound, sensual young men were revolutionary because they equated underwear with sex (something European manufacturers had been doing all along). Jockey had actually preempted the sex-appeal approach in 1981 with ads featuring the Baltimore Oriole pitcher Jim Palmer sporting seductively tight briefs, but the photographs were discreetly airbrushed; Klein's ads, to the dismay of many men, showed far less restraint.

Whatever the misconceptions and mismeasurements involved in calculating penis size, Rosenstein found that virtually none of his patients was truly undersized; most were simply, and unhappily, average. Just as physical imperfection had subtly evolved into physical deformity, penile ordinariness had become penile insufficiency. For men unwilling to accept this supposed defect, phalloplasty offered a solution.[5]

The Ultimate Male Surgery

Penis lengthening was first performed fifty years ago on babies born with deformed or extremely retracted penises. Augmentation technology for cosmetic purposes was developed by a Chinese surgeon, Long Doachau, a specialist in correction of microphallic penises (a rare condition in which the penis may be less than an inch in length). In the course of his work in the mid-1980s, Long encountered patients with penises somewhat smaller than average, though not abnormally so, who voiced as much despair about their organ size as his microphallic patients. Knowing that approximately one-third of total penis length lies within the body cavity, Long cut the ligament attaching the penis to the pubic bone, pulling several inches of internal length to the outside of the body.

Long's first operation was performed on a neighbor's son whose penis had been almost completely severed by a dog bite, leaving him too embarrassed to have sex and therefore unlikely to carry on his family lineage; subsequent patients typically included men so sensitive about their small penises that they bordered on suicide. Long operates only on men with "real" problems—not vanity cases. In China, the cost for penis-enlargement surgery ranges from 800 to 1,000 yuan, about U.S. $149–$186. Though extremely cheap by American standards, this operation costs the equivalent of an average month's salary for working Chinese and is not undertaken frivolously.

News of Long's work soon spread outside China, and in the United States, Dr. Melvyn Rosenstein would become the supreme architect of penis enlargement. During his urology residency at

New York University in the early 1970s, Rosenstein learned how to do penis implants. While implants are remedies for real physical problems that cause impotence, Rosenstein discovered, as had Long before him, that less tangible psychological issues could be equally disturbing to men. Clearly the link between the size of the male organ and sexual prowess was a powerful one. After spending his early professional life specializing in operations on boys whose testicles had not descended, Rosenstein moved into the relatively unexplored field of phalloplasty, initially offering operations free of charge to clients willing to undergo experimental procedures. Shortly thereafter, he founded the Men's Institute of Cosmetic Surgery and opened twenty-six marketing offices nationwide.

Most of Rosenstein's patients were thirtyish. They didn't fall into any particular racial or socioeconomic categories, and single or married men were equally likely to seek his services. The ratio of gay to heterosexual patients paralleled that in the general population. Rosenstein's crosstown rival, the Beverly Hills urologist Rodney Barron, who ranked second only to Rosenstein in the number of penis-augmentation operations performed annually, said that the ages of his patients ranged from eighteen to mid-seventies.

American doctors use the same procedure pioneered by Long. Rosenstein claimed that 90 percent of his patients add two inches, with the largest length increase being three inches; Barron reported similar results, with the largest increase—admittedly unusual— being four inches. For men in search of width as well as length, the penis can be widened by injecting the shaft with fat liposuctioned from buttocks and stomach, a procedure pioneered by the Miami liposuctionist Richard Samatier.

Fat injection became widely used by surgeons in combination with penis lengthening. Rosenstein's method, condemned by other physicians as excessive, consisted of injecting sixty cubic centimeters of fat into the penis shaft to ensure maximum retention, because the body naturally absorbs part of its own fat. Though reputable physicians caution against overinjection not only for medical reasons but also to maintain, as the Los Angeles plastic surgeon Gary Alter put it, "a reasonable aesthetic proportion" between the shaft and glans of the penis, some men opt for massive injections and apparently are pleased with the results: a grotesquely enlarged penis shaft. In a more advanced technique known as dermal-graft augmentation, strips of fat are removed from the groin or buttocks and transplanted into the penis. Because it comes intact with its blood supply, much like a strip of hair in a transplantation procedure, fat in a dermal graft has a much higher survival rate than injections of loose fat globules.

Some of the most enthusiastic advocates of penis enlargement aren't doctors. In 1987, Gary Griffin founded Added Dimensions Publishing to market his book *Penis Enlargement Methods.* Within a few years, the volume of response encouraged Griffin to promote a catalog of books on male sexuality, especially enlargement methods, and to begin publication of *Penis Power Quarterly,* described as "the only journal dedicated to reporting the underground breakthroughs in genital enlargement." Griffin's publications also provide information on scrotum enlargement through vacuum pumping, silicone injections, and saline infusions. In addition, Griffin organizes group tours to fly to Miami for "unforgettable" weekends of sight-seeing, beachgoing, stone-crab dining, and, as the pièce de résistance, penis-enlargement surgery.

Men's determination to add as little as an inch of penile length contributed to a $200,000-per-week gross for Rosenstein's practice. The fee for penis lengthening was $3,500; widening cost $3,500; and the deluxe package including both procedures was $5,900. According to his office records, 75 percent of Rosenstein's patients opted for both procedures; 16 percent chose only lengthening, 9 percent chose only widening. Barron's prices are similar, but his specialty, the sophisticated dermal-graft augmentation, cost a hefty $6,900 in 1998. Some doctors find such prices appalling: according to one urologist, the fee for a one-hour penis operation equals what would normally be charged for an eight-hour surgery.

Between 1991 and 1996, by his own estimate, Rosenstein performed more than five thousand surgeries, taking in at least $30 million dollars. He was able to perform up to ten a day. His self-proclaimed goal: to make penis enlargement as common as breast implants, on which American women spent $350 million in 1996 alone.

When Rosenstein's practice was reaching the height of its popularity, a Toronto plastic surgeon expressed outrage that any man would have such dangerous and "ridiculous" surgery—with the possible exception, he added, of men in Los Angeles, where "everyone is vain." He was wrong to assume the surgery would appeal only to Los Angelenos. The eleven thousand patients of a successful Virginia-based phalloplasty clinic came from every state and many foreign countries. It is therefore small wonder that the American Academy of Phalloplastic Surgeons was optimistic about its future: "It's a vain society out there," observed one of its doctors.[6]

If the cost of phalloplasty was not a deterrent, potential risk might be. In 1990, Samatier was imprisoned for manslaughter after one of his patients bled to death following surgery. Fat injections per se weren't the culprit—the patient, unbeknownst to Samatier, had been taking anticoagulant drugs following heart surgery. Throughout the 1990s, the American Society for Aesthetic Plastic Surgery repeatedly warned that existing data on phalloplasty were insufficient for determining its safety. Though most of the approximately forty U.S. physicians who regularly perform the operation are urologists and plastic surgeons, not all are board certified, and, as with other lucrative new areas like hair transplantation, more doctors enter the field each month. Reputable physicians require patients to sign comprehensive consent forms, offering the sobering reminder that "patients have only one penis."

Rosenstein insisted that he informed all patients of potential risks and never told them that "everything would be perfect—that this was magic wand therapy." Nevertheless, by 1996, the number of complications had increased, along with lawsuits against doctors performing the operations. Problems ranged from nerve damage, scarring, inhibited erection, and lowered erectile angle to penis shafts marred by concave areas, nodules, or benign fatty tumors. Rare but frightening complications could also develop from the inner root of the penis failing to hold its new position, causing it to swivel disconcertingly. Patients sometimes suffered pain so excruciating that they became addicted to painkillers. But perhaps worst of all was the impact on self-image: men were repelled by the sight of their own penises. Some talked about suicide; most "just settled into chronic depression."

One thirty-one-year-old Los Angeles man had the surgery because his penis was so thin that it bent during erections. "I thought if I thickened it up, I'd have more power," he explained. The result of his surgery was not a thicker penis but a "clumpy" one covered with odd knots. A television writer suffered so much pain after the surgery that he was bedridden for two months, virtually unable to move; Rosenstein assured him that he was "one in a million." One of the most publicized cases of phalloplasty gone awry was that of Ron Nance, a forty-seven-year-old carpenter who opted for surgery when his girlfriend of a year seemed to be losing interest in their relationship. The surgery, performed by Rosenstein, promised to "make me feel better about my aging self" and to make Nance a member of the enviable fraternity of the well endowed. Within a day after the purportedly "flawless, painless" procedure, Nance was feverish, infected, and racked with pain; when he flew back to Los Angeles for medical attention, he was so ill on arrival at the airport that paramedics had to rush him to emergency treatment. To counter the swelling and infection, it was necessary to cut substantial amounts of skin away from Nance's penis, pushing the penile shaft back into his abdomen and making the penis shorter than it had been prior to surgery, as well as misshapen. The urologist Ajay Nehra notes that in the majority of cases, cutting the ligaments will create scar tissue, causing the penis to retract instead of lengthen. Subsequent treatments included emergency circumcision to relieve pressure from a constricted foreskin, weights to correct retraction and bending, and hormone injections. After the surgery, Nance was unable to have an erection. When he went to three other urologists, all of whom were appalled by his condition, none would do additional surgery; one told Nance to forget about his penis and "go to church to pray for peace."

Some of the most damaging testimony against Rosenstein came from his office staff. A surgical technologist claimed that he rushed through surgeries, spending less than thirty minutes on procedures requiring an hour or more. Operations became testing grounds, she claimed, for the doctor to see if he could beat his own speed records, with little apparent regard for patient safety (and a record time of twenty minutes for one operation). Patients were whisked into surgery so quickly that operating rooms weren't properly cleaned between procedures; the *Los Angeles Times* reported that "blood was left on the floor, and occasionally fat would fly out of the liposuction machine and splatter on walls and cabinets and not be cleaned up." The doctor remained resolutely optimistic in the face of postoperative problems, assuring patients that their condition was normal even when the penis looked mangled.

In 1993, the Doctors Company, California's major malpractice insurer, informed physicians that they wouldn't be covered for malpractice if they used fat injections to increase penis width. Dr. Mark Gorney, the firm's medical director, stated that most physicians regarded penile fat injections "with a combination of amusement and contempt." A 1997 report by the Department of Urology at University of California, San Francisco stated that many surgeons were seeing "penis cripples" who, after phalloplastic surgery, were "emotionally, psychologically, socially and sexually impaired due to a deformed penis."

Arguments commonly brought to bear against cosmetic surgery in general were also invoked. Some inveighed against penis augmentation because its only purpose is "to cosmetically change a perceived deficiency in body image." Claiming that most men who had the surgery were dissatisfied by the results, a New York urologist insisted that all potential augmentation patients be given psychiatric clearance, while another suggested that it would be cheaper and safer for them to buy a Porsche.

Rosenstein adamantly denied the horror stories. Nevertheless, in February 1996, the State Medical Board of California prohibited him from advertising and performing penis surgery pending further investigation. The board called the operations "an immediate danger to the public health, safety and welfare," based on allegations that he grossly misrepresented the risk. As of August 1996, approximately eighty former patients had brought lawsuits against Rosenstein; attorneys believed there were a good many more potential cases but that the men feared public ridicule. Two weeks later, the state board suspended Rosenstein's medical license.

Given the potential dangers of penis surgery, men's unwillingness to admit having it done, and its lack of advantage in the business world, why have an estimated fifteen thousand American men had this operation? Rosenstein has stated that he doesn't believe men would have had penis enlargements prior to the 1970s, even had the technology been available. If a face-lift was considered unacceptably vain, cosmetically changing the penis carried an infinitely heavier psychic burden, to say nothing of social disapproval. Before the 1960s, middle-class men were also more secure in their social and workplace roles, so methods of self-actualization didn't go to such extremes. The biggest motivation for phalloplasty, doctors agree, is low self-esteem; "regardless of where the knife goes in," says a Colorado surgeon, "the primary benefit is to the brain." Dr. Gary Alter, who is well versed in the art of phalloplasty, justifies the procedure on the basis that it "improves a normal form and enables the patient to better accept himself"; he recommends that it be done by plastic surgeons because urologists aren't "aesthetically oriented." Good aesthetic results are important, Alter adds, because "dissatisfied male patients can become violent."

Fears about penile inadequacy may be stimulated by advertising and locker-room comparisons, but there are other influences as well, including pornography. Beginning in the 1930s, public discourse on sexuality was intensified by a series of Supreme Court decisions narrowing the definition of obscenity and eroding barriers to the representation of sex in literature, film, and other media. As a result, a flood of books, films, videos, magazines, and songs glamorizing and commodifying sex, often quite explicitly, entered public entertainment. The most graphic displays of all came from pornography, which paralleled the sexual revolution and became widely available during the 1970s. Unlike *Playboy*, hard-core magazines like *Hustler* didn't try to ameliorate their portrayal of naked women by promoting a lifestyle or philosophy or pretending the girls were just like the ones next door: they were about sex, and sex only.

Twenty-five years ago, the total retail value of all hard-core pornography in the United States was between five and ten million dollars. In the mid-1990s, Americans were spending eight billion dollars on hard-core videos, adult cable programming, computer porn, and sex magazines—an amount much larger than Hollywood's entire domestic box-office take. In 1996, 665 million porn videos were rented, and 8,000 new hard-core porn movies were produced, making the United States the world leader in the production of pornography.

Thanks to the popularity of VCRs, the vast majority of pornography is consumed not in seedy theaters or at stag parties but in private homes. It is viewed by millions of ordinary men who can hardly help making invidious comparisons between themselves and the actors on-screen, who are both well endowed and sexually insatiable. Pornography therefore holds up an unrealistic standard of both physical appearance and performance.

Sex therapists have found that many men with potency problems are porn viewers. The therapist Lou Paget, a fierce critic of the distorted and damaging images of sexuality portrayed by the porn industry, points out that porn is "scripted, acted, voiced over, and edited," and thus impossible to compare with real sex. It is as unrealistic for the average man to emulate a model in a porn video, she argues, as for the average woman to look like an eighteen-year-old starlet. In reality, few male porn stars can perform consistently—Susan Faludi, in her account of the porn industry, describes the anguish of waiting for an erection while camera and cast stand in the wings. But, of course, the male audience doesn't see this aspect.[7]

"Henceforth the Earth Will Move for Everyone": Viagra

Viagra is produced by the Pfizer Corporation, a pharmaceutical giant founded in 1849. Like minoxidil, Viagra evolved from laboratory experiments in which drugs designed to combat one set of ailments—angina and hypertension—were discovered to have other, unexpected consequences: they promoted erections. Pfizer's scientists toiled for ten years before the Food and Drug Administration (FDA) certified Viagra safe and viable on March 27, 1998; in the wings, Wall Street watched and waited, while shares of Pfizer stock more than doubled within a year in anticipation of the oncoming Viagra stampede. Launched in April with fanfare and publicity more suitable to the opening of a Hollywood blockbuster than a pill, Viagra would quickly eclipse penicillin, the polio vaccine, and the birth-control pill as the most talked about drug of the century. And what a dialogue it would be, spanning popular culture, media hype, medical ethics, social policy, gender bias, and even sex crimes. Investors made millions on its stock; insurance companies squabbled over how much, if any, of its cost should be covered, and within weeks of its introduction, lawyers launched suits related to both its successes and its failures. Later, doctors wrestled with the moral dilemma of whether to prescribe it for men who might drop dead from taking it, and Bob Dole hawked it on prime-time television.

Aside from the boom in Pfizer's share prices and a nonstop stream of jokes on late-night television, Viagra's largest impact initially was among consumers. The first day the pill became available, an Atlanta urologist wrote out three hundred prescriptions, resorting to a rubber stamp when his hand began to ache. The urologist Michael Moran wrote his first prescription for a seventy-seven-year-old patient who asked for a thousand pills (Moran gave him thirty). Nationwide, urologists were inundated with patients complaining of "emergency" problems that, when they gained entry to the doctors' offices, turned out to be requests for Viagra. Within one month after its introduction, doctors had written 598,000 prescriptions, and Pfizer raked in more than $400 million in worldwide first-quarter sales—most of them in the United States, since few other countries had approved the drug. A thriving black market sprang up, as fake pills made of flour and cornstarch found their way across national borders and over the Internet, selling for as much as sixty dollars a pill in Taiwan and eight hundred dollars per bottle in Turkey. Japanese travel agencies offered "Viagra Specials"—three-day trips to Hawaii, including paid-for doctor's visits and two bottles of Viagra. Tiny San Marino—population twenty-five thousand—was one of the few places outside the United States where Viagra was legally available, and hordes of men from neighboring Italy flocked across the border to buy the new miracle drug. Within Italy, where the drug wasn't legal, ice cream vendors did a brisk business selling a blue gelato named "Viagra." On America's own borders, Canadians stampeded into upstate New York and Vermont; to the south, the owner of a small Mexican drugstore reported that five hundred Mexican men came in every day asking for Viagra—not for impotence, she hastened to say, but for use in "sexual marathons."

Initially, Viagra seemed too good to be true. It came along just at the right time. By the late 1990s, estimates of impotence had been adjusted upward to thirty million. It was beginning to look like a circular malady—the more it was talked about, the more of it there was. Men who had never breathed the word "impotence," much less consulted a doctor about it, burst out of their collective closets to climb on the Viagra bandwagon. It wasn't guaranteed to work for every man—in trials, about 80 percent had a positive response—but no group of men tested had a totally negative response, even those with the most hopeless forms of impotence like victims of spinal injury or diabetes. These positive findings, combined with the enthusiasm of Wall Street and men the world over, seemed to promise endless good things for Pfizer. But clouds soon appeared on this sunny horizon.[8]

To begin with, almost as soon as Viagra hit the market it was confronted with impostors like Viagro and Vaegra, forcing Pfizer into a series of lawsuits. Despite the company's insistence that the drug be prescribed only after urological analysis, Viagra was sold over the Internet by organizations that handed out prescriptions on the basis of fifty-dollar cyberspace consultations. And although Pfizer warned that only urologists should prescribe the drug, escalating demand prompted general practitioners, gynecologists, and even anesthesiologists to churn out prescriptions.

Stories also surfaced about strange side effects. During initial testing, some men had complained of blinding headaches, which may have seemed a reasonable price to pay for instant virility. More alarming than these "Viagra hangovers" were vision distortions that developed in about 3 percent of users, prompting the Airline Pilots Association to issue warnings to its members about blurred vision, blue tingeing, and halo effects. In July, a fifty-three-year-old man filed a $110 million lawsuit against Pfizer after blue hazing in his vision caused him to crash his car. Worst of all, by May 21, only weeks after the introduction of Viagra, the FDA had confirmed reports of 6 user deaths—a figure that had risen to 130 by the end of 1998. Most victims were older men suffering from

heart problems, a condition for which Viagra had been contraindi-
cated in label warnings, but the deaths did help to cool the initial
buying binge. Sales, projected by some enthusiastic analysts in
April to reach $1 billion annually by the year 2000, with some
optimists predicting global revenues as high as $20 billion, slumped
from $411 million in Pfizer's second quarter to $141 million in the
third—only six months after Viagra's spectacular debut. In October, the widow of Charles Mastroianni of the Bronx filed the first
wrongful-death suit against Pfizer. Lawsuits based on Viagra's
physical side effects, however, were only the tip of the iceberg.
This was, after all, a drug that dealt with a problem that was not
only physical but related to emotions, relationships, and self-
esteem. The prospects for disaster were great.

Pfizer had tried to anticipate as many potential issues as possible. It even sent a delegation to the Vatican to find out how the
Roman Catholic Church would respond to the pill (the Church
gave its blessings on the basis of Viagra's contribution to improving
family relations). While awaiting FDA approval, the company
convened ethics panels to discuss possible problem areas—for
instance, what if rapists used Viagra? All the planning in the world,
however, couldn't have anticipated the multitude of issues raised
by the little blue pill. One of the biggest debates arose among
insurance companies.

Asked whether she thought prescriptions for Viagra should be
covered by health insurers, a Pfizer spokeswoman answered that of
course they should. What, after all, was the difference between
Viagra and medications for conditions like allergies and arthritis,
neither of which was life threatening but both of which eroded
the quality of life if left untreated? She was addressing questions of
great importance for the future of the medical and insurance professions: How far should insurers go toward paying for drugs that
were not so much treatment as enhancements? And how, exactly,
was the health profession going to define medical need?

Besieged with requests for the new drug, insurers scrambled to
formulate policies. Cigna declared that until it came up with a

permanent policy, it would pay for only six pills a month, and then only for a "preexisting, documented condition of organic impotence which is currently being treated by other medical means" (no psychological cases, in other words). Kaiser Permanente, the nation's largest HMO, aroused a furor by initially declaring it wouldn't pay for Viagra, but then backed off and said it would pay for half the cost. But the cost of how many pills? How many were enough? What if the patient was a one-hundred-year-old man? Blue Cross came up with a formula of eight Viagra pills every thirty days, thereby certifying itself willing to pay for sex twice a week—a decision that prompted an outcry about the intrusion of insurers into American bedrooms. Another HMO was criticized by a female member of its board who argued that Viagra was being overprescribed. Authorizing more Viagra than necessary was tantamount, she claimed, to "sexual swaggering" on the part of the company's predominantly male administration. Oxford Health Plans, a Connecticut-based HMO, decided to avoid the issue altogether by refusing to cover Viagra—and promptly became the first insurer to be sued by an irate client.

The debate over medical coverage even spread to the Pentagon, where it was estimated that Viagra could gobble up one-fifth of the entire pharmaceutical budget of the Veterans Affairs Department—roughly the cost, a Pentagon spokesman pointed out, of "two new Marine Corps Harrier Jets or 45 Tomahawk Cruise Missiles." By the end of 1998, the military's 1.2 million troops and 5 million dependents and retirees had been given the word: No more than six pills a month, and only for doctor-diagnosed erectile dysfunction. "Lost, stolen, or destroyed" pills, the Pentagon added cryptically, would not be replaced.

Very quickly, the issue of who would pay for Viagra expanded to include questions about social justice. If insurers refused to pay, the benefits of sexual enhancement—and, by extension, self-esteem—would be limited to those who could afford them. Here was a drug that could turn men into what they dreamed of being—but only if they had enough money. "Now I can't even afford sex," one man was overheard telling another on a Brooklyn subway. For that matter, added a growing chorus of family-planning organizations—and women—why should Viagra be a covered medical benefit if contraception was not? That insurers paid for Viagra, "a drug used mainly by men beyond the normal child-rearing age, and thus to simply make life more enjoyable," was to some "a clear reflection of who runs the nation's economy."

Women's indignation was not only directed at the inequities of the health-care system. Men and women had very different points of view about the desirability of revving up males who had been quiescent for years. Although much of the demand for Viagra, at least initially, was believed to be fueled by hopeful wives, not every woman was pleased by the prospect of rejuvenated male libidos. "We don't need any more senior male citizens thinking they're virile teenagers; we have enough of that already," complained one in a *Newsweek* editorial. "Why not birth control for men? That's what women want!" Even Ann Landers had to address female indignation: "The minute he walks in the door with those Viagra pills, I'm walking out!" declared one of thousands of anti-Viagra letters she received. Landers later published the results of a poll of more than ninety thousand women, nearly three-quarters of whom declared they would be happy to forget about intercourse altogether. For some women, erectile dysfunction was seen as protection against the possibility of infidelity or even divorce. Men, too, didn't always have entirely romantic views about Viagra: as one told his urologist, "I don't want to have sex with my wife, but I want to be able to say, 'I can, but I won't,' rather than have her tell me, 'I won't, and you can't.'"

If a man was with a woman who had lost interest in sex and Viagra restored his potency, where would he turn for sexual satisfaction? The divorce lawyer Raoul Felder cynically predicted that men would be most likely to use Viagra with mistresses and girlfriends, not wives. A sixty-one-year-old woman, for example, sued her companion of ten years for two million dollars when, reinvigorated by Viagra, he left her for a younger woman. The drug raised concerns about excessive lust, infidelity, and older men trying to keep pace with young women. When a thirty-four-year-old Florida woman was beaten to death by an eighty-nine-year-old man who, reportedly invigorated by Viagra, made advances to her and was spurned, concerns about sex crimes were added to the list.

Although urologists made it clear that Viagra wouldn't do anything for men who were already functioning properly—"If your tank is full, your tank is full," advised one doctor—many saw it as a potency booster rather than a potency restorer. Men who didn't have erection problems claimed it made them "better" at sex; others used it to counter the effects of drugs like MDMA (ecstasy) and crystal meth, which stimulated sexual desire while inhibiting the erectile process. Men may have thought these benefits made them better lovers, but Viagra had the same problems as other medical solutions for impotence. Too many men, the sex therapist Karen Martin warned, expected their little blue pills to do everything. They needed to "*try* harder, not just take a pill." Viagra might be a miracle drug, but it wouldn't compensate for poor technique or emotional emptiness.

In some ways, Viagra is most significant as the preeminent member of a proliferating class of medications best described as lifestyle drugs. Their purpose is not to save lives but to enhance the quality of life. Although lifestyle enhancement through chemistry didn't begin with Viagra—tranquilizers did the same thing fifty years ago, as does Prozac today—Viagra represents a quantum leap, along with cosmetic surgery and other technologies, toward blurring the lines between medical necessity and self-esteem.

In 1998, the journalist Michael Risher asked why Viagra isn't a controlled substance. Since it's illegal to take steroids to look more virile, why is it *not* illegal to take a pill to become virile? Even more troubling is the question of how sexual "normalcy" is being redefined in the wake of miracle drugs like Viagra. Preventive health care, improved diet, fitness, and the cult of youth have created a population healthier and more body-conscious than any of its predecessors. Men in early generations generally didn't expect to be sexually active in their later years. Nineteenth-century doctors cautioned that sexual activity for men after the age of fifty was likely to bring on severe physical disabilities, including paralysis and apoplexy. In the mid-twentieth century, Dr. Alfred Kinsey estimated that 10 percent of men were impotent by the time they turned fifty, with the incidence doubling for every subsequent decade. But Kinsey's research was conducted at a time when doctors warned men not to play more than nine holes of golf if they were over forty. As the baby-boomer generation grows older, impotence will increase. Yet contemporary expectations about health, fitness, and sexuality have pushed men to maintain youthful performance in all aspects of their lives. Even if men were content to live with erectile failure, women probably wouldn't accept cutting short their own sex lives.

But what happens to the man or woman who doesn't want to take drugs to enhance sexuality, who is content to age without the benefit of pills and potions? How far are we willing to go in our public discourse about how much sex is enough, what constitutes "good" sex, and how central a role sex should play in relationships? Medical advances and healthier lifestyles offer men hope for longer and more potent sex lives than at any other time in history, but expectations are likely to continue to outpace reality. Not even Viagra can guarantee sexual success to all men, all the time. What it can guarantee is a continuing moral and ethical debate.[9]

The Unkindest Cut

If it is fair that men's bodies are being scrutinized, just as women's have been, it's questionable whether the new visibility of men's most private parts has had an altogether salutary effect on American culture. Making the penis public reached its apex on June 23,

1993, in Manassas, Virginia, when twenty-four-year-old Lorena Bobbitt took a twelve-inch kitchen knife and sliced off her husband's penis. John Wayne Bobbitt was lucky. Had the penis not been recovered by police, the surgeon would simply have sewn him up. Furthermore, the huge blood clot that formed over the wound prevented him from bleeding to death. He also became famous.

Nearly two-thirds of the American public followed the trial. Outside the packed courtroom, T-shirts emblazoned with logos like LOVE HURTS sold briskly; some were even autographed by the victim himself. After the trial was over, the gravy train kept rolling for quick-thinking entrepreneurs, like the shameless creator of the Bobbitt paperweight, a bronze casting of a penis sporting a large bronze bandage.

Everyone associated with the incident became a minor celebrity, including the urologist James Sehn, who reattached Bobbitt's penis in a grueling nine-and-a-half-hour operation, teamed with a surgeon who specialized in reattaching severed fingers. Newspapers, talk shows, and cocktail party habitués elicited minute details about the surgery. Sehn was astounded by his celebrity; prior to his involvement with Bobbitt, guests at cocktail parties had drifted away after a few moments of urology chat. Though he was showered with interview requests, Sehn gained little monetary profit and few new patients. The surgery was "too weird," he believed, to help his private urology practice, and Bobbitt never paid his fifty-thousand-dollar surgical fee, although he did scrape together enough cash to have his reattached penis enlarged by Rosenstein in 1995.

The plight of John Wayne Bobbitt can perhaps be seen as a metaphor for the declining fortunes of American men and the severed penis as a shocking symbol of loss of power. Many women expressed grim satisfaction about the incident, in no small part because Lorena Bobbitt claimed to have done the deed in retaliation against spousal abuse. It suggests as well deep resentment about the different valuations of male and female bodies. Kim Gaudy, the executive vice president of the National Organization for Women, expressed the sentiments of many women when she commented that because a man's body had been violated and exposed, "suddenly it's a big deal."

More significantly, Bobbitt's ordeal represents yet another celebration of the self. When the trial was finally over and a verdict of temporary insanity rendered, a reporter was overheard saying, "There is considerable joy in the prospect that the word 'penis' can now be reserved for special occasions." But he was wrong. Thanks to the publicity that surrounded the trial, the barriers around this most private body part were irrevocably lowered. For the first time, it was acceptable to use the word "penis" in polite society.

As for Bobbitt, he took full advantage of his misfortune to become a "celebrity." He embarked on a career as a porn star, made nationwide promotional tours, wrote a book about his experience, and intends to pursue a mainstream film career; Bobbitt "fans" can choose from thousands of photographs of him on the Internet. Not all men feel so positively about the new sexual standards. They have discovered what women have known for a long time: once the body becomes public, it is subject to admiration and lust, but also to critical scrutiny and judgment.[10]

In 1986, the writer Pete Hamill interviewed young men on the subject of relationships. He found that though a few seemed to realize that adjusting to life with another person might entail some sacrifices, many believed that with some luck they could "have it all." Having it all *is* the American dream—and for many of us, the path to "having it all" means "buying it all."

As lifestyles and the market for goods became increasingly segmented after World War II, consumerism offered ordinary Americans the ability to have leisure, beauty, and self-esteem at their fingertips, tailored to their individual needs. But consumerism has another, darker side: by creating insatiable desire, it also creates unappeasable discontent.

Desire has become more than a craving for consumer goods. In our quest for the new, we search restlessly for new relationships, new love objects—even a new "me." We have come to believe that all of these can be obtained, at least theoretically, by transforming ourselves in order to attract others. The struggle to look good is no longer gender specific, and for both women and men it mirrors a relentless search for happiness based on an often-illusory image.

For no group of Americans has this been more true than for the seventy-six million baby boomers. Because of their sheer numbers, and because they came of age at a time when national prosperity held out promises of self-fulfillment unimaginable to earlier generations, the baby boomers have been the center of attention throughout their lives—in no small part because of their role as consumers. Imbued with expectations far exceeding those of any previous generation, these children of postwar abundance were unprepared for the social changes and economic reverses of the 1970s and 1980s. One of the most treasured assumptions of all is that youth, vitality, and self-fulfillment are permanent entitlements. But as it turns out, none of us has been able to "have it all." Coming to terms with these realities hasn't been easy; according to the American Psychiatric Association, the most common question of baby boomers entering middle age is "Why haven't I got what I expected?"

Although every age-group appears to be subject to body-image worries, those most vulnerable are Americans crossing the threshold into middle age and beyond. At the beginning of the century, there were about three million people over the age of sixty-five in the United States, about 4 percent of the population. Today there are thirty-one million, 12 percent of the total population, and by the time the last baby boomer reaches sixty-five, there will be fifty-five million of these senior citizens, or 18 percent of the population. In 1982, the *Saturday Evening Post* suggested there was little reason to expect that "the baby-boomers will be any more docile or malleable in old age than they have been in youth or adulthood"—or, as a corollary, that their influence will wane or their expectations dim.

If Americans are aging, a trend over which they have no control, there is another trend that seems likely to continue by choice: the propensity for adults to spend longer periods, and perhaps their entire lives, as singles. Since 1970, the number of single Americans has increased 85 percent, compared with only a 19 percent increase in the number of married couples. Though the divorce rate has declined slightly from its high in the mid-1970s, nearly half of all marriages and an even higher proportion of second marriages still end in divorce. As of 1992, more than one out of every three baby boomers between the ages of twenty-five and forty-four was single, a statistic starkly at odds with the 1950s, when practically every adult American, no matter what his age, was married. At all ages, being single generally imposes higher standards for physical appearance and keeps both genders anxiously peering into the mirror and contemplating their shortcomings.

As a nation, we spend more money on fitness and cosmetics than on education or social services. In 1990 alone, Americans spent thirty-three billion dollars on diets and diet-related services, much of this on fad diets with high failure rates. Eating the "right" foods and running the proper number of miles daily have been vested with an almost mystical power. Writing for *Lears* in 1990, Barbara Ehrenreich asked whether we were confusing health with goodness. Like runners sprinting to a higher consciousness, she suggested, Americans were redefining virtue as health, holding up firm bodies as evidence of moral superiority in a world that seemed to have lost its moral compass.

Though there may be some virtue in adhering to rigorous fitness routines—as one twenty-four-year-old banker put it, "fitness is a way of signaling to people that you're serious"—it is nevertheless true that since the fitness revolution began in the 1970s, health objectives have tended to become secondary to remaking bodies for purely aesthetic ends. Virtue, in this case, is superseded by the quest for self-esteem, which makes the moral component of fitness questionable. Morality notwithstanding, there is nothing further from health than obsessive dieting, bingeing and purging, and plastic surgery.

The subtle melding of health and beauty is obvious to the successful dermatologist Dr. Howard Murad, who explains that to be truly healthy, people must have a sense of well-being. If having "fewer wrinkles or a little more hair is going to make you feel better," Murad suggests, "that can add to your health"—a point of view that defines where all of us, men and women alike, are today.[11]

NOTES

INTRODUCTION

Epigraph: Warren I. Susman, *Culture as History: The Transformation of American Society in the Twentieth Century* (New York: Pantheon, 1984), 271.

1. Statistics from American Academy of Cosmetic Surgery, 1997, and Alan Farnham, "You're So Vain," *Fortune* (September 9, 1996); Barbara Ehrenreich, *The Worst Years of Our Lives: Irreverent Notes from a Decade of Greed* (New York: Pantheon, 1990), 135; Elisabeth Badinter, *XY: On Masculine Identity* (New York: Columbia University Press, 1995), 130.

   Statistics on age at first marriage and marriage rates from Peter N. Carroll, *It Seemed Like Nothing Happened: The Tragedy and Promise of America in the 1970s* (New York: Holt, Rinehart and Winston, 1982), 279; survey results in William H. Chafe, *The Unfinished Journey* (New York: Oxford University Press, 1999), 436; Brown cited by John D'Emilio and Estelle Freedman, *Intimate Matters: A History of Sexuality in America* (New York: Harper and Row, 1988), 303; Greer cited by Norman F. Cantor, *The American Century: Varieties of Culture in Modern Times* (New York: HarperCollins, 1997), 480.

   Erik H. Erikson, *Childhood and Society* (New York: Norton, 1963), 261; Diane Barthel, *Putting on Appearances: Gender and Advertising* (Philadelphia: Temple University Press, 1988), 1; Daniel Boorstin, *The Image; or, What Happened to the American Dream* (New York: Atheneum, 1962), 186; Christopher Lasch, *The Culture of Narcissism: American Life in an Age of Diminishing Expectations* (New York: Norton, 1979), 48–63; Margaret Morganroth Gullette, "All Together Now: The New Sexual Politics of Midlife Bodies," *Michigan Quarterly Review* (Fall 1993); statistics on baby boomers in Jeff Ostroff, "Targeting the Prime-Life Consumer," *American Demographics* (January 1991), 30, and Landon Jones, "The Baby-Boom Legacy," *Saturday Evening Post* (May–June 1982), 20.

1: LOOKING GOOD

Epigraph: David Nap in Amy Spindler, "It's a Face-Lifted, Tummy-Tucked Jungle Out There," *New York Times* (June 9, 1996), sec. C, p. 8.

1. For detailed history of hairstyles, treatments, and wigs in Europe and America and attitudes about hair, see Wendy Cooper, *Hair: Sex, Society, and Symbolism* (New York: Stein and Day, 1971), and Richard Corson, *Fashions in Hair: The First Five Thousand Years* (New York: Hastings House, 1965). History of hair treatments and potions in Fred Setterberg, "In Search of Bald Perfection," *Los Angeles Reader* (April 1, 1994), 9; Bosley Medical Group, *The Art and Science of Hair Restoration* (1994), 3–4; Bill Heavey, "For Men Only," *Washingtonian* (May 1993), 87; Lynn Darling, "A Generation Comes to Terms with Hair," *Esquire* (Fall 1987), 65; Michael Segell, "The Bald Truth about Hair," *Esquire* (May 1994), 115; Jeff Stevenson, "Making Headway," *Men's Health* (May 1993), 25; "bigwig" derivation in John Berendt, "The Toupee," *Esquire* (June 1990), 57; advertising from Kevin White, *The First Sexual Revolution* (New York: NYU Press, 1993), 23; observations on hair etiquette in Corson, *Fashions in Hair,* and Robert Tomes, *The Bazar Book of Decorum* (New York: Harper, 1877); Harvard College Book in *New York Times* (April 9, 1967), 126–27.

2. Arnaldo Testi, "The Gender of Reform Politics: Theodore Roosevelt and the Culture of Masculinity," *Journal of American History* (March 1995), 1520–23; Mark Dyreson, "The Emergence of Consumer Culture and the Transformation of Physical Culture: American Sport in the 1920s," *Journal of Sport History* (Winter 1989), 261–62; Joel Sayre, "The Body Worshippers of Muscle Beach," *Saturday Evening Post* (May 25, 1957), 34; Jim Bebbington, "Getting Classic with Arnold," *Saturday Evening Post* (July/August 1993), 36–37. Brady in James Trager, *Foodbook* (New York: Grossman, 1970), 459–60; antebellum diet and alcoholism in William J. Rorabaugh, "Estimated U.S. Alcohol Beverage Consumption, 1790–1860," *Journal of Studies on Alcohol* (March 1976), 360–61, and William J. Rorabaugh, *The Alcoholic Republic* (New York: Oxford, 1979); influence of motion-picture industry on body ideals in Robert Sklar, *Movie-Made America* (New York: Vintage, 1994); somatotypes and women's reactions to men's body types in W. Wells and B. Siegel, "Stereotyped Somatotypes," *Psychological Reports* 8 (1961), 77–78, and K. T. Strongman and C. J. Hart, "Stereotyped Reactions to Body Build," *Psychological Reports* 23 (1968), 1175.

3. I. Kelman Cohen, Andrea L. Pozez, and Joseph E. McKeown, "Gynecomastia," in Eugene H. Courtiss, ed., *Male Aesthetic Surgery* (St. Louis: Mosby Press, 1991), 373, 376, 383; John O. Roe, "The Deformity Termed 'Pug Nose' and Its Correction by a Simple Operation" (paper presented at the Medical Society of the State of New York, February 1, 1887), 114; George B. Monks, "Correction, by Operation, of Some Nasal Deformities and Disfigurements," *Boston Medical and Surgical Journal* (1898), 262.

Paré described by Harry Hayes, Jr., *An Anthology of Plastic Surgery* (Rockville, Md.: Aspen Publishers, 1986), 134–36; Joanna Bourke, *Dismembering the Male: Men's Bodies, Britain, and the Great War* (Chicago: University of Chicago Press, 1996), 33; Richard Battle, "Plastic Surgery in the Two World Wars and in the Years Between," *Journal of the Royal Society of Medicine* (November 1978); "Miracles of Surgery on Men Mutilated in War," *New York Times Magazine* (January 16, 1916), 6; Jacob Sarnoff, "What to Expect of Plastic Surgery," *Medical Record* (July 15, 1936), 62; Barnes cited by Katherine Lyle Stephenson, "The 'Mini-Lift': An Old Wrinkle in Face-Lifting," *Plastic and Reconstructive Surgery* (September 1970), 234; surgeons' responses to male patients in Roland H. Berg, "Face-Lifts for Men," *Look* (December 1, 1970), 80, and Walter C. Alvarez, "Face Lifting . . . for What, for Whom, for How Much?" *Good Housekeeping* (September 1957), 189.

4. S. J. Aston, "What I Tell My Patients," *Aesthetic Surgery* (Winter–Spring 1989), 6 7; Thomas J. Baker and Howard Gorden, "The Temporal Face-Lift ('Mini-Lift')," *Plastic and Reconstructive Surgery* 47, no. 3 (March 1971), 313; poem from Correspondence to the Editor, "Blepharoplasty: A Surgeon's Perspective," *Plastic and Reconstructive Surgery* 76, no. 5 (November 1985). Earl Calvin Padgett, *Plastic and Reconstructive Surgery* (Springfield, Ill.: Charles Thomas, 1948), 4. Face-lifting surgery described by John R. Lewis, ed., *The Art of Aesthetic Plastic Surgery* (Boston: Little, Brown, 1989), 663; Baker and Gorden, "Temporal Face-Lift"; and personal observation and discussions with Dr. Harold Clavin, Santa Monica, Calif.; Alvarez, "Face Lifting . . . for What?" 86; doctors' views about women's need for plastic surgery in Robert Goldwyn, *The Patient and the Plastic Surgeon* (Boston: Little, Brown, 1991), 63.

5. Historical discussion of impotence in Carol Groneman, "Nymphomania: The Historical Construction of Female Sexuality," *Signs* 19, no. 2 (Winter 1994), 353, 358; Alfred C. Kinsey, Wardell B. Pomeroy, and Clyde E. Martin, *Sexual Behavior in the Human Male* (Philadelphia: W. B. Saunders, 1948), 237, 580; and Vern L. Bullough and Bonnie Bullough, *Sexual Attitudes* (Amherst, N.Y.: Prometheus, 1995). Data on primates from Michael Segell, "Man's Primal Urge," *Muscle & Fitness* (October 1994), 119.

Lesley A. Hall, *Hidden Anxieties: Male Sexuality, 1900–1950* (Cambridge, U.K.: Polity Press, 1991), 67; Bernie Zilbergeld, *The New Male Sexuality* (New York: Bantam, 1992), 408; Eric Carlton, *Sexual Anxiety: A Study of Male Impotence* (New York: Barnes and Noble, 1980), 58–59; Hugh Drummond, "The Ultimate Erector Set," *Mother Jones* (February–March 1987), 8; Donald W. Hastings, *Impotence and Frigidity* (Boston: Little, Brown, 1963), 24; Elaine Tyler May, *Barren in the Promised Land: Childless Americans and the Pursuit of Happiness* (New York: Basic Books, 1995), 39; John Demos, "The American Family in Past Times," *American Scholar* (1974), 424–26; Kevin J. Mumford, " 'Lost Manhood' Found: Male Sexual Impotence and Victorian Culture in the United States," in John J. Fout and

Maura Shaw Tantillo, eds., *American Sexual Politics* (Chicago: University of Chicago Press, 1993), 77–78; Michael S. Kimmel, "Consuming Manhood: The Feminization of American Culture and the Recreation of the Male Body, 1832–1920," *Michigan Quarterly Review* (Winter 1994), 23; Michael S. Kimmel, *Manhood in America: A Cultural History* (New York: Free Press, 1996), 128, 133; George M. Beard, *Sexual Neurasthenia* (New York: E. B. Treat, 1883), 149–50; Alan H. Bennett, *Management of Male Impotence* (Baltimore: Williams and Wilkins, 1982), 46–47.

William Robinson, *Sexual Impotence: A Practical Treatise on the Causes, Symptoms and Treatment of Impotence and Other Sexual Disorders in Men and Women* (New York: Critic and Guide Co., 1912), 114; van de Velde in Barbara Ehrenreich, Elizabeth Hess, and Gloria Jacobs, *Remaking Love: The Feminization of Sex* (New York: Anchor, 1986), and "The Cold Woman," *Time* (June 26, 1950), 80; Stekel cited in Lynn Segal, *Slow Motion: Changing Masculinities, Changing Men* (New Brunswick, N.J.: Rutgers University Press, 1990), 219; Gorer in William Atwood, "The American Male: Why Does He Work So Hard?" *Look* (February 25, 1958), 73.

2 : THE ORGANIZATION MAN

Epigraph: Ralph Knight, "The Vain Sex Is Men!" *Saturday Evening Post* (December 25, 1954), 28.

1. Quotes from contemporary sources include Lynda Schor, "What Women Love about Men's Bodies," *Mademoiselle* (April 1982), 82; "Tell Us, Ladies, How Should Men Look?" (November 1991), 252; Barry Glassner, *Bodies: Overcoming the Tyranny of Perfection* (Los Angeles: Lowell House, 1992), 25; Germaine Greer, "What Turns Women On?" *Esquire* (July 1989), 89; Judith Chase Churchill, "What Women First Notice about Men," *Ladies' Home Journal* (March 1951), 51, 114; Orr cited by Nancy Friday, *The Power of Beauty* (New York: HarperCollins, 1992), 382, 391.

2. Corporate-military comparisons in Anthony Sampson, *Company Man: The Rise and Fall of Corporate Life* (New York: Random House, 1995), 93; Sloan quoted by Reinhard Bendix, *Work and Authority in Industry* (Berkeley: University of California Press, 1974), 307; Olivier Zunz, *Making America Corporate, 1870–1920* (Chicago: University of Chicago Press, 1990), 39, 126; business leaders cited by Ely Chinoy, *Automobile Workers and the American Dream* (Urbana: University of Illinois, 1992), 7; Vance Packard, *The Pyramid Climbers* (New York: McGraw-Hill, 1962), 96–98; Merton system described on p. 101 of *The Pyramid Climbers.*

3. Presley discussed by Peter Guralnick, *Last Train to Memphis: The Rise of Elvis Presley* (Boston: Little, Brown, 1994), 81; film historian Michael Malone discusses Elvis and beauty parlors in *Heroes of Eros: Male Sexuality in the Movies* (New York: Dutton, 1979), 160; Nelson described by Sara

Davidson, *Real Property* (New York: Simon and Schuster, 1969), 130; crew cuts as suitable only for convicts from Bernard Rudofsky, *The Unfashionable Human Body* (New York: Doubleday, 1971), 132; Herbert Mitgang, "About—Men's Haircuts," *New York Times Magazine* (June 2, 1957), 26.

4. Gerald Walker, "Baldness Unbared," *New York Times Magazine* (January 4, 1959), 62; John Berendt, "The Toupee," *Esquire* (June 1990), 57; Sears campaign in "Proper Toppers," *Time* (March 30, 1959), 82; "Rug Boomlet," *Newsweek* (May 2, 1949), 52; "Does He or Doesn't He?" *Time* (January 25, 1963), 71; salesmen's experiences related by Fred Sparks, "I'm Glad I Bought a Toupee," *Saturday Evening Post* (December 15, 1956), 64–65; Robert Wallace, "Divots, Doilies, and Rugs," *Life* (December 7, 1954), 85; toupee maker Herb Yerman in Beth Ann Krier, "Hair Raising Tales of Baldness," *Los Angeles Times* (October 12, 1976), sec. 4, p. 1; *Playboy* advertising discussed in Gay Talese, *Thy Neighbor's Wife* (New York: Doubleday, 1980), 73; *Playboy* advertising director Howard Lederer quoted in "Think Clean," *Time* (March 3, 1967), 78; Lancelot Designs advertising in *Esquire* (October 1970), 200.

5. "Thirty-four Million Fatties," *Time* (March 23, 1953), 64; Dublin in "Fat and Unhappy," *Time* (May 23, 1952), 64, and Roberta Pollack Seid, *Never Too Thin* (New York: Prentice-Hall, 1989), 120; W. H. Sebrell, Jr., "Obesity Is Now No. 1 U.S. Nutritional Problem," *Science Newsletter* (December 27, 1952), 408. In his charts, Dublin set ideal weight for a man five feet ten within a range of 151–62 pounds, and for the six-footer, it was 160–72 pounds. Dublin's chart also set weights for women: for women five feet four, ideal weight was 127–37; for five feet six, 133–43. These are, of course, considerably higher than prevailing ideals of women's weight today.

On executive exercise programs, see Walter McQuade, "Why Are They Running, Stretching, Starving?" *Fortune* (August 1970), 136; "Fat People's Fight against Job Bias," *U.S. News & World Report* (December 5, 1977), 78; "Man's Week at the Golden Door Spa in Escondido," *Business Week* (December 22, 1962), 23; Betty Leddick, "Fat Farm Turns to Weightier Matters," *Los Angeles Times* (December 26, 1973), sec. 4, p. 1.

6. Articles on men's diets include Samuel W. Bryant, "Keeping Executives Healthy," *Fortune* (April 1963), 122; "Executive Health," *American Mercury* (September 1960), 109; "If You Want to Stay Healthy," *Nation's Business* (February 1969), 56–60; Dana L. Farnsworth, "The Way to Stay Healthy: A Doctor's Advice to Businessmen," *U.S. News & World Report* (August 1963), 72–74. Articles with advice to women include Frederick J. Stare, "How to Keep a Husband Alive," *McCall's* (October 1953), 80; Hannah Lees, "Our Men Are Killing Themselves," *Saturday Evening Post* (January 28, 1956), 114; "How to Kill a Husband," *Time* (March 7, 1960), 47.

Women's magazines told women "how to feed a hungry family while *you* take off that extra weight" and extolled the virtues of the "secret French-style diet" that allowed a wife to shed pounds while preparing meals that her husband could enjoy. Louis Dublin, "Stop Killing Your Husband," *Reader's Digest* (July 1952), 107–9; "Diets for Men," *Time* (March 26, 1951), 63–64; "The Drinking Man's Danger," *Time* (March 5, 1962), 72; Robert Werrick, "I Wrote the Drinking Man's Diet," *Saturday Evening Post* (May 22, 1965), 84; "Diet Full of Cheer," *Newsweek* (January 11, 1965), 54; McQuade, "Why Are They Running," 134–38; Johanna T. Dwyer, Jacob J. Feldman, and Jean Mayer, "The Social Psychology of Dieting," *Journal of Health and Social Behavior* 11 (1970), 280; Seid, *Never Too Thin*, 135.

7. "How Not to Commit Suicide," *Time* (November 7, 1960), 96; "A New Approach to Stress," *Newsweek* (December 3, 1956), 55; Hans Selye, "Stress and Disease," *Science* (October 7, 1955), 625–31; Barbara Ehrenreich, *The Hearts of Men: American Dreams and the Flight from Commitment* (New York: Anchor Press, 1983), 83; C. D. Jenkins, "Psychological and Social Precursors of Coronary Disease," *New England Journal of Medicine* 284 (1977), 244; "Coronary Candidates," *Newsweek* (November 4, 1963), 63; psychiatrists cited by McQuade, "Why Are They Running," 134–35. For recommendations about women's responsibilities toward their husbands, see Alice Lake, "Five Husbands Who Might Have Lived," *McCall's* (November 1964), 126; Gerald J. Barry, "The Care and Feeding of Busy Executives . . . Who Know Now They Are Not 'Supermen,' " *Newsweek* (May 11, 1959), 88; and William Atwood, "The American Male: Why Does He Work So Hard?" *Look* (February 25, 1958), 73.

8. Hans Kraus and Ruth P. Hirschland, "Muscular Fitness and Health," *Journal of Health, Physical Education, and Recreation* 24, no. 10 (December 1953), 17–19; studies of Japanese versus American girls, and comments of General Marshall, cited by George A. Silver, "Fits over Fitness," *Nation* (June 9, 1962), 516–17; "Are We Becoming Soft? Why the President Is Worried about Our Fitness," *Newsweek* (September 26, 1955), 35–37; Donald P. Zingale, " 'Ike' Revisited on Sport and National Fitness," *Research Quarterly* 48, no. 1 (1977), 17; programs for children described in John B. Kelly, "Are We Becoming a Nation of Weaklings?" *Reader's Digest* (July 1956), 29. Kennedy's statement appeared in an article he wrote for *Sports Illustrated* in 1960 titled "The Soft American," cited by Patricia A. Eisenman and C. Robert Barnett, "Physical Fitness in the 1950s and 1970s: Why Did One Fail and the Other Boom?" *Quest* 31, no. 1 (1979), 116; John F. Kennedy, "Physical Fitness: A Report of Progress," *Look* (August 13, 1963), 82; "Suck in That Gut, America," *Esquire* (November 1962), 82; Shoup's fitness programs described in "Physical Fitness on the New Frontier," *U.S. News & World Report* (February 18, 1963), 54; Gallup poll on men's fitness cited by ad for Relax-A-cizor in *Newsweek* (June 8, 1959).

9. Dublin in "Fat and Unhappy," 64; Peter J. Steincrohn, "You Don't Have to Exercise!" *Reader's Digest* (May 1952), 86–87; Frank P. Foster, "Warning against a 'Physical Fitness Mania,' " *New York Times* (February 9, 1964), 15; Larsen in Harry Gilroy, "Beneficial Exercise," *New York Times* (December

21, 1952), 12; "How Not to Commit Suicide," 96; Relax-A-cizor in Inge-
borg de Beausacq, "It Changes Your Shape," *Mademoiselle* (July 1954), 12;
"Name the Spot," *Vogue* (August 15, 1956), 130; "An Eminently Suitable
Offer," *Vogue* (March 1, 1968), 88; Richard Gehman, "Toupees, Girdles,
and Sun Lamps," *Cosmopolitan* (May 1957), 42; "Electrical Reducing
Devices Banned from Market," *Science Newsletter* (October 1966), 262;
Joseph P. Davis, "How Effective Are Those 'No Work' Exercise Devices,"
Good Housekeeping (August 1970), 146; Jean Carper, "Beware of Those
'Quick Reducing' Gadgets," *Reader's Digest* (August 1971), 63.

Tone-O-Matic in *New York Times* (May 19, 1971), 40; Yoga Slim
Wheel described in "Off the Fat of the Land," *Newsweek* (April 20, 1970),
86–87; Chris Chase, *The Great American Waistline: Putting It On and Taking It
Off* (New York: Coward, McCann and Geohagen, 1981), 256–58; advertis-
ing for Hot Pants from *Esquire* magazine, various 1960s issues; for Sauna
Belt from *Esquire* (June 1970); for Relax-A-cizor, "Name the Spot," 130.
Other no-effort exercise products are described in "A Mechanized War on
the Waistline," *Life* (January 6, 1961), 72–73; "Spontaneous Reduction,"
Time (October 1971), 46.

10. Charles Gaines, *Yours in Perfect Manhood: Charles Atlas* (New York: Simon
and Schuster, 1982); Michael S. Kimmel, "Consuming Manhood: The
Feminization of American Culture and the Recreation of the Male Body,
1832–1920," *Michigan Quarterly Review* (Winter 1994); letters from Atlas
customers in Gaines; Anna Quindlen, "Kicking Sand in the Face of Time,"
New York Times (June 30, 1982), sec. B, p. 3; interviews with Seymour
Konig and Barry Lieberman in Venice, Calif., March 7, 1999; "Atlas Was
Right All Along," *Life* (April 17, 1964), 47.

11. Sir Harold Gillies and Ralph Millard, Jr., *The Principles and Art of Plastic
Surgery* (Boston: Little, Brown, 1957), 395; Rodney Barker, *The Hiroshima
Maidens* (New York: Penguin, 1985), 33; "Young Ladies of Japan," *Time*
(October 24, 1955); Walter C. Alvarez, "Face Lifting . . . for What, for
Whom, for How Much?" *Good Housekeeping* (September 1957), 86–87;
Robert Potter, "Farewell to Ugliness," *American Weekly* (March 31, 1946);
Dixie Dean Harris, "Now You Can Have Your Hair Restored ($1 a Hair),
Your Eyelids Tightened ($500), Wrinkles Erased ($750), Jowls Trimmed
($1000), Blood Rinsed ($1000), Energies Revived ($2000 and Up),"
Esquire (November 1965), 189; papal restrictions cited by Irving B. Gold-
man, ed., "Religious Views on Cosmetic Surgery," *Eye, Ear, Nose, and
Throat Monthly* (December 1961), 856–57; for the Jewish view, see Irving B.
Goldman, ed., "Religious Views on Cosmetic Surgery," *Eye, Ear, Nose, and
Throat Monthly* (March 1962), 220–21.

For the history of the professionalization of plastic surgery after World
War II, see Elizabeth Haiken, *Venus Envy: A History of Cosmetic Surgery* (Bal-
timore: Johns Hopkins University Press, 1997), 47–48, 132–34, 142–44;
Geri Trotta, "The Wish to Be Beautiful," *Harper's Bazaar* (June 1960), 101;

patient demographics in Johns Hopkins University study cited by Milton T. Edgerton, William Webb, Jr., Regina Slaughter, and Eugene Meyer, "Surgical Results and Psychosocial Changes following Rhytidectomy," *Plastic and Reconstructive Surgery* 33, no. 6 (June 1964), 503–14; face-lifts as alternatives to other luxuries in "The Imagined Image," *Vogue* (September 15, 1961), 173, 213; Harris, "Now You Can Have," 134; and Anonymous, "Diary of a Face Lift," *San Francisco Chronicle* (December 9, 1969), 26; John Medelman, "The Illusion of a Future," *Esquire* (November 1965), 137.

12. Quote from Eugene D. Fleming, "New Light on the Most Vexing Problems of Married Life," *Cosmopolitan* (October 1958), 30; Diana Trilling, "The Case for the American Woman," *Look* (March 10, 1959), 52; J. Robert Moskin, "The American Male: Why Do Women Dominate Him?" *Look* (February 4, 1958), 80; Eleanor Harris, "Men without Women," *Look* (November 22, 1960), 125; "Some Persons Should Stay Single," *Science Digest* (May 1956), 26, 104; Paul Gallico, "You Don't Know How Lucky You Are to Be Married," *Reader's Digest* (July 1956), 134; AMA statistics on frigidity in "The Cold Woman," *Time* (June 26, 1950), 80.

13. "Female Frigidity a Neurotic Illness," *Science Digest* (September 1950), 47; Edmund Berglor, "Frigidity in the Female: Misconceptions and Facts," *Marriage Hygiene* 1, no. 1 (1947), 16–21; Philip Polatin, "The Frigid Woman," *Medical Aspects of Human Sexuality* 4, no. 8 (August 1970), 21; Herbert D. Lawson, "Are Our Women Frigid?" *International Journal of Sexology* 3 (1950), 162–67; Ralph R. Greenson, "On Sexual Apathy in the Male," *Medical Aspects of Human Sexuality* 3, no. 8 (August 1969), 34; Kinsey in Donald W. Hastings, *Impotence and Frigidity* (Boston: Little, Brown, 1963), 68. Therapy for sexual dysfunction in J. Richard Udry, *The Social Context of Marriage* (Philadelphia: J. B. Lippincott, 1966), 547; Benita Eisler, *Private Lives: Men and Women of the Fifties* (New York: Franklin Watts, 1986), 274, 277; and Alan S. Gurman and David P. Kniskern, eds., *Handbook of Family Therapy* (New York: Brunner and Mazel, 1981), 11–12; "The Doctor Talks about Frigidity," *McCall's* (April 1957), 4; Daniel A. Sugarman, "Male Impotence: What Every Woman Should Know," *Reader's Digest* (September 1973), 91–94; Moskin, "The American Male," 78; study of "frigid" women cited by Myrtle Mann Gillette, "Normal Frigidity in Women: A Plea to the Family Physician," *International Journal of Sexology* 5 (1951), 34–35; Fleming, "New Light," 32; Solomon in Jerry Adler, Renee Michael, and Nikke Fiuke Greenberg, "You're So Vain," *Newsweek* (April 14, 1986), 55.

3: "FINDING THE REAL ME"

Epigraph: Fritz Perls in Jane Howard, *Please Touch* (New York: McGraw-Hill, 1970), 64.

1. Central Park hippie described by Hal Higdon, "Jogging Is an In Sport," *New York Times Magazine* (April 14, 1968), 36; Steven M. Tipton, *Getting*

Saved from the Sixties: Moral Meaning in Conversion and Cultural Change (Berkeley: University of California Press, 1982), 16; Judson Gooding, "The Accelerated Generation Moves into Management," *Fortune* (March 1971), 102–3; discussion of encounter groups and human potential movement in Howard, *Please Touch,* 49–64, and Martin L. Gross, *The Psychological Society* (New York: Random House, 1978), 293–300, 317; Tom Wolfe, "The Me Decade and the Great Awakening," *New York* (August 23, 1976), 26.

2. George H. Douglas, *The Smart Magazines* (New York: Archon Press, 1991), 176, 204–6; Alan Nourie and Barbara Nourie, eds., *American Mass-Market Magazines* (New York: Greenwood Press, 1990), 110, 113; Thomas Weyr, *Reaching for Paradise: The* Playboy *Vision of America* (New York: Times Books, 1978), 3; Benjamin de Bott, "The Anatomy of *Playboy,*" *Commentary* (August 1962), 113; "An Empire Built on Sex," *Life* (October 29, 1965), 68–69; "Playboy Puts a Glint in the Admen's Eye," *Business Week* (June 28, 1969), 146; "Urbunnity," *Newsweek* (January 6, 1964), 48; Bill Davidson, "Czar of the Bunny Empire," *Saturday Evening Post* (April 28, 1962), 34, 38.

3. Relationship between masculinity and Vietnam in John Wheeler, *Touched with Fire: The Future of the Vietnam Generation* (New York: Avon, 1984), 79, and Susan Jeffords, *Hard Bodies: Hollywood Masculinity in the Reagan Era* (New Brunswick, N.J.: Rutgers University Press, 1994), 7; "Youths Lose Hair for Ideal," *New York Times* (May 4, 1966), 45; Richard H. Parke, "Connecticut Boy Loses Appeal to Wear Bangs," *New York Times* (December 16, 1964), 45; Jagger cited by Claudia Brush Kidwell, ed., *Men and Women: Dressing the Part* (Washington, D.C.: Smithsonian Press, 1989), 153. With regard to rock stars and style, one cutting-edge designer, discussing the state of male fashion in 1997, identified rock musicians, especially Jagger, David Bowie, and the members of Oasis, as the greatest influence on male dress outside of the basic business suit men were still wearing to work. The rock world, he pointed out, offered men "distinctive style"—no matter how ugly that style might be ("Generation Next," *Los Angeles Times* [May 22, 1997], sec. E, p. 1). Judy Klemesrud, "Tired of a Toupee?" *New York Times* (April 15, 1968), 38; Donald H. Dunn, ed., "The Ins and Outs of Hair Weaving," *Business Week* (July 13, 1981), 85; Charles G. Bennett, "City Plans to Look into Hair-Weaving Complaints," *New York Times* (November 23, 1968), 36; Remar Sutton, *Body Worry* (New York: Viking, 1987), 164; "The Perm," *New York Times* (October 13, 1976), sec. C, p. 1.

4. "Without Moving a Muscle," *Time* (January 1, 1964), 38–39; Robert R. Spackman, "Exercises You Can Do Wherever You Are," *Reader's Digest* (June 1969), 113; George Walsh, "Get Trim and Strong in Seconds," *Sports Illustrated* (December 4, 1961), 34; "Oof," *Newsweek* (January 15, 1962), 78; "How to Live to Be a Hundred!" advertisement in *Esquire* (December 1963); "Getting Fat by Making Others Slim," *Business Week* (March 22, 1969), 146. For discussion of isometrics, see Bullworker advertisement in

Esquire (January 1975), 167; "Oof," 78; Walsh, "Get Trim and Strong in Seconds"; studies of effects of isometrics on weight lifters by Dr. Alexander C. Lund in "The Perils of Muscle Beach," *Time* (July 20, 1970), 46.

5. Barney Lefferts, "Swanky Sweatshops," *New York Times* (March 23, 1958), 47; Richard Gehman, "Toupees, Girdles, Sun Lamps," *Cosmopolitan* (May 1957), 42; "Tannyed and Fit," *Time* (February 10, 1961), 76; Peter Bunzel, "Health Kick's High Priest," *Life* (September 29, 1958), 71–73; Smith in William Overend, "Flocking to the Body Temples with the Gym Generation," *Los Angeles Times* (May 6, 1981), sec. 5, p. 1; Severin and Peggy Peterson, "Something New for Your Peace of Mind," *Ladies' Home Journal* (February 1968), 112; Sara Davidson, "The Rush for Instant Salvation," *Harper's* (July 1971), 41.

   Donald P. Zingale, " 'Ike' Revisited on Sport and National Fitness," *Research Quarterly* 48, no. 1 (1977), 16–17; "Ike on the Links," *Newsweek* (August 31, 1953), 60; "Don't Just Sit There: Walk, Jog, Run," *Time* (February 23, 1968), 45; "Getting Fat by Making Others Slim," 140–41; London study in John Medelman, "The Loneliness of the Long-Distance Runner over Forty," *Esquire* (June 1966), 120; "Off the Fat of the Land," *Newsweek* (April 20, 1970), 86–87.

6. "Plastic Surgery: It's No Longer Reserved for the Vain and Rich," *New York Times* (September 27, 1971), sec. 1, p. 30; Dixie Dean Harris, "Now You Can Have Your Hair Restored ($1 a Hair), Your Eyelids Tightened ($500), Wrinkles Erased ($750), Jowls Trimmed ($1000), Blood Rinsed ($1000), and Energies Revived ($2000 and Up)," *Esquire* (November 1965), 189; Patrick M. McGrady, "The Art of Manly Face-Lifting," *Vogue* (June 1969), 117; Arthur J. Snider, "Psychiatrist Warns Cosmetic Surgeons," *Science Digest* (August 1973), 48–49; Wayne Jacobson, Milton T. Edgerton, Eugene Meyer, Arthur Canter, and Regina Slaughter, "Psychiatric Evaluation of Male Patients Seeking Cosmetic Surgery," *Plastic and Reconstructive Surgery* 26, no. 4 (1960), 356; Milton T. Edgerton and Norman J. Knorr, "Motivational Patterns of Patients Seeking Cosmetic (Esthetic) Surgery," *Plastic and Reconstructive Surgery* 48, no. 6 (December 1971), 554; David William Horan, "Limiting Risk of Medical Liability—A Lawyer's View," in Eugene H. Courtiss, ed., *Male Aesthetic Surgery* (St. Louis: Mosby, 1991), 24; Thomas G. Baker and Howard Gordon, "Rhytidectomy in Males," *Plastic and Reconstructive Surgery* 44, no. 2 (August 1969), 219; E. Horace Klabunde and Edward Falces, "Incidence of Complications in Cosmetic Rhinoplasties," *Plastic and Reconstructive Surgery* 34, no. 2 (August 1964).

7. John Kronenbergh, "The Singles Scene," *Look* (February 2, 1968), 80; David S. Glenwick, Leonard A. Jason, and Donald Elman, "Physical Attractiveness and Social Contact in the Singles Bar," *Journal of Social Psychology* 105 (1978), 311–12; Paul J. Lavrakas, "Female Preferences for Male Physiques," *Journal of Research in Personality* 9, no. 4 (1975), 333; Jill

Niemark, "The Beefcaking of America," *Psychology Today* (November/December 1994), 35, 38; women's response to male earning in Ellis Cose, *A Man's World: How Real Is Male Privilege—and How High Its Price?* (New York: HarperCollins, 1995), 33; Farrell cited by Nancy Friday, *The Power of Beauty* (New York: HarperCollins, 1992), 59; discussion of occupations in singles bars in Diana Newell, "Singles Scene: All Those Lonely People," *Los Angeles Times* (March 18, 1976), sec. 4, p. 1; "Rise of the 'Singles'—40 Million Free Spenders," *U.S. News & World Report* (October 7, 1974), 54–55; "The Ways 'Singles' Are Changing U.S.," *U.S. News & World Report* (January 31, 1977), 59; "Games Singles Play," *Newsweek* (July 16, 1973), 53–58.

8. Robert W. Kistner, "What 'The Pill' Does to Husbands," *Ladies' Home Journal* (January 1969), 66–68; Masters and Johnson's research in "Repairing the Conjugal Bed," *Time* (May 25, 1970), 49–52, and "Two Sex Researchers on the Firing Line," *Life* (June 24, 1966), 43–44; Riesman in Vance Packard, *The Sexual Wilderness* (New York: Pocket Books, 1970), 110; Colette Downing and Patricia Fahey, "The Calculus of Sex," *Esquire* (May 1966), 123; David Cort, "Sexual Happiness for All," *Nation* (September 2, 1961), 119; Wolfe, "Me Decade."

4: A CULTURE OF NARCISSISM

Epigraph: Rudy Smith in William Overend, "Flocking to the Body Temples with the Gym Generation," *Los Angeles Times* (May 6, 1981), sec. 5, p. 1.

1. Daniel Yankelovich, "New Rules," *Psychology Today* (April 1981), 36; definitions and descriptions of narcissism from discussions with Dr. Thomas Crocker, private practitioner, March 1997, and Dr. Mauricio Mazon, University of Southern California, April 1997; Christopher Lasch, *The Culture of Narcissism: American Life in an Age of Diminishing Expectations* (New York: Norton, 1979); Rubin in Robert Coles, "Unreflecting Egoism," *New Yorker* (August 27, 1979), 98.

   Description of corporations in Anthony Sampson, *Company Man: The Rise and Fall of Corporate Life* (New York: Random House, 1995), 251; changes in earnings expectations in Frank Levy and Richard Michel, "An Economic Bust for the Baby Boom," *Challenge* (March–April 1986), 33–39; Paula Leventman, *Professionals Out of Work* (New York: Free Press, 1981), xv, 30–31; Katherine Newman, *Falling from Grace: The Experience of Downward Mobility in the American Middle Class* (New York: Free Press, 1988), 23; diminished value of college degree in "Growing Pains at Forty," *Time* (May 19, 1986), 22.

2. Bureau of Labor Statistics information on work segmentation from Michael Maccoby, *The Leader: A New Face for American Management* (New York: Ballantine, 1981), 38; profile of executive qualities in Robert S. Diamond, "Self-Portrait of the Chief Executive," *Fortune* (May 1970), 181; Judson Gooding, "The Fraying White Collar," *Fortune* (December 1970),

80; Judson Gooding, "The Accelerated Generation Moves into Management," *Fortune* (March 1971), 102; Steven Levy, "Working in Dilbert's World," *Newsweek* (August 12, 1996), 56; Maccoby, *Leader,* xiv, 38.

3. Divorce rates from Michael F. Myers, *Men and Divorce* (New York: Guilford, 1989), 4–5, and Judith T. Younger, "Love Is Not Enough," *New Republic* (June 19, 1976), 8–9; Stan L. Albrecht, "Correlates of Marital Happiness among the Remarried," *Journal of Marriage and the Family* 41 (November 1979), 858; Alan Booth and John N. Edwards, "Starting Over: Why Remarriages Are More Unstable," *Journal of Family Issues* (June 1992), 179; Teresa Castro Martin and Larry L. Bumpass, "Recent Trends in Marital Disruption," *Demography* 26 (February 1989), 37; Lynn K. White, "Determinants of Divorce: A Review of Research in the 1980s," *Journal of Marriage and the Family* 52 (November 1990), 906; Albrecht, "Correlates of Marital Happiness among the Remarried," 858.

Childlessness is discussed in "The First Baby," *Life* (December 24, 1956); "Three's a Crowd," *Newsweek* (September 1, 1986); "The Dilemma of Childlessness," *Time* (May 2, 1988), 88; "Childless and Unfettered," *U.S. News & World Report* (October 4, 1976), 60; Benita Eisler, "Who Doesn't Want Children and Why," *Glamour* (November 1983), 250; Ellen Peck, *The Baby Trap* (New York: Bernard Geis, 1971), 9, 131; college professor quoted by Elaine Tyler May, *Barren in the Promised Land: Childless Americans and the Pursuit of Happiness* (New York: Basic Books, 1995), 197–98; statistics cited by Peter N. Carroll, *It Seemed Like Nothing Happened: The Tragedy and Promise of America in the 1970s* (New York: Holt, Rinehart and Winston, 1982), 279; Tia Gindrich, "After 50 Dating Game Is More Dilemma Than Delight," *Los Angeles Times* (April 4, 1982), sec. 7, p. 1; Manhattan doctor in Nancy Friday, *The Power of Beauty* (New York: HarperCollins, 1992), 392.

4. Shirley Lord, "Has He or Hasn't He?" *Harper's Bazaar* (March 1972), 127; importance of "natural" substances in Warren J. Belasco, *Appetite for Change: How the Counterculture Took on the Food Industry* (Ithaca, N.Y.: Cornell University Press, 1989), 204, and Beth Ann Krier, "Confidence Sprouts in Hair Transplantation," *Los Angeles Times* (October 13, 1976), sec. 4, p. 1; Helsinki formula and evolution of chemical hair-loss treatments in Mark Stuart Gill, "Splitting Hairs," *Los Angeles Times* (November 10, 1991), 19–22; FDA ban in "Hope Sprouts Eternal," *Time* (January 28, 1985), 92.

Harold Crocker in Beth Ann Krier, "Hair Raising Tales of Baldness," *Los Angeles Times* (October 12, 1976), sec. 4, p. 4; Harry Nelson, "Doubts Grow on Safety of Hair Implants," *Los Angeles Times* (February 22, 1979), sec. 1, p. 1; T. Gerard Aldhizer, Thomas M. Krop, and Joseph W. Dunn, *The Doctor's Book on Hair Loss* (Englewood Cliffs, N.J.: Prentice-Hall, 1983), 16; Amy Dunkin, ed., "The Battle against Baldness: A Progress Report," *Business Week* (June 11, 1990), 85.

5. "Executives on an Exercise Kick," *Business Week* (June 3, 1972), 44; "The Art of Aerobics," *Time* (March 18, 1971), 60; "Top Joggers, Top Jobs," *Newsweek* (July 8, 1968), 60–61; "Ready, Set—Sweat," *Time* (June 6, 1977), 90; Philadelphia doctor in "Exercise Not Always Beneficial," *Science Digest* 73 (March 1973), 55; Martin Hochbaum, "Requiem for Yesterday's Gym," *New York Times* (October 27, 1984), sec. A, p. 27; health-club interviewees in Holly Brubach, "Musclebound," *New Yorker* (January 11, 1993), 37, and Wanda Urbanska, *The Singular Generation* (New York: Doubleday, 1986), 97–101; Barry Glassner, "Men and Muscles," in Michael S. Kimmel and Michael Messner, eds., *Men's Lives* (New York: Macmillan, 1989), 315; William E. Geist, "The Mating Game and Other Exercises at the Vertical Club," *New York Times* (May 19, 1984), sec. L, p. 25; Randi Blaun, "A Hard Act to Follow," *GQ* (December 1988), 180; Smith cited by William Overend, "Flocking to the Body Temples with the Gym Generation," *Los Angeles Times* (May 6, 1981), sec. 5, p. 1; Hal Higdon, "Stalking the Jock-Macho Dilettante," *Chicago* (November 1980), 216; Blair Sabol, *The Body of America* (New York: Arbor House, 1986), 45.

6. "More People, More Speed," *Runner's World* (February 1975), 23; Hal Higdon, "The AAU: Kingdom in Crisis," *Runner* (September 1979), 57; Hal Higdon, "Jogging Is an In Sport," *New York Times Magazine* (April 14, 1968), 36; "Billy Graham's Amazing Physical Fitness Program," *Reader's Digest* (July 1965), 61; Bassler's study published in *New England Journal of Medicine* and cited by Muriel R. Gillick, "Health Promotion, Jogging, and the Pursuit of the Moral Life," *Journal of Health Politics, Policy, and Law* (Fall 1984), 373, 379; executive claims of benefits in Marilyn Wellemeyer, "Addicted to Perpetual Motion," *Fortune* (June 1977), 58; demographic profile of runners in James Curtis and William McTeer, "Toward a Sociology of Marathoning," *Journal of Sport Behavior* 4, no. 2 (June 1981), 79; running as antidote to Vietnam in John Wheeler, *Touched with Fire: The Future of the Vietnam Generation* (New York: Avon, 1984), 108.

Sacks and Frankfurt cited in Dinitia Smith, "The New Puritans: Deprivation Chic," *New York* (June 11, 1984), 24–29; Frankfurt interviewed by Susan Bordo, *Unbearable Weight: Feminism, Western Culture, and the Body* (Berkeley: University of California Press, 1993), 150; Jim Fixx cited by Jonathan Maslow, "Jogging Mania: Enough Already," *Saturday Review* (June 10, 1978), 47; Michael Spino, *Running Home* (Millbrae, Calif.: Celestial Arts, 1977); *Runner* survey results in Colman McCarthy, "Runners Make Lousy Lovers," *Los Angeles Times* (October 19, 1983), sec. 2, p. 7; Christopher Nyerges, "Running to Olympus," *Los Angeles Times* (February 8, 1981), sec. 5, p. 5.

7. "Ready, Set—Sweat," 86, 90; "Jogging for the Mind," *Time* (July 24, 1978), 42; Beth Ann Krier, "Joy of Jogging: Sexual Desire Increases," *Los Angeles Times* (February 28, 1982), sec. 5, p. 1; Chicago club owners interviewed by Higdon, "Stalking the Jock-Macho Dilettante," 181–82; Charles

Edgley, Betty Edgley, and Ronny E. Turner, "Changes in Runners' Vocabularies of Motive: Physical Fitness as Religion," *Free Inquiry in Creative Sociology* 12 (May 1984), 100–4; Arnold M. Cooper, "Masochism and Long Distance Running," in Michael H. Sacks, ed., *The Psychology of Running* (Champaign, Ill.: Human Kinetics, 1981), 271; Brenda Loree, "Runner Beware—the Ego You Nurture Is Only Your Own," *Los Angeles Times* (May 6, 1984), sec. 4, p. 5; T-shirts in Carol Galginaitis, "To Corporations, Name's the Game," *Advertising Age* (August 27, 1979), sec. 5, p. 2.

8. Robert M. Goldwyn, *The Patient and the Plastic Surgeon* (Boston: Little, Brown, 1991), 54; Truman S. Blocker, "Plastic Surgery in America: A Progress Report," *Plastic and Reconstructive Surgery* 38, no. 2 (August 1956); Eugene H. Courtiss, "Doctor, Am I Being Vain?" *Plastic and Reconstructive Surgery* 65, no. 6 (June 1980), 819; "A Happy Specialty," *Newsweek* (May 31, 1971), 40; normalcy of male patients in Eugene H. Courtiss, *Male Aesthetic Surgery* (St. Louis: Mosby, 1991), xiii, 12; study of industrial societies by Eleanor Maxwell and Robert Maxwell, "Explanation for Contempt Expressed toward Old People" (paper presented at the thirty-second annual Scientific Meeting of Gerontological Society, Washington, D.C., November 1979); Amy Spindler, "It's a Face-Lifted, Tummy-Tucked Jungle out There," *New York Times* (June 9, 1996), sec. C, p. 8; Alfred C. Kinsey, Wardell B. Pomeroy, and Clyde E. Martin, *Sexual Behavior in the Human Male* (Philadelphia: W. B. Saunders, 1948), 298–99.

9. NYU professor William Barrett in David Boroff, "Among the Fallen Idols: Virginity, Chastity, and Repression," *Esquire* (June 1962); George L. Ginsberg, William A. Frosch, and Theodore Shapiro, "The New Impotence," *Archives of General Psychiatry* 26 (March 1972), 218–19; Philip Nobile, "What Is the New Impotence and Who's Got It?" *Esquire* (October 1972), 95; B. Lyman Stuart, "Is Impotence Increasing?" *Medical Aspects of Human Sexuality* 6, no. 6 (October 1971), 34; Mark S. Kroop, "When Women Initiate Sexual Relations," *Medical Aspects of Human Sexuality* 20, no. 2 (February 1986), 28; Deborah Phillips, "The Sex Revolution Bows to Boredom," *Los Angeles Times* (October 10, 1980) sec. 5, p. 6; co-ed cited in "Impotence: The Result of Female Aggressiveness—or What?" *Mademoiselle* (February 1972), 124; "Impotent Males Increasing?" *Science Digest* (October 1972), 52; Seymour L. Halleck, "Sex and Power," *Medical Aspects of Human Sexuality* 3 (October 1969), 14.

Anne Koedt, "The Myth of the Vaginal Orgasm," in Anne Koedt, ed., *Radical Feminism* (New York: Quadrangle, 1973), 202–3; Greer cited in John Heidenry, *What Wild Ecstasy: The Rise and Fall of the Sexual Revolution* (New York: Simon and Schuster, 1997); Shere Hite, *The Hite Report: A Nationwide Study of Female Sexuality* (New York: Macmillan, 1976), 95–109, 366; Farber in Malcolm Muggeridge, "Down with Sex," *Esquire* (February 1965), 72–74 ; Herbert J. Freudenberger, "Today's Troubled Men," *Psychol-

ogy Today (December 1987), 46–47; studies of U.S. sexual patterns in Robert T. Michael, John H. Gagnon, Edward O. Laumann, and Gina Kolata, *Sex in America: A Definitive Survey* (Boston: Little, Brown, 1994), 111, 126–27, 131, and Terence Monmanly, "Study Finds Widespread Sexual Problem," *Los Angeles Times* (February 10, 1999), sec. A, pp. 3, 16.

10. Anslinger cited by George R. Gay and Charles W. Sheppherd, "Sex in the Drug Culture," *Medical Aspects of Human Sexuality* 6, no. 10 (October 1972), 28; Eric Goode, "Sex and Marijuana," in Leonard Gross, ed., *Sexual Behavior* (New York: Spectrum, 1974), 159, 163; David J. Powell and Robert W. Fuller, "Marijuana and Sex: Strange Bedpartners," *Journal of Psychoactive Drugs* 16 (October/December 1983), 269–80; Alfred M. Freedman, "Drugs and Sexual Behavior," *Medical Aspects of Human Sexuality* 1 (November 1967), 30; James L. Mathis, "Sexual Aspects of Heroin Addiction," *Medical Aspects of Human Sexuality* 4 (August 1970); Lester Grinspoon and James B. Bakalar, "Cocaine: A Social History," *Psychology Today* (March 1977), 37, 77–78; Patrick T. MacDonald, Daniel Waldorf, Craig Reinarman, and Sheigla Murphy, "Heavy Cocaine Use and Sexual Behavior," *Journal of Drug Issues* 18, no. 3 (Summer 1988), 437; James M. Cocores, "Substance Abuse and Sexual Dysfunction," *Medical Aspects of Human Sexuality* 23, no. 1 (January 1989), 22.

   Macbeth 2.3; Eric Carlton, *Sexual Anxiety: A Study of Male Impotence* (New York: Barnes and Noble, 1980), 48, 104; D. M. Gallant, "The Effects of Alcohol and Drug Abuse on Sexual Behavior," *Medical Aspects of Human Sexuality* 20, no. 1 (January 1968), 36; Matti Valimaki and Ylikhari Elein, "The Effect of Alcohol on Male and Female Sexual Function," *Alcohol and Alcoholism* 18, no. 4 (1983), 313–20; Raul C. Schiavi, "Chronic Alcoholism and Male Sexual Dysfunction," *Journal of Sex and Marital Therapy* 16 (Spring 1990), 27; D. Van Thiel and R. Lester, "The Effect of Chronic Alcohol Abuse on Sexual Function," *Clinics in Endocrinology and Metabolism* 8 (1979), 499–510; effects of over-the-counter medications in Keith Mano, "The Dick Clinic," *Playboy* (January 1996), 96, and Alan J. Wein and Keith N. Van Arsdalen, "Drug-Induced Male Sexual Dysfunction," *Urologic Clinics* 15, no. 1 (February 1988), 23–26.

11. Gorm Wagner and Richard Green, *Impotence: Physiological, Psychological, Surgical Diagnosis and Treatment* (New York: Plenum Press, 1981), 34; Morton M. Golden, "Acute Attack of Impotence," *Medical Aspects of Human Sexuality* 6, no. 7 (July 1972), 74; Stuart, "Is Impotence Increasing?" 34; interview with sex therapist Bryce Britten, June 18, 1996; "Sexual Dysfunction: An Executive Malady?" *Industry Week* (April 1, 1985), 46; "Impotents Anonymous," *Psychology Today* (June 1984), 12; John Racy, "How the Work Ethic Impacts Sexuality," *Medical Aspects of Human Sexuality* 8, no. 4 (April 1974), 90; Charles William Wahl, "Do Women Understand Men's Sexuality Better Than Men Understand Women's?" *Medical Aspects of Human Sexuality* 11, no.

1 (January 1977), 37; Dennis Brisset and Lionel S. Lewis, "Guidelines for Marital Sex: An Analysis of Fifteen Popular Marriage Manuals," *Family Coordinator* (January 1970), 41; Lionel S. Lewis and Dennis Brisset, "Sex as Work," *Social Problems* (Summer 1967), 9–10. Lewis and Brisset examined more than fifty popular sex manuals and found a technical, businesslike approach to lovemaking to be standard. This would change in the 1970s, when women began writing sex manuals.

5: BINGEING AND BUFFING UP

Epigraph: Bodybuilder quoted in Andrew Sullivan, "Muscleheads," *New Republic* (September 15–22, 1986), 24–25.

1. Remar Sutton, *Body Worry* (New York: Viking, 1987); "Rebuilding Remar Sutton," *Time* (April 6, 1987), 72; Hendrik Hertzberg, "The Short Happy Life of the American Yuppie," *Esquire* (February 1988), 100–9; "The Year of the Yuppie," *Newsweek* (December 31, 1984), 14–15; Jerry Adler, "Call It Yuppie Love," *Newsweek* (December 31, 1984), 25; Haynes Johnson, *Sleepwalking through History: America in the Reagan Years* (New York: Norton, 1991), 139–51; Neal Gabler, *Life: The Movie* (New York: Knopf, 1998), 109–10.

   Psychological analysis of personal ads in Catherine Cameron, Stuart Oskamp, and William Sparks, "Courtship American Style: Newspaper Ads," *Family Coordinator* (January 1977), 27, and Rosemary Bolig, Peter J. Stein, and Patrick McKevey, "The Self-Advertisement Approach to Dating: Male-Female Differences," *Family Relations* (October 1984), 591; in *Los Angeles,* from January 1982 to December 1989, out of 3,370 women, 1,035 specify physical characteristics. This trend continued into the 1990s: in the *Los Angeles Times,* from June 30 to September 8, 1995, out of 4,966 women, 1,679 specify physical characteristics.

2. Robert Steinbrook, "Putting Hair Back Where It Belongs," *Los Angeles Times* (September 21, 1986), sec. 1, p. 1; experiments with mynah birds in Gerald Walker, "Baldness Unbared," *New York Times* (January 4, 1959), 62; Michael Castleman, "Losing It All," *Ms.* (September 1986), 51–53, 87; feminizing aspect of Rogaine cited in interview with Dr. John Williams, Aesthetica Plastic Surgery, Beverly Hills, Calif., January 9, 1996; sales and marketing figures for Rogaine in Mark Stuart Gill, "Splitting Hairs," *Los Angeles Times* (November 10, 1991), 22; William G. Flanagan and David Stix, "The Bald Truth," *Forbes* (July 22, 1991), 309; Amy Dunkin, "The Battle against Baldness: A Progress Report," *Business Week* (June 11, 1990), 84; Linda Roch Monroe, "The Rub in a Hair Remedy," *Los Angeles Times* (March 12, 1990), sec. 3, p. 1; Adam Smith, "Upjohn's Bald Ambitions," *Esquire* (October 1986), 73; Sherl Stolberg, "Hair-Loss Drug Rogaine OKd for Counter Sales," *Los Angeles Times* (February 13, 1996), sec. A, p. 14;

Propecia in Robert Langreth, "Bulletins from the Battle of the Baldness Drugs: Merck Readies a Media Blitz for Its New Pill," *Wall Street Journal* (December 19, 1997), sec. B, pp. 1, 12; Yumiko Ono, "Sports Figures Tout Rogaine for Pharmacia," *Wall Street Journal* (December 19, 1997), sec. B, pp. 1, 12.

3. History of Japanese hair transplantation in Samuel J. Stegman, Theodore A. Thomovitch, and Richard G. Glogau, *Cosmetic Dermatologic Surgery* (Chicago: Year Book Medical Publishers, 1990), and T. Gerard Aldhizer, Thomas M. Krop, and Joseph W. Dunn, *The Doctor's Book on Hair Loss* (Englewood Cliffs, N.J.: Prentice-Hall, 1983), 110; Thomas D. Cronin, "Use of Hair-Bearing Punch Grafts for Partial Traumatic Losses of the Scalp," *Plastic and Reconstructive Surgery* 44, no. 5 (November 1969), 446.

Interview with Bosley Medical Group, Beverly Hills, Calif., February 3, 1994; Bosley Medical Group, *The Art and Science of Hair Restoration,* 1994; for effects on women, see Sharon Doyle Driedger, "Coping with Hair Loss," *Maclean's* (May 21, 1990), 59.

Balloon techniques are described by Guy Blanchard and Bernard Blanchard, "Obliteration of Alopecia by Hair-Lifting: A New Concept and Technique," *Journal of the National Medical Association* 69, no. 9 (1977), 639; Dr. Thomas D. Rees, *More Than Just a Pretty Face: How Cosmetic Surgery Can Improve Your Looks and Your Life* (Boston: Little, Brown, 1987), 237; Walter Sullivan, "Hair-Loss Experts Cite Innovations," *New York Times* (June 17, 1984), sec. 1, p. 21; Thomas H. Mangh II, "Swelled Head First Step in Surgical Baldness Cure," *Los Angeles Times* (March 12, 1990), sec. B, p. 3.

4. S. Roll and J. S. Verinis, "Stereotypes of Scalp and Facial Hair as Measured by the Semantic Differential," cited by Thomas F. Cash, "Losing Hair, Losing Points? The Effects of Male Pattern Baldness on Social Impression Formation," *Journal of Applied Social Psychology* 20, no. 12 (1990), 154–63; Stephen L. Franzoi, Joan Anderson, and Stephen Frommelt, "Individual Differences in Men's Perceptions of and Reactions to Thinning Hair," *Journal of Social Psychology* 130 (April 1990), 210; Thomas F. Cash and Thomas Pruzinsky, eds., *Body Images: Development, Deviance, and Change* (New York: Guilford, 1990), Table 3.4, "Percentage of Balding Men Attributing Specific Experiences to Hair Loss"; Paul Chance, "That Bald Feeling," *Psychology Today* (July/August 1988), 16; Sandra Blakeslee, "Bald Facts about Male Self-Esteem," *American Health* (September 1991), 24; Felipe Coiffman, "Use of Square Scalp Grafts for Male Pattern Baldness," *Plastic and Reconstructive Surgery* 60, no. 2 (August 1977), 228.

Anne Tolstoi Wallach, "Hairpower," *New York Times* (September 20, 1987), sec. 6, pp. 86, 88; Owen Edwards, "Hair Apparent," *Saturday Review* (April 12, 1980), 13; William Harris, "Grey's Elegy," *Forbes* (September 13, 1982), 224; Trish Hall, "Ssssh: More Men Are Coloring Their Hair," *New York Times* (July 15, 1990), sec. A, p. 32; search firm executive cited by Amy

Spindler, "It's a Face-Lifted, Tummy-Tucked Jungle out There," *New York Times* (June 9, 1996), sec. C, p. 1; Bill Heavey, "I Feel Pretty," *Washingtonian* (May 1993), 90.

5. K. T. Strongman and C. J. Hart, "Stereotyped Reactions to Body Build," *Psychological Reports* 223 (1968), 1175; Paul J. Lavrakas, "Female Preferences for Male Physiques," *Journal of Research in Personality* 9, no. 4 (1975), 332. Economic penalties of being overweight in Laurie Baum, "Extra Pounds Can Weigh Down Your Career," *Business Week* (August 3, 1987), 96; "Fat People's Fight against Job Bias," *U.S. News & World Report* (December 5, 1977), 78; N. Allon, "The Stigma of Overweight in Everyday Life," in Benjamin B. Wolman and Stephen DeBerry, eds., *Psychological Aspects of Obesity* (New York: Van Nostrand Reinhold, 1982), 130; "Weighty Problem," *Newsweek* (March 31, 1975), 64.

Hopeful Recoverer, "Guys Have Eating Disorders Too," *ANAD* (Highland Park, Ill.: National Association of Anorexia Nervosa and Associated Disorders), June 1993, 1; Paul E. Garfinkel and David M. Garner, *Anorexia Nervosa: A Multi-dimensional Perspective* (New York: Brunner/Mazel, 1978), 2; Leslie Knowlton, "Silence and Guilt," *Los Angeles Times* (May 23, 1995), sec. E, p. 1; National Association of Anorexia Nervosa and Associated Disorders, *ANAD*, June 1995; Maureen O'Donnell, "Fear of Food," *Chicago Sun-Times* (October 27, 1991), 1, 36; Joseph A. Silverman, "An Eighteenth-Century Account of Self-Starvation in a Male," *International Journal of Eating Disorders* 6 (1987), 431–32; Jean Seligmann, Patrick Rogers, and Peter Annin, "The Pressure to Lose," *Newsweek* (May 2, 1994), 60; Grahl in "I Wanted To Eat But I Couldn't," *Woman's World* (July 26, 1994), 12; Patrick Engelmann and male bulimic cited by Gabriella Stern, "The Anorexic Man Has Good Reason to Feel Neglected," *Wall Street Journal* (October 18, 1993), sec. A, p. 1; Mardie E. Burckes-Miller and David R. Black, "Eating Disorders: A Problem in Athletics," *Health Education* (February–March 1988), 22; Flanery in Knowlton, "Silence and Guilt"; Andersen in *Males with Eating Disorders* (New York: Brunner/Mazel, 1990) and telephone discussions, August 1995; Alayne Yates, Kevin Leehey, and Catherine M. Shisslak, "Running—an Analogue of Anorexia?" *New England Journal of Medicine* 308, no. 5 (February 3, 1983), 253; Adam Drewnowski and Doris Yee, "Men and Body Image: Are Men Satisfied with Their Body Weight?" *Psychosomatic Medicine* 49, no. 6 (November–December 1987), 627; Jack L. Katz, "Long-Distance Running, A.N., and Bulimia: A Report of Two Cases," *Comprehensive Psychiatry* 27, no. 1 (January/February 1986), 74–76; Adams and Flanery cited in Knowlton, "Silence and Guilt."

6. Popularity of bodybuilding in Kim Brizzolara, "Bodybuilding Business Bulks Up," *New York Times* (March 27, 1989), sec. C, p. 11, and Alan M. Klein, "Of Muscles and Men," *Sciences* (November/December 1993), 32;

Gaines in Lynn Darling, "How Much Bigger Can Arnold Get?" *Esquire* (March 1985), 130; Arnold on bodybuilding as performance in Edward W. L. Smith, *Not Just Pumping Iron: On the Psychology of Lifting Weights* (Springfield, Ill.: Charles Thompson, 1989), 10; Vicki Goldberg, "Body Building," *New York Times* (November 30, 1975), 46; David Davis, "Muscle, Inc.," *Los Angeles Weekly* (January 26–February 1, 1996), 21–23; Leonard Kriegel, "The Purpose of Lifting," *New York Times* (April 12, 1987), 60; Richard W. Johnston, "The Men and the Myth," *Sports Illustrated* (October 14, 1974), 109, 118; statistics on male hustling from Alan Klein, *Little Big Men: Bodybuilding Subculture and Gender Construction* (Albany: State University of New York Press, 1993), 133.

Reverse anorexia was first diagnosed in the early 1990s by Dr. Harrison Pope, a Harvard psychiatrist and a bodybuilder. In addition to Pope's research, Dr. William N. Taylor, an expert on anabolic steroids, found that steroid users also develop distorted body images so that they perceive their reflections in the mirror as smaller than they actually are; Taylor called his discovery megarexia.

7. Brizzolara, "Bodybuilding Business Bulks Up," sec. C, p. 11; David Wallis, "Overpumped," *Details* (September 1995), 128; nutrition and early death rates discussed by Dr. Barry Brenner, professor of medicine, in Sullivan, "Muscleheads," 24; Greek diet in Terry Todd, "Anabolic Steroids: The Gremlin of Sport," *Journal of Sports History* 14 (Spring 1987), 90; Sam Fussell, *Muscles: Confessions of an Unlikely Bodybuilder* (New York: Poseidon, 1991), 115, 118, and Sam Fussell, "Bodybuilder Americanus," *Michigan Quarterly Review* (Fall 1993), 586; 1991 report on injuries in Mary Roach, "Pumping Iron III: The Emergency Room," *Esquire* (March 1993), 59; David Porter, "No Pain, No Gain: An Ethnography of Bodybuilders" (master's thesis, California State University, 1988), 8, 51.

For a discussion of gay influence, see George Chauncey, *Gay New York: Urban Culture and the Making of the Gay Male World, 1890–1940* (New York: Basic Books, 1994); Dan Shaw, "Mirror, Mirror," *New York Times* (1994), sec. C, p. 6; Steven Gaines and Sharon Churcher, *Obsession: The Lives and Times of Calvin Klein* (New York: Carol Publishing Group, 1994), 162–63, 209.

Pageants described by Johnston, "Men and the Myth," 109; Fussell, "Bodybuilder Americanus," 583; Michael Malone, *Heroes of Eros: Male Sexuality in the Movies* (New York: Dutton, 1979), 96; interview with Michael in Marina del Rey, Calif., August 1998; physiology of muscles in Goldberg, "Body Building," 52.

8. Unemployment statistics in Katherine Newman, *Falling from Grace: The Experience of Downward Mobility in the American Middle Class* (New York: Free Press, 1988), 23, and Frank Levy and Richard Michel, "An Economic Bust for the Baby Boom," *Challenge* (March–April 1986), 33–39; Jeffrey

Madrick, *The End of Affluence* (New York: Random House, 1995), 89; Spindler, "Face-Lifted, Tummy-Tucked Jungle," sec. C, p. 8; Jonathan Kaufman, "A Middle Manager, 54 and Insecure, Struggles to Adapt to the Times," *Wall Street Journal* (May 5, 1997), sec. A, pp. 1, 6; Michael J. Mandel, "This Time, the Downturn Is Dressed in Pinstripes," *Business Week* (October 1, 1990), 130–31; Jonathan Kaufman, "For Richard Thibeault, Being a 'Manager' Is a Blue-Collar Life," *Wall Street Journal* (October 1, 1996), sec. A, p. 1; Hal Lancaster, "For Some Managers, Hitting Middle Age Brings Uncertainties," *Wall Street Journal* (April 20, 1999), sec. B, p. 1.

9. Jerry Adler, "New Bodies for Sale," *Newsweek* (May 27, 1985), 65; New York surgeon Norman Pastorek cited in Elizabeth Mehren, "Facing the 80s with New Eyes—A New Nose," *Los Angeles Times* (January 25, 1985), sec. 5, p. 1; Susan Heller Anderson and Sara Rimer, "The Face of the 80s," *New York Times* (January 16, 1985), sec. B, p. 2; Everett R. Holles, "Face-Lifting Erases Age in Men, Too," *New York Times* (June 28, 1971), 26.

    Milt Freudenheim, "As Insurers Cut Fees, Doctors Shift to Elective Procedures," *New York Times* (August 24, 1996), sec. A, pp. 1, 11; advertisement for Bel Age Plastic Surgery Center, Washington, D.C., in *Washingtonian* (May 1993), 89; San Francisco surgeon Ronald Iverson in Rodney Ho, "Men Try to Put a New Face on Careers," *Wall Street Journal* (August 28, 1991), sec. B, p. 1; Irene Hanson Frieze, Josephine E. Olson, and Jane Russell, "Attractiveness and Income for Men and Women in Management," *Journal of Applied Social Psychology* 21, no. 13 (1991), 1021; Lee Berton, "A Rising Stock Market Also Lifts Faces, Noses, Tummies, and Necks," *Wall Street Journal* (February 24, 1997), sec. B, p. 1; Alexander Alger, "Nipping and Tucking," *Forbes* (December 4, 1995), 290; J. Gabka and E. Vaubel, "The First Blepharoplasty," in Frank MacDowell, ed., *Source Book of Plastic Surgery* (Baltimore: Williams and Wilkins, 1977), 156; Thomas T. Baker and Howard Gordon, "Rhytidectomy in the Male," *Plastic and Reconstructive Surgery* 44, no. 2 (August 1969), 219; interviews with Dr. John Williams, January 1996.

10. David Stafford-Clark, "The Etiology and Treatment of Impotence," *Practitioner* (April 1954), 184; Leonore Tiefer, "In Pursuit of the Perfect Penis," *American Behavioral Scientist* 29 (May/June 1986), 587, 595; psychological approaches of Masters and Johnson, as well as Kaplan, discussed in Irwin Goldstein and Larry Rothstein, *The Potent Male* (Los Angeles: The Body Press, 1990), 49, and Randi Blaun, "Dealing with Impotence," *New York* (March 30, 1987), 52; Alex L. Finkle, "Sexual Impotence: Current Knowledge and Treatment," *Urology* 16, no. 5 (November 1980), 449; Lawrence M. Martin, Drogo Montague, Robert E. James, Jr., and Victor G. DeWolffe, "Diagnosis, Evaluation, Classification, and Treatment of Men with Sexual Dysfunction," *Urology* 14, no. 6 (December 1979), 545; Dennis

J. Krauss, Larry Lantinga, and Christine M. Kelly, "In Treating Impotence Urology and Sex Therapy Are Complementary," *Urology* 36, no. 1 (November 1990), 469; Saul Boyarsky and Gail Spector Lewis, "Can a Urologic Nurse Contribute to Management of Secondary Impotence in an Office Setting?" *Urology* 35, no. 1 (January 1990), 25–26; Alex L. Finkle, "Psychosexual Problems of Aging Males: A Urologist's Viewpoint," *Urology* 13, no. 1 (January 1979), 41–43; Ronald M. Podell, "Sexual Science: Bridging the Discipline Lines," *Urology* 31, no. 1 (January 1988), 90.

Karl Menninger, "Impotence and Frigidity from the Standpoint of Psychoanalysis," *Journal of Urology* 34, no. 1 (1935), 166; Candace Talmadge, "Selling the Unsellable," *Forbes* (June 16, 1986), 142; Leonore Tiefer, "The Medicalization of Impotence: Normalizing Phallocentrism," *Gender and Society* 8 (September 1994), 363–77; Barry A. Bass, "In Further Pursuit of the Perfect Penis: The Comprehensive Urology Center and the Medicalization of Male Sexual Dysfunction," *Journal of Sex and Marital Therapy* 20, no. 4 (Winter 1994), 318–19; Keith Mano, "The Dick Clinic," *Playboy* (January 1996), 96; NPT procedures described by Peter Metz and Gorm Wagner, "Penile Circumference and Erection," *Urology* 18, no. 3 (September 1981), 268–70.

Implants described in Wayne M. Sotile, "The Penile Prosthesis," *Journal of Sex and Marital Therapy* 5, no. 2 (Summer 1979), 101; John E. Heller and Paul Gleich, "Erectile Impotence: Evaluation and Management," *Journal of Family Practice* 26, no. 3 (March 1988), 323; W. F. Gee, "A History of Surgical Treatment of Impotence," *Urology* 5, no. 3 (1975), 401; and Helene M. Cole, ed., "Diagnostic and Therapeutic Technology Assessment: Penile Implants for Erectile Impotence," *Journal of the American Medical Association* 260, no. 7 (August 19, 1988), 998–99. Injection therapy in Robert J. Krane, Irwin Goldstein, and Inigo Saenz de Tejada, "Impotence," *New England Journal of Medicine* 21, no. 24 (December 14, 1989), 1654; Josephine Novak, "Impotence Not Always a Psychological Problem," *Los Angeles Times* (December 16, 1981), sec. 5, p. 19; "Overcoming Impotence," *Newsweek* (June 18, 1984), 103; Joel Marmar, "Non-Surgical Treatment of Impotence," *Medical Aspects of Human Sexuality* (April 1989), 44; Stanley E. Althof et al., "Self-Injection of Papaverine and Phentolamine in the Treatment of Psychogenic Impotence," *Journal of Sex and Marital Therapy* 15, no. 3 (Fall 1989), 163–76; Adrian W. Ziogniotti, "Update on Pharmacological Erection," *Medical Aspects of Human Sexuality* (January 1989), 28; and Stanley E. Althof et al., "Self-Injection of Papaverine," 164, 173.

Interview with Paul in Malibu, Calif., January 1999; Martin quoted by Douglas Martin, "The Pill That Revived Sex," *New York Times* (May 3, 1998), WK-3; John Leland, "Not Quite Viagra Nation," *Newsweek* (October 26, 1998), 68.

6: "NO MAN EVER NEEDS TO FEEL INADEQUATE AGAIN"

Epigraph: David Barton cited by Dan Shaw, "Mirror, Mirror," *New York Times* (1994), sec. C, p. 6.

1. Singles quoted by Susan Littwin, *The Postponed Generation* (New York: William Morrow, 1986), 219; Denise Hamilton, "Love through the Ages," *Los Angeles Times* (January 9, 1995), sec. E, p. 1; Margaret Morganroth Gullette, "All Together Now: The New Sexual Politics of Midlife Bodies," *Michigan Quarterly Review* (Fall 1992), 685; Steinem in Teri Agins, "Belly Roll Blues," *Wall Street Journal* (October 25, 1994), sec. A, p. 1.

2. Harry Nelson, "Hair Transplant Techniques Assailed by Plastic Surgeons," *Los Angeles Times* (April 24, 1972), sec. 2, pp. 1, 5; William Allen, "The Last Strand," *Esquire* (October 1992), 88; Gary Anthony, "The Hair Transplant Scam," unpublished manuscript, 14; Chris Byron, "Hair Raising," *Men's Health* (July–August 1995); "An Honest Account of Hair Transplantation," Web site reprinted and distributed by HairArt, Los Angeles, Calif.; correction rate from interview with Dr. Mark Rifkin, Bosley Medical Center, February 3, 1994; James Kelly, "Cosmetic Lib for Men," *New York Times* (September 24, 1977), 132; descriptions of outcomes based on observations of surgeries and interviews in the offices of Dr. Randall Sword, Torrance, Calif., August 1, 1997; Stephen Sobek, "Snap On, Snap Off," *Houston Chronicle* (December 6, 1996), sec. D, p. 8; Alex Cukan, "Plastic Surgeon Pleads Guilty," *Buffalo News* (June 8, 1999); Ivari Centre in Byron, "Hair Raising."

3. Popularity of weight lifting in Andrew Sullivan, "Muscleheads," *New Republic* (September 15–22, 1986), 24, and Alan Klein, "Pumping Irony," *Sociology of Sport Journal* (June 1986), 115; *Family Feud* contest in Sam Fussell, *Muscle: Confessions of an Unlikely Bodybuilder* (New York: Poseidon, 1991); Phillips in Stephen S. Hall, "The Bully in the Mirror," *The New York Times Magazine* (August 22, 1999), 33, 35; Pope in Natalie Angier, "Drugs, Sports, Body Image, and G.I. Joe," *New York Times* (December 22, 1998), sec. F, p. 1.

   History of steroid use in Terry Todd, "Anabolic Steroids: The Gremlins of Sport," *Journal of Sport History* (Spring 1987), 91, 95–96, 101; William N. Taylor, *Macho Medicine: A History of the Anabolic Steroid Epidemic* (Jefferson, N.C.: McFarland, 1991), 10–18; Bill Gilbert, "Drugs in Sport: Problems in a Turned-On World," *Sports Illustrated* (June 23, 1969), 71; use by Arnold and other bodybuilders in David Davis, "Muscle, Inc.," *LA Weekly* (January 26–February 1, 1996), 25. Steroid use among boys in Oliver Fultz, "Roid Rage," *American Health* (May 1991), 60–61; Bruce Bower, "Pumped Up and Strung Out," *Science News* (July 13, 1991), 31; Anastasia Toufexis, "Shortcut to the Rambo Look," *Time* (January 30, 1989), 78; Davis, "Muscle, Inc.," 27; HGH in Joanne M. Schropf, "Pumped Up," *U.S. News & World Report* (June 1, 1992), 56, 59–62; Alzado in Schropf, "Pumped Up," 62, and Jim Bebbington, "Getting Classic with Arnold," *Saturday Evening Post* (July/August 1993), 59; gym interviewees in Skip Rozin, Julia Flynn, and Cynthia Durcanin, "Steroids: A Spreading Peril," *Business Week* (June 19, 1995), 138–39; interview with Seymour Konig, Venice, Calif., March 7, 1999; Lockwood in Gerald Secor Couzens, "Surgically Sculpting Athletic Physiques," *Physician and Sports Medicine* 20 (February 1992), 157; Jacqueline Bueno, "Bodybuilding Gets New Contestants: Old Guys Muscle In," *Wall Street Journal* (August 23, 1996), sec. A, pp. 1–4.

4. Iverson in Rodney Ho, "Men Try to Put a New Face on Careers," *Wall Street Journal* (August 28, 1991), sec. B, p. 1; interview with Dr. Harold Clavin, Santa Monica, Calif., March 15, 1995; "If Narcissus Managed a Mutual Fund," *Fortune* (September 9, 1996), 70; statistics from American Academy of Cosmetic Surgeons in Alan Farnham, "You're So Vain," *Fortune* (September 9, 1996), 69, 82; interview with Dr. Lawrence David, Institute of Cosmetic Laser Surgery, Hermosa Beach, Calif., November 1995.

San Francisco surgeon Dr. Bruno Ristow in Helen Bransford, *Welcome to Your Facelift* (New York: Doubleday, 1997), 173. Alloplastic facial reshaping described by Edward O. Terino, "Implants for Male Aesthetic Surgery," *Clinics in Plastic Surgery* (Philadelphia: Harcourt-Brace-Jovanovich, 1991), 731–32; Ian T. Jackson, "Skeletal Alterations," in Eugene H. Courtiss, ed., *Male Aesthetic Surgery* (St. Louis: Mosby Press, 1991), 245.

Bahman Teimourian, *Suction Lipectomy and Body Sculpturing* (St. Louis: Mosby, 1987); Nora Underwood, "Sculpting the Body," *Maclean's* (October 9, 1989), 58; Kenneth D. Christman, "Death following Suction Lipectomy and Abdominoplasty," *Plastic and Reconstructive Surgery* 78, no. 3 (September 1986), 428; endocrinologist Robert H. Eckel cited by Judith Gingold, "Adventures in Liposuction," *Atlantic Monthly* (March 1996), 104.

Implants described by Steve Schwade, "Body Shop," *Muscle & Fitness* (January 1993), 211, Brian H. Novack, "Alloplastic Implants for Men," in Courtiss, ed., *Male Aesthetic Surgery*, 797, 848; Jill Gerston, "How Men Really Feel about Their Bodies," *Redbook* (October 1994), 100–5; interview with Dermott, May 1997, Malibu, Calif.; Adrian E. Aieache, "Male Chest Correction," *Clinics in Plastic Surgery* (October 1991), 823; Emily Yoffe, "Valley of the Silicone Dolls," *Newsweek* (November 26, 1990), 72; Bircoll interviewed by Martha Sherrill, "Breast Him-Plants: The Joy of Pecs," *Washington Post* (March 8, 1992), sec. F, p. 2.

5. Kathrin Perutz, *Beyond the Looking Glass: America's Beauty Culture* (New York: William Morrow, 1970), 119. All information on Dr. Melvyn Rosenstein, unless otherwise noted, obtained in interviews at his offices in Culver City in May and June 1995; national statistics from Lisa Banion, "How a

Risky Surgery Became a Profit Center for Some Los Angeles Doctors," *Wall Street Journal* (June 6, 1996), sec. A, p. 1; measurements in Peter Lehman, *Running Scared: Masculinity and the Representation of the Male Body* (Philadelphia: Temple University Press, 1993), 138–39, and Kenneth Purvis, "The Phallic Connection," *Cosmopolitan* (April 1992) 104, 108; Joyce Brothers, "Does He Measure Up?" *Cosmopolitan* (July 1982), 120; Germaine Greer, "What Turns Women On?" *Esquire* (July 1989), 88; Patricia Flood, "Body Parts," *Esquire* (July 1981) 42–43; Michael Barson, "Penis Size: A Sexual or Political Issue," *Cosmopolitan* (March 1984), 224, 225; Cosby cited in Bernie Zilbergeld, *New Male Sexuality* (New York: Bantam, 1992), 32–33.

6. Lina H. Sun, "A Growth Industry in China," *Washington Post* (November 17, 1991), sec. F, p. 1; Kevin Cook, "Is Bigger Better?" *Vogue* (April 1995), 268; Andrea Gross, "The Ultimate Sex Operation," *Ladies' Home Journal* (March 1993), 94; interview with office of Dr. Rodney Barron, Beverly Hills, Calif., February 29, 1995; Gary Alter, "Augmentation Phalloplasty," *Urologic Clinics of North America* (November 1995), 887–901; Gary Griffin, *A Celebration of Manhood—1996 Collection* (Palm Springs, Calif: Added Dimensions Publishing, 1996); *Penis Power Quarterly* (October 1992 and April 1993); interview with Toronto surgeon Dr. Oakley Crocker, March 1996, and representatives of the Men's Cosmetic Surgery Center, July 1998; academy surgeon cited in Banion, "Risky Surgery," sec. A, p. 1.

7. Brian D. Johnson, "When Dr. Stubbs Met Mr. Long," *Maclean's* (January 31, 1994), 41; Douglas P. Shuit, "Penile Enlargement Patients Sue," *Los Angeles Times* (March 5, 1996), sec. B, p. 2; C. E. Brietzke, "The Long and Short of It," *Men's Health* (April 1994), 67; H. Wessels, T. F. Lue, and J. W. McAninch, "Complications of Penile Lengthening and Augmentation Seen at One Referral Center," *Journal of Urology* 155, no. 5 (May 1996), 1617–20; Ahmed I El-Sakka and Tom F. Lue, "Penile Augmentation: Myths and Realities," *Focus on Surgery,* Department of Urology, University of California, San Francisco, April 1997; Edmund Newton, "Dr. Dick," *Los Angeles View* (August 8–14, 1996), 6; Nance interviewed by Amy Chen Mills, "Dicked Around," *San Jose Metro* (February 8–14, 1996); Nehra cited in "Penile Enlargement Surgery: Results Less Than Expected," Mayo Foundation for Medical Education and Research, 1998; Leslie Knowlton, "New Surgeries—Just for Men," *Los Angeles Times* (March 30, 1994), sec. E, pp. 1–2; Douglas P. Shuit, "Doctor Agrees to Stop Doing Penile Surgery," *Los Angeles Times* (February 6, 1996), sec. B, p. 1; Darrin Hosteter, "A Groin Concern," *New Times* (January 5–11, 1994); M. G. Lord, *Barbie: The Unauthorized Biography of a Real Doll* (New York: William Morrow, 1994), 251; Gary Alter, "Augmentation Phalloplasty," *Urologic Clinics of North America* (November 1995), 887–88; Eric Schlosser, "The Business of Pornography," *U.S. News & World Report* (February 10, 1997), 44–45; Susan Faludi, "The Money Shot," *New Yorker* (October 30, 1995), 70.

8. Viagra was initially tested on forty-five hundred men aged nineteen to eighty-seven suffering from erectile dysfunction for at least five years from causes ranging from anxiety to diabetes. Quote in section heading from Russell Watson, Ron Moran, et al., "The Globe Is Gaga for Viagra," *Newsweek* (June 22, 1998), 44; Joseph Weber et al., "Viagra: The New Era of Lifestyle Drugs," *Business Week* (May 11, 1998), 97; Irwin Goldstein et al., "Oral Sildenafil in the Treatment of Erectile Dysfunction," *New England Journal of Medicine* (May 14, 1998), 1397; "Pfizer Hires Bob Dole for TV Ad Campaign," *Los Angeles Times* (December 12, 1998), sec. C, p. 2.

The biggest-selling new drug to date (as of early 1999) is Lipitor, a cholesterol-lowering drug jointly produced by Warner-Lambert and Pfizer that generated one billion dollars in sales in its first year. Bruce Handy, "The Viagra Craze," *Time* (May 4, 1998), 51; Jerry Adler, "Take a Pill and Call Me Tomorrow," *Newsweek* (May 4, 1998), 48; Daniel McGinn, "Viagra's Hothouse," *Time* (December 21, 1998), 46; black-market sales in Watson, Moran, et al., "The Globe Is Gaga"; Mexican sales in M. B. Sheridan, "Men around the Globe Lust After Viagra," *Los Angeles Times* (May 26, 1998), sec. A, pp. 1–2. Viagra test results in Robert Langreth and Michael Waldholz, "Pfizer Pins Multibillion Dollar Hopes on Impotence Pill," *Wall Street Journal* (March 19, 1998), sec. B, pp. 1, 9; and Arnold Mann, "Cross-Gender Sex Pill," *Time* (April 6, 1998), 62; John Greenwald, "Drug Quest: Magic Bullets for Boomers?" *Time* (May 4, 1998), 54.

9. Andrea Petersen, "Get Ready for the Viagra Wannabes," *Wall Street Journal* (April 30, 1998), sec. B, p. 1; Andrea Petersen and Robert Langreth, "Stampede Is On for Impotence Pill," *Wall Street Journal* (April 30, 1998), sec. B, p. 1; Greg Borzo, "Viagra Raises Demand, Questions," *American Medical News* (June 1, 1998), 25; Marilyn Chase, "A Reality Check: Viagra Won't Help Absolutely Everyone," *Wall Street Journal* (May 4, 1998), sec. B, p. 1; lawsuit filed by motorist Joseph Moran and report of six initial deaths in McGinn, "Viagra's Hothouse"; Andrea Petersen and Robert Langreth, "The Morning After: Sales of Viagra Cool Down," *Wall Street Journal* (October 15, 1998), sec. B, p. 1.

Ethics of Viagra in Langreth and Waldholz, "Pfizer Pins Multibillion Dollar Hopes"; Peter Coy, "Is This RX Necessary?" *Business Week* (May 11, 1998), 98; David Olmos, "Viagra Shows the Potency of Insurers," *Los Angeles Times* (June 7, 1998), sec. A, p. 2; HMO board member in "Speaking the Unspeakable," *New York Times* (June 6, 1998), sec. A, p. 1; Michael Slezak, "From Bob Dole to Godzilla, It's a Viagra Stampede," *American Druggist* (June 1998), 22; "Viagra Is a $50M Pentagon Budget Item," *Los Angeles Times* (October 3, 1998), sec. A, p. 23.

Brooklyn man and therapist Karen Martin in Douglas Martin, "The Pill That Revived Sex, or at Least Talking about It," *New York Times* (May 3, 1998), WK-3; Viagra as drug to make life more enjoyable in Olmos, "Viagra Shows Potency," sec. A, p. 28; women's responses to Viagra in Letters to

Editor, *Newsweek* (December 8, 1997), 22; Ann Landers columns in *Los Angeles Times,* 1999; quote in Lynne Lambert, "New Drug for Erectile Dysfunction Boon for Many, 'Viagravation' for Some," *Journal of the American Medical Association* (September 9, 1998), 867. It should be noted that of the 72 percent of women respondents to Ann Landers's poll who declared themselves uninterested in sex, 40 percent were under the age of forty.

Felder in Martin, "Pill That Revived Sex"; Charles W. Henderson, "Woman Says Lust Drug Broke Up Relationship," *Male Health Weekly* (June 22, 1998), 13; sex crimes in Watson, Moran, et al., "The Globe Is Gaga"; Geoffrey Cowley, "Is Sex a Necessity?" *Newsweek* (May 1, 1998), 62; urologist Andrew McCullough in Avery Comaron, "Viagra Tale," *U.S. News & World Report* (May 4, 1998), 64; Joseph Weber, Amy Barrett, Michael Mandel, and Jeff Laderman, "Viagra: The New Era of Lifestyle Drugs," *Business Week* (May 11, 1998); Michael Risher, "Controlling Viagra Mania," *New York Times* (July 20, 1998), sec. A, p. 15; Dr. T. L. Nichols, an American physician writing in 1873, in Lesley A. Hall, *Hidden Anxieties: Male Sexuality, 1900–1950* (Cambridge, U.K.: Polity Press, 1991), 64.

10. Kate Rounds, "The Penile Code," *Ms.* (September/October 1993), 94; Lawrence Kaltman, "Artful Surgery," *New York Times* (July 13, 1993), sec. C, p. 1; interviews with Steve Shannon on Bobbitt paperweight, 1996; Tony Horwitz, "Urology Was Boring until Dr. Sehn Met John Wayne Bobbitt," *Wall Street Journal* (August 11, 1993), sec. A, p. 1; Gaudy in "Hanging by a Thread," *Newsweek* (November 22, 1993), 50–51; reporter quoted in Banion, "Risky Surgery," sec. A, p. 1.

11. Pete Hamill, "Great Expectations," *Ms.* (September 1986), 36; APA in "When a Generation Turns 40," *U.S. News & World Report* (March 10, 1986), 61; Landon Jones, "The Baby-Boom Legacy," *Saturday Evening Post* (May–June 1982), 20; Paula M. DeWitt, "All the Lonely People," *American Demographics* (April 1992), 44; Barbara Ehrenreich, "The Naked Truth about Fitness," *Lears* (September 1990), 96; Mimi Avins, "When the Dr's Office Is Also a Day Spa," *Los Angeles Times* (April 2, 1999), sec. E, p. 1.

BIBLIOGRAPHICAL ESSAY

In recent years, male body image has been the subject of lively discussion in virtually every popular magazine and newspaper and on television. To date, however, no Big Picture has been drawn to explain why looking good has become so important to American men. In writing this book, I've tried to do two things: chronicle the changes in attitudes about and standards for male body image in postwar society, and provide a comprehensive analysis of why these changes have taken place. My research has consisted of three hundred books and more than two thousand articles; to cover areas of discussion as disparate as plastic surgery and bodybuilding, impotence and eating disorders, I've relied on input from historians, economists, sociologists, psychologists and psychiatrists, journalists, sex therapists, medical doctors, and students of popular culture, as well as interviews with both providers and recipients of procedures to enhance the male body. The following brief synopsis of my sources will, I hope, prove helpful.

At the core of my analysis is a historical overview of American society since World War II—the social, cultural, economic, and political currents that have shaped the nation in the past half century. The roots of much of this change lie in the late nineteenth and early twentieth centuries, when America began shifting from a culture based on character to one based on personality. As the century progressed, questions about the effects of that shift, as well as about the material benefits of consumerism and changing notions of success, engaged scholars and social critics. In the midst of postwar affluence, the *Fortune* editor William Whyte and the sociologists David Riesman and C. Wright Mills expressed concern about the effects of white-collar life and cultural conformity, especially with regard to the workplace. The historian Daniel Horowitz, in *The Morality of Spending* (Baltimore: Johns Hopkins University Press, 1985), addresses the debates aroused by consumerism, pointing out that since colonial times Americans have been concerned about the declining of "economic virtue" and have wrestled with the "moral consequences of new patterns of consumption and . . . the consequences of comfort, affluence, and luxury." The historians Daniel Boorstin, in *The Image; or, What Happened to the American Dream* (New York: Atheneum, 1962), and Warren I. Susman, in *Culture as History: The Transformation of American Society in the Twentieth Century* (New York: Pantheon, 1984), debate the influence of a consumption-oriented culture on the national character. More recently, Neal Gabler has updated Boorstin's critiques of the pervasiveness of image and celebrity in *Life: The Movie* (New York: Knopf, 1998).

Consumerism couldn't have penetrated the American consciousness as thoroughly as it has without advertising. Stuart Ewen's *Captains of Consciousness: Advertising and the Social Roots of the Consumer Culture* (New York: McGraw-Hill, 1976) and, with Elizabeth Ewen, *Channels of Desire: Mass Images and the Shaping of American Consciousness* (New York: McGraw-Hill, 1982) present classic interpretations of how consumerism and advertising have turned attention to the self. Roland Marchand's *Advertising the American Dream* (Berkeley: University of California Press, 1985) and Diane Barthel's *Putting on Appearances: Gender and Advertising* (Philadephia: Temple University Press, 1988) are especially good at showing how desire is created by focusing on body image—and worries about it.

American masculinity prior to the twentieth century is discussed in depth by E. Anthony Rotundo, in *American Manhood: Transformations in Masculinity from the Revolution to the Modern Era* (New York: Basic Books, 1993), and Michael Kimmel, in *Manhood in America: A Cultural History* (New York: Free Press, 1996). Gay influence on lifestyle and body image is described by Dennis Altman in *The Homosexualization of America* (Boston: Beacon, 1982), while Robert Sklar's *Movie-Made America: A Cultural History of American Movies* (New York: Vintage, 1994) shows how movies transformed society from the bottom up while setting forth new ideals about body image and fitness through the promotion of celebrity and beauty.

Male body image mirrors women's body image, about which there is an abundance of excellent information. Lois Banner's *American Beauty* (New York: Knopf, 1983), Naomi Wolf's *The Beauty Myth: How Images of Beauty Are Used against Women* (New York: Anchor, 1991), and Susan Faludi's *Backlash: The Undeclared War against American Women* (New York: Crown, 1991) have been essential in shaping my thoughts about the pervasive culture of beauty in America, which for so long was the special burden of women—until now. Although popular books have focused more on women, there is an abundance of professional information available about men. Psychological and sociological journals, including *Psychosomatics, Medical Aspects of Human Sexuality, American Health, Journal of Clinical Psychology, Journal of Applied Social Psychology, Journal of Research in Personality,* and *Psychosomatic Medicine,* provided case studies dealing with body image, the relationship between physical appearance and success, and social perceptions of physical attractiveness. The popular press offered images and representations of the male body via advertising, product marketing, and articles written for and about men. *Playboy, Esquire, GQ,*and *Men's Health* dealt directly with men and male products, but more generalized sources like *Look, Life, Saturday Evening Post, Time, Newsweek,* and *U.S. News & World Report* also provided a longitudinal chronicle of men's fashions, social roles, and consumerism. The psychologist Thomas F. Cash is the leading contemporary authority on body-image issues and has edited books, including, with Thomas Pruzinsky, *Body Images: Development, Deviance, and Change* (New York: Guilford, 1990), in addition to publishing numerous surveys and studies in popular and scholarly journals; especially useful for this analysis were "Losing Hair, Losing Points? The Effects of Male Pattern Baldness on Social Impression Formation" (*Journal of Applied Social Psychology,* 1990) and "Body Image Survey Report: The Great American Shape-Up" (*Psychology Today* 20, no. 4, 1996) 30–37. A wide-ranging and thorough overview of the subject is provided by Elaine Hatfield and Susan Sprecher in *Mirror, Mirror: The Importance of Looks in Everyday Life* (Albany: State University of New York Press, 1986).

A major cause of men's heightened concern about physical appearance is fear of aging, which has both social and economic consequences. General information on demographic trends, especially with regard to the baby-boomer generation, is available in the journals *American Demographics* and *Demography.* Howard P. Chudacoff's *How Old Are You? Age Consciousness in American Culture* (Princeton, N.J.: Princeton University Press, 1989) traces the evolution of aging from a positive process to a negative one, especially in the twentieth century, while Margaret Morganroth Gullette's "All Together Now: The New Sexual Politics of Midlife Bodies" (*Michigan Quarterly Review,* Fall 1993) is unusual in its focus on midlife *male* bodies.

Beginning in the late 1960s, men's body-image concerns were heightened by women's growing self-confidence and rejection of the notion that only they had to have good bodies; a key article on this topic is Paul J. Lavrakas's "Female Preferences for Male Physiques" (*Journal of Research in Personality,* 1975). Much of the impetus for women's changing attitudes came from second-wave feminism and is documented in popular periodicals like *Ms., Cosmopolitan,* and *Psychology Today.* America's singles culture is analyzed in *Journal of Marriage and the Family,* including statistics on divorce, remarriage, and success rates of remarriage as well as attitudes about divorce, being single, dating, and other social consequences of the liberated post-1960s society. In *Lonely in America* (New York: Simon and Schuster, 1976), the sociologist Suzanne Gordon offers a penetrating look at the realities of singles life in the 1970s, including the heightened importance of looking good to attract a mate and male resentment against new female freedoms. The journalists Sara Davidson, in *Real Property* (New York: Simon and Schuster, 1969), and Lindsey Maracotta, in *The Sad Eyed Ladies* (New York: Simon and Schuster, 1977), document body-image anxieties of men and women in their firsthand accounts of Manhattan and Los Angeles singles bars; *Journal of Social Psychology* and *Journal of Applied Social Psychology* offer studies correlating physical attractiveness and success in the singles-bar scene. As the purchasing power of single people became evident, business magazines began to publish demographic statistics and evaluate spending patterns. Especially useful were personal ads, where I found a surprisingly high interest among women in looks and money. Journals as disparate as *Personality and Social Psychology Bulletin, International Journal of Eating Disorders,* and *National Review* have published articles on the body-image connection in personal ads—a connection applicable to both genders.

For statistics related to the gross national product, salaries, employment categories, unemployment rates, women's representation in the workplace, education, and general economic trends, I am indebted to the historians William Chafe, in *The American Woman: Her Changing Social, Economic, and Political Roles, 1920–1970* (New York: Oxford University Press, 1972) and *The Unfinished Journey: America since World War II* (New York: Oxford University Press, 1999), Carl Degler, in *At Odds: Women and the Family in America from the Revolution to the Present* (New York: Oxford University Press, 1980), and James T. Patterson, in *Grand Expectations: The United States, 1945–1974* (New York: Oxford University Press, 1996). Douglas T. Miller and Marilyn Nowack provide an introspective and engaging look at families, culture, and society in the 1950s in *The Fifties: The Way We Really Were* (New York: Doubleday, 1977). Elaine Tyler May, in *Homeward Bound: American Families in the Cold War Era* (New York: Basic Books, 1988), looks at the internal dynamics of family life in the 1950s in the context of the Cold War, consumerism, divorce, and sexuality. All of these books were invaluable as well for providing statistics on social and economic trends.

Traditional white male dominance in the white-collar workplace came under siege in the 1970s, a trend that escalated in the 1980s and was exacerbated by economic decline. To track the disintegration of men's fortunes in the workplace I relied on a wide selection of readings in history, economics, and business. Changes in the workplace, especially the corporation, in the postwar period have affected management techniques, profit levels, organizational patterns, corporate psychology, and desired worker attributes. Classic definitions of corporate culture and historical analysis of the corporation and its ethos are provided by scholars like Olivier Zunz in *Making America Corporate: 1870–1920* (Chicago, University of Chicago Press, 1990), and Louis Galambos, in *America at Middle Age: A History of the United States in the Twentieth Century* (New York: McGraw-Hill, 1983). The historian Daniel T. Rodgers, in *The Work Ethic in Industrial America, 1850–1920* (Chicago: University of Chicago Press, 1974), traces the evoultion of the work ethic and the meanings of work for American men.

For a more specific view of white-collar employees in the postwar period, particularly in terms of the image they are expected to project, the approaches of sociologists and psychologists are a helpful adjunct to those of the historian.

In 1962, the social critic and journalist Vance Packard wrote *The Pyramid Climbers* (New York: McGraw-Hill) to describe the typical manager; in the 1970s and 1980s, the psychologist Michael Maccoby's *The Gamesman* (New York: Simon and Schuster, 1976) and *The Leader: A New Face for American Management* (New York: Ballantine, 1981) and Anthony Sampson's *Company Man: The Rise and Fall of Corporate Life* (New York: Random House, 1995) show how radically this ideal changed in the face of escalating foreign competition and declining American profits.

Shrinking American prosperity and the travails of the workplace are described by the economists Frank Levy, in *Dollars and Dreams: The Changing American Income Distribution* (New York: Russell Sage Foundation, 1987), Bennett Harrison and Barry Bluestone, in *The Great U-Turn: Corporate Restructuring and the Polarizing of America* (New York: Basic Books, 1988), and Jeffrey Madrick, in *The End of Affluence: The Causes and Consequences of America's Economic Dilemma* (New York: Random House, 1995). Katherine Newman's *Falling from Grace: The Experience of Downward Mobility in the American Middle Class* (New York: Free Press, 1988) and *Declining Fortunes: The Withering of the American Dream* (New York: Basic Books, 1993) place particular emphasis on dislocations to the middle class, especially men. For data on the economy, corporate culture, and the general climate of business in America, I relied heavily on *The Wall Street Journal, Forbes, Fortune, Duns, Business Week,* and *The New York Times.*

The turbulent 1960s brought a backlash against the conformity of the preceding decade and a reevaluation of American values and society. These are well documented by Steven M. Tipton, in *Getting Saved from the Sixties* (Berkeley: University of California Press, 1982), Peter Clecak, in *America's Quest for the Ideal Self: Dissent and Fulfillment in the 60s and 70s* (New York: Oxford University Press, 1983), and Edward P. Morgan, in *The Sixties Experience: Hard Lessons about Modern America* (Philadelphia: Temple University Press, 1991). Jane Howard, in *Please Touch* (New York: McGraw-Hill, 1970), and Martin L. Gross, in *The Psychological Society* (New York: Random House, 1978), examine the rise of the human potential movement, the foundation for the historian Christopher Lasch's culture of narcissism.

Lasch's work, especially *The Culture of Narcissism* (New York: Norton, 1979), provides an essential core to my analysis. Although I don't agree with all his propositions, Lasch offers a provocative articulation of the troubling change in the American psyche that emerged in the 1970s. America's shifting values, along with demographic statistics, are provided by Peter N. Carroll, in *It Seemed Like Nothing Happened: The Tragedy and Promise of America in the 1970s* (New York: Holt, Rinehart and Winston, 1982), and Robert Bellah et al., in *Habits of the Heart: Individualism and Commitment in American Life* (Berkeley: University of California Press, 1985). The historian Elaine Tyler May, in *Great Expectations: Marriage and Divorce in Post-Victorian America* (Chicago: University of Chicago Press, 1980) and *Barren in the Promised Land: Childless Americans and the Pursuit of*

Happiness (New York: Basic Books, 1995), and Michael F. Myers, in *Men and Divorce* (New York: Guilford, 1989), examine changes in family life and social values. May's incisive historical analysis combined with statistical information provided invaluable background for the 1950s, 1960s, and 1970s as well as for the late nineteenth century. Similarly, the historian Stephanie Coontz, in *The Way We Never Were: American Families and the Nostalgia Trap* (New York: Basic Books, 1992), by looking closely at the "perfect" family life of the 1950s, uncovers the roots of the social dysfunction of succeeding decades. In *The Divorce Culture* (New York: Knopf, 1997), Barbara Dafoe Whitehead uses sociological and psychological research to provide a historical perspective of divorce, with particularly compelling insights into how an institution once seen as a last resort had become, by the 1970s, an "individual prerogative and source of personal growth and new opportunity."

In addition to these sources for my general historical overview, I also consulted sources specific to each area of male body image: hair, weight and fitness, cosmetic surgery, and impotence.

The history of hair, from styling to cultural interpretations, can be found in Richard Corson, *Fashions in Hair: The First Five Thousand Years* (New York: Hastings House, 1965), and Wendy Cooper, *Hair: Sex, Society, and Symbolism* (New York: Stein and Day, 1971). For background on how the growing passion for fitness, health, and organized sport reflected American society, politics, and even religion in the late nineteenth and early twentieth centuries, I relied on a number of excellent historical sources, especially Harvey Green's *Fit for America: Health, Fitness, Sport, and American Society* (Baltimore: Johns Hopkins Universtiy Press, 1986), James C. Wharton's *Crusaders for Fitness: The History of American Health* (Princeton, N.J.: Princeton University Press, 1982), and Elliot Gorn and Warren Goldstein's *A Brief History of American Sports* (New York: Hill and Wang, 1993). Elliot Gorn's *The Manly Art: Bare Knuckle Prize Fighting in America* (Ithaca, N.Y.: Cornell University Press, 1986) offers a fascinating analysis of how the popularity and legitimization of boxing reflected the evolution of urban entertainment and spectator sports, as well as the role of class and gender. David L. Chapman's *Sandow the Magnificent: Eugen Sandow and the Beginnings of Bodybuilding* (Urbana: University of Illinois Press, 1994) documents the life and times of the "father of modern bodybuilding," a promotional genius who combined muscularity with showmanship and laid the foundations for the popularity of physical culture in the 1970s and 1980s.

On the little-known topic of male eating disorders, *International Journal of Eating Disorders, Psychosomatic Medicine, Comprehensive Psychiatry,* and *Health Education* were good sources for case studies and background information. The psychiatrist Arnold E. Andersen, the leading authority in the field, generously answered questions about male bulimics and anorectics, as did the National Association of Anorexia Nervosa and Associated Disorders in Illinois. Dr. Linda

Blakely, a clinical psychologist who specializes in body-image and eating disorders, and Dr. Elizabeth Weinberger, a specialist in diet and eating disorders who has worked extensively with male patients in a variety of experimental programs, were also very helpful.

On the other end of the eating spectrum for men are dieting and weight control. Books written primarily about women and weight provide an interesting counterpoint to men's experience; Kim Chernin's *The Obsession: Reflections on the Tyranny of Slenderness* (New York: Harper and Row, 1981) and Susan Bordo's penetrating cultural analysis in *Unbearable Weight: Feminism, Western Culture, and the Body* (Berkeley: University of California Press, 1993) are good examples. For a historical analysis of dieting and eating habits that includes men, see Hillel Schwartz's *Never Satisfied: A Cultural History of Diets, Fantasies, and Fat* (New York: Free Press, 1986) and Roberta Pollack Seid's excellent *Never Too Thin* (New York: Prentice-Hall, 1989). A classic work on the costs of being overweight in American society is Jean Mayer's *Overweight: Causes, Cost, and Control* (Englewood Cliffs, N.J.: Prentice-Hall, 1968). While Mayer delineates the worries about being overweight that surfaced in the 1950s, Warren Belasco takes an interesting position on the role of food in culture, and moves the dialogue into the 1960s and 1970s, in *Appetite for Change* (New York: Pantheon, 1989). Most useful in tracing men's love-hate affair with diet and weight loss were news magazines and sources like *Fortune* and *Duns* that discuss the costs of being overweight in the business world.

Bodybuilding has a long and somewhat checkered history in the United States, beginning as an expression of male resistance to the overcivilizing effects of urban life and the threat of foreign domination in the form of both immigration and European imperialism. The great turning point for bodybuilding in the twentieth century came with Arnold Schwarzenegger, who transformed the sport into a middle-class pastime and set a whole new standard for male bodies. Prior to Schwarzenegger, the best-known twentieth-century icon of the sport was Charles Atlas. Charles Gaines's biography of Atlas, *Yours in Perfect Manhood* (New York: Simon and Schuster, 1982), intertwines class, ethnicity, and popular culture and includes a fascinating collection of letters written to Atlas by grateful customers of his bodybuilding program.

The preeminent authority on the cultural role of bodybuilding is Dr. Alan Klein, a professor of anthropology at Northeastern University and the author of *Little Big Men: Bodybuilding Subculture and Gender Construction* (Albany: State University of New York Press, 1993). Klein's articles, as well as those of other scholars concerned with bodybuilding and strength training, have appeared in *The Sciences, Sociology of Sport Journal, Society and Leisure, Journal of Personality and Social Psychology, Society,* and *Play and Culture,* which also look at the relationship between muscular strength and mental health and the role of muscularity in shaping male identity. A great deal of information on the bodybuilding subculture has appeared in the popular press since Schwarzenegger's phenomenal rise to popularity in the mid-1970s, much of which serves to show the sport's evolution from developing strength and physical power to a concern with *looking* powerful; *Muscle & Fitness,* along with other Joe Weider publications, is an excellent source for tracing these changes. For a psychological perspective on bodybuilding, see Edward W.L. Smith, *Not Just Pumping Iron: On the Psychology of Lifting Weights* (Springfield, Ill.: Charles Thompson, 1989).

For the middle class's engagement in what was formerly seen as a primarily working-class activity, one of the most interesting sources is *Muscle: Confessions of an Unlikely Bodybuilder* (New York: Poseidon, 1991), an autobiographical account of how Sam Fussell, the son of two upper-middle-class New York academics, plunged into the world of professional bodybuilding in the 1980s. Fussell and other writers deal not only with the bodybuilding subculture but also with steroid abuse, an important issue that highlights the strange dichotomy in a sport presumably dedicated to improving the body, not harming it. Along with many articles on steroids available in popular periodicals, William N. Taylor's *Macho Medicine: A History of the Anabolic Steroid Epidemic* (Jefferson, N.C.: McFarland, 1991) provides both a historical and a scientific perspective.

Cosmetic surgery is one of the most intriguing of men's ventures into looking good because of its association with feminine vanity. Only at the far end of the historical spectrum do men begin venturing into the offices of plastic surgeons in significant numbers. The profession itself was long beset with negative imagery; not until narcissism took on positive connotations in the late twentieth century would cosmetic surgery find widespread acceptance.

The medical research libraries at the University of Southern California and University of California, Los Angeles provided a wealth of information on the history of cosmetic surgery that allowed me to trace how unique, and recent, the shift to male aesthetic surgery actually is, as well as the tortuous path the profession has followed to respectability. Fine histories of the plastic surgery profession are provided by Frank McDowell, *Source Book of Plastic Surgery* (Baltimore: Williams and Wilkins, 1977), Paul Regnault and Rollin K. Daniel, *Aesthetic Plastic Surgery* (Boston: Little, Brown, 1984), and Harry Hayes, Jr., *An Anthology of Plastic Surgery* (Rockville, Md.: Aspen Publishers, 1986). History, procedures, and techniques are described in Earl Calvin Padgett's seminal *Plastic and Reconstructive Surgery* (Springfield, Ill.: Charles C. Thomas, 1948), Mario Gonzalez-Ulloa, *The Creation of Aesthetic Plastic Surgery* (New York: Springer-Verlag, 1976), and Samuel Stegman, Theodore A. Tromovitch, and Richard G. Glogam, *Cosmetic Dermatologic Surgery* (Chicago: Year Book Medical Publishers, 1990, 2nd ed). The history of battlefield surgery and responses of other medical specialties to cosmetic surgery are documented in Harvey Graham's *The History of Surgery* (New York: Doubleday, 1939) and Frederick W. Cartright's *The Development of Modern Surgery* (New York: Thomas Crowell, 1967). Insights into wartime surgery, a turning point in the profession's prestige and proficiency, are especially to be found in the writings of the preeminent surgeon of the World

War I battlefield, Sir Harold Gillies, in Gillies and Ralph Millard, Jr., *The Principles and Art of Plastic Surgery* (Boston: Little, Brown, 1957), while the historian Joanna Bourke, in *Dismembering the Male: Men's Bodies, Britain, and the Great War* (Chicago: University of Chicago Press, 1996), and Elizabeth Haiken, in her excellent history of cosmetic surgery, *Venus Envy* (Baltimore: Johns Hopkins University Press, 1997), provide historical perspectives of the war and its effects on the male body and male self-esteem.

Some of the best accounts of the specialty's history, as well as the evolution of its acceptance in modern society, are provided by practitioners. Notable in this regard is Maxwell Maltz, who began his practice in New York in the 1930s, when plastic surgery was still widely regarded as frivolous and unnecessary—attitudes Maltz documents in *New Faces, New Futures: Rebuilding Character with Plastic Surgery* (New York: Richard R. Smith, 1936), *The Evolution of Plastic Surgery* (New York: Froken, 1946), and *Dr. Pygmalion: Autobiography of a Plastic Surgeon* (New York: Thomas Crowell, 1953). A more recent perspective on procedures and patients is provided by Dr. Robert Goldwyn, a pioneer in the modern profession and currently editor of *Plastic and Reconstructive Surgery*, in *Beyond Appearance: Reflections of a Plastic Surgeon* (New York: Dodd, Mead, 1986), and *The Patient and the Plastic Surgeon* (Boston: Little, Brown, 1991). Anthropological interpretations of body-image alteration can be found in Robert Brain's *The Decorated Body* (New York: Harper and Row, 1979), which offers a fascinating look at how body-image ideals vary among cultures, and Bernard Rudofsky's *The Unfashionable Human Body* (New York: Doubleday, 1971).

Professional journals, especially in their editorial sections, show how the cosmetic part of the profession, vis-à-vis purely reconstructive practice, gradually gained ascendancy and chart the ambivalence displayed by surgeons themselves about performing nonessential work. Concerns about body-image alteration and its effects on the psyche effectively limited the number of cosmetic procedures performed before the 1970s; the research and clinical experiences of Dr. John Goin and Dr. Marcia Goin, in *Changing the Body: Psychological Aspects of Plastic Surgery* (Baltimore: Williams and Wilkins, 1981), and Jean Ann Graham and Albert M. Kligman, in *The Psychology of Cosmetic Treatments* (New York: Praeger, 1985), contribute to some of the best books on this subject. *Plastic and Reconstructive Surgery* refers frequently to the need to screen prospective patients carefully—especially if they were men. Not until negative perceptions were ameliorated was it possible for men fully to embrace cosmetic surgery.

Men are reluctant to admit to having plastic surgery, but I found a number who were willing to talk to me about their experiences. Cosmetic surgeons proved more forthcoming, and I interviewed more than a dozen doctors and observed face-lift, eye-lift, laser eye correction, and liposuction surgery. I interviewed doctors, nurses, technicians, and patients at the Bosley, Randall Sword, Elliott and True, and Petersen hair-transplantation centers in Los Angeles and observed a half-dozen surgical procedures in various stages of hair replacement.

Seminars intended to explain procedures and stimulate business for practitioners also provided information on the latest advances in hair transplantation and cosmetic surgery, as well as the marketing strategies used by providers.

Plastic and Reconstructive Surgery, Aesthetic Surgery, and *Annals of Plastic Surgery* are the leading professional journals for the speciality. In reviewing all issues between 1950 and 1995, I was looking for several things: first, the evolution of plastic surgery to the point where purely cosmetic procedures became more common; second, the profession's shift away from being almost entirely geared to women; and finally, the techniques and enhancements developed during the past half century. *The New York Times, Los Angeles Times,* and *The Wall Street Journal,* along with major news, women's, and specialty magazines like *Psychology Today,* have featured many articles on plastic surgery that deal with procedures offered and their social and psychological ramifications.

Phalloplasty, or penis augmentation, is a subset of cosmetic surgery that became popular in the early 1990s. Information and advertising about the procedures is readily available in the popular press—*The Wall Street Journal* and *Los Angeles Times* were especially good sources—but I found it necessary to talk with practitioners, including the most prolific, Dr. Melvyn Rosenstein, to find out who was getting the surgery and why. For a detailed medical description of the procedure, see Gary J. Alter, "Augmentation Phalloplasty," in *Urologic Clinics of North America* (Impotence Series, 1995). Dr. Bernic Zilbergeld's *New Male Sexuality* (New York: Bantam, 1992) also provides useful background on male sexuality, potency, and concerns about penis size, as does Willard Gaylin's *The Male Ego* (New York: Viking, 1992).

Of course, phalloplasty has become popular because of men's concerns about impotence, and I consulted numerous sources on impotence and male sexuality more generally. A classic work on the causes and treatment of impotence is Dr. William Robinson's *Sexual Impotence: A Practical Treatise on the Causes, Symptoms and Treatment of Impotence and Other Sexual Disorders in Men and Women* (1912). Robinson's book is notable not only for forthrightly addressing the topic of impotence but for laying much of the blame for it on women—a view that would prevail for many years. Vern Bullough and Bonnie Bullough, in *Sexual Attitudes: Myths and Realities* (Amherst, N.Y.: Prometheus Books, 1995), offers a historical overview of sexuality, and Lynn Segal combines culture and history in *Slow Motion: Changing Masculinities, Changing Men* (New Brunswick, N.J.: Rutgers University Press, 1990).

In the 1950s, impotence was a largely unrecognized phenomenon, while frigidity raised national concerns. Two decades later, journals like *Psychological Abstracts* and *Medical Aspects of Human Sexuality* showed a sharp decline in articles on frigidity and an increase in articles on impotence. Women's magazines and advice columnists, as well as *Esquire* and other men's magazines, also show how frigidity, the "new" impotence of the 1970s, and other forms of sexual "dysfunction" were viewed at different periods of time. Dr. Alfred Kinsey's ground-breaking study of male sexuality, *Sexual Behavior in the Human Male* (Philadelphia: W. B. Saunders, 1948), and Dr. William H. Masters and Dr. Virginia Johnson's studies of human sexual response *Human Sexual Response* (Boston: Little, Brown, 1966) and *Human Sexual Inadequacy* (Boston: Little, Brown, 1970) were essential to understanding both the realities of and changing attitudes about sexual dysfunction.

The debate as to whether impotence is physical or psychological in origin made it necessary to look at both medical and psychological journals. To see how impotence has been identified and treated by doctors, I reviewed all issues of *Urology*, which began publication in 1972, *Urologic Clinics,* and *Journal of Urology* dating back to the 1950s. General medical journals, including *Journal of the American Medical Association, New England Journal of Medicine,* and *Practitioner,* also gave increasing coverage to impotence in the 1980s and 1990s. The best sources for looking at impotence from a psychological perspective were *Medical Aspects of Human Sexuality, International Journal of Sexology, American Sociological Review,* and *Journal of Sex and Marital Therapy.* Articles by the most outspoken critics of the medicalization of impotence, Dr. Leonore Tiefer and Dr. Barry Bass, appear in *American Behavioral Scientist, Gender and Society,* and *Medical Aspects of Human Sexuality.*

In the twentieth century, Kinsey and Masters and Johnson are central to the study of sexuality. In the 1970s, a number of studies were aimed at popular audiences, including Shere Hite's surveys of male and female sexuality. *Sex in America: A Definitive Study* (1994) by Robert T. Michael, John H. Gagnon, et al. is the first national study to look at America's sexual habits and the sociocultural milieu in which they have developed since Kinsey's seminal research of the late 1940s and early 1950s. Also important in showing attitudinal changes among laymen are feminist writings like Anne Koedt's classic "The Myth of the Vaginal Orgasm," in Anne Koedt, ed., *Radical Feminism* (New York: Quadrangle, 1973).

Because impotence is sometimes related to drug use, I referred to *Alcohol and Alcoholism, Journal of Psychoactive Drugs,* and *Journal of Drug Issues;* the relationship between impotence and the stresses of workplace and home is discussed in sociological journals, including *Social Problems* and *Family Coordinator.* I interviewed sex therapists and psychologists who specialize in sexual issues in order to get current insights into the prevalence and treatment of impotence. The arrival of Viagra in early 1998 prompted an outpouring of articles, along with enormous speculation as to the drug's role in medical, social, economic, and even political issues; *The Wall Street Journal* and *The New York Times* have been particularly useful sources on the new male wonder drug.

INDEX